"I love this book. Behrendt and Le Donne model for [...] at its best—witty, respectful, and full of substance. [...] the ongoing conversation between the two faiths, a conversation that I can hope will become increasingly commonplace."

—Pete Enns
Abram S. Clemens Professor of Biblical Studies, Eastern University
Author of *The Bible Tells Me So* and *The Sin of Certainty*

"*Sacred Dissonance* marks an important step forward in Jewish-Christian discourse. The essays are candid and probing, the dialogues rigorous, insightful, and devoid of the platitudes so typical in interfaith encounters. Jews and Christians wishing to learn more about each other—and themselves—will enjoy the opportunity to eavesdrop on these rich conversations. I know I did."

—Rabbi Joshua D. Garroway
Associate Professor of Early Christianity & Second Commonwealth
Hebrew Union College-Jewish Institute of Religion

"This provocative book will change the way we look at interfaith dialogue. It is both intellectually challenging and personally moving—a story not only of two traditions but also, and even more, about two people. At this particular moment, when current political dialogue is so dissonant, so focused on winning or losing, this book offers a model of a different way to talk and a different way to listen. That in itself is sacred."

—Rabbi Laura Geller
Rabbi Emerita, Temple Emanuel of Beverly Hills

"Conversations between Jews and Christians have never been more productive. So, aren't we done with Jewish-Christian dialogue already? In this book, Anthony Le Donne and Larry Behrendt answer this question with an emphatic no. By embracing rather than papering over the complex differences between Christians and Jews, Larry and Anthony show how an exploration of the things that divide us can lead to deeper faith and friendship."

—Dana Evan Kaplan
Rabbi, Springhill Avenue Temple
Faculty, Springhill College, Mobile, Alabama

"From both a deeply personal and an intellectually honest place, the authors invite us into a world of sacred conversation and learning between Christian and Jew. Now more than ever, dialogue—the ability to be mutually transformed and informed through conversation—is a tool we need to cultivate in our lives and in our communities. The authors reflect Divine Light in their ability to listen, learn and share with the reader the strength and vitality that comes from honest and compassionate exchange."

—Yohanna Kinberg
Rabbi, Congregation Kol Ami, Woodinville, Washington

"Honest conversations between Jews and Christians are as important now as any time in the past 2,000 years. *Sacred Dissonance* marks an important point in that sometimes difficult, sometimes joyous journey of mutual understanding, enhancement, and coexistence. In this book, we are privileged to read the conversations between two brave friends, one Jew and one Christian, who made themselves vulnerable to each other in the hard process of exploring the dissonances between their theological outlooks. The authors are masterful in their honest engagement, handling tough issues with critical poise and careful presentation. Here theological integrity is matched by an ethos of rhetorical integrity—a rare and exquisite accomplishment."

—Bruce W. Longenecker
Professor of Religion and W. W. Melton Chair, Baylor University
Author of *Hitler, Jesus, and Our Common Humanity*

Sacred Dissonance

Sacred Dissonance

THE BLESSING OF DIFFERENCE
IN JEWISH-CHRISTIAN DIALOGUE

Anthony Le Donne *and* Larry Behrendt

**Sacred Dissonance: The Blessing of Difference
in Jewish-Christian Dialogue**

© 2017 by Anthony Le Donne and Larry Behrendt

Hendrickson Publishers Marketing, LLC
P. O. Box 3473
Peabody, Massachusetts 01961-3473
www.hendrickson.com

ISBN 978-1-68307-067-2

Printed in the United States of America

First Printing—December 2017

Library of Congress Cataloging-in-Publication Data

A catalog record for this title is available from the Library of Congress
Hendrickson Publishers Marketing, LLC ISBN 978-1-68307-067-2

Dedicated to Sarah and Stephanie

Contents

Conclusions

Foreword

Amy-Jill Levine

Academics have *debates*. The academic life is often a blood sport where careers begin at a "defense" and the battles continue through tenure and promotion. When academics debate, the result can be a negative review, a quashed grant application, or an attack at a conference.

Participants in formal gatherings have *dialogues*. Dialogue participants tend to avoid very difficult subjects lest a comment be taken as an insult. Much of their kind of dialogue is show-and-tell rather than give-and-take. In dialogue, speakers often agree to disagree, and then move quickly to the next subject.

Friends have *conversations*. If the friendship is strong enough, the conversations move beyond politeness to challenge and even discomfort. Friends can say, "I really don't like this about your . . . and we need to talk about it." They can enter this dangerous ground because they know that the friendship will continue.

In this remarkable study, Anthony Le Donne and Larry Behrendt allow us to listen to their conversations and invite us to participate in them. While Anthony and Larry—by the second chapter, readers will likely feel that they are friends of and on a first-name basis with the authors—are friends, they often disagree, fiercely, even as they learn more about and grow closer to each other. They have academic *bona fides*, which they do display on occasion, but they also engage in conversation, which means they talk *to* each other and not past each other. Anthony and Larry are at the vanguard of a new genre, the *Jewish/Christian schmooze*.[1]

---

1. Michael Wex notes that *schmooze* in real Yiddish means an informal, friendly conversation. Since entering English vocabulary, it takes on slightly sinister connotations, as in to chat in order to curry favor, make a business connection, or network. See his *Born to Kvetch: Yiddish Language and Culture in All of Its Moods* (New York: Harper Perennial, 2005), appendix, 12.

With the trust built up over years, they have moved Jewish/Christian relations beyond the academic debate supported by lots of footnotes and beyond the dialogue of "Let's get to know each other but let's go carefully" and "Let's see if I can understand your belief and practice in my own terminology." They take the conversation to the risky familiarity of "Here's what bothers me about what (some) Christians, or (some) Jews, say or do; indeed, here's what bothers me about what you just said." Their comments and their responses ring true to me.

In conversation marked by pain, pathos, and occasional puns, they ask what individual Christians and Jews, and what they themselves, *really* think about each other, and each other's traditions. They discuss not just the Shoah, but how to talk about it, including its distinct effects on Jewish and Christian social and personal memory. Larry forthrightly expresses his concerns about what he sees as the dangers in Christianity, from evangelical attempts to convert Jews to Gospel passages he thinks should be excised. Anthony opens with two forceful, and dissonant, points: Christians generally like Jews and many of those same Christians have anti-Jewish tendencies. He then takes us through how, from ignorance, such tendencies manifest themselves.

Anthony notes, correctly, that the academic study of Jews and Judaism is insufficient preparation for real-world encounters; Larry observes, correctly, that as a whole, most Jews would prefer to be left alone rather than to engage Christians in an interreligious dialogue, let alone "interfaith" dialogue where the questions of G-d and salvation are of no interest to some Jews. They talk about alienation from and disappointment with their own communities; they talk about wrestling with Scripture, and then they get into the ring to show how this wrestling is done.

The schmoozing, because it is personal, allows for moments where one participant is jarred by what is normative for another: Anthony's shock at armed guards at Larry's synagogue coupled with his recognition that, statistically, there are more anti-Semites in the world than there are Jews; Larry's experience at a "bring a friend to church day," where songs of Jesus' suffering— "thirty minutes of angst" as he puts it—made going to church feel like a trip to the intensive care ward. And yet, he also realized how meaningful and sustaining that same church experience was for members of the congregation.

At points, I laughed out loud. Larry's comments about the pervasive but nominal Christianity of television characters neatly summarize network offerings in the '50s and '60s. As he puts it, "At least I assumed they were Christian; they certainly weren't Jewish. But they never built a church on *Gilligan's Island.*" Well, of course not, is my (Jewish) response: had there been

Jews, or at least Jewish-identified characters on the island, not only would they have figured a way off, they would not have booked a three-hour cruise on the *Minnow* in the first place. The producer of *Gilligan's Island*, Sherwood Schwartz, planned to be a medical doctor, but the quota system restricting Jews kept him out of NYU Medical School. Tina Louise (Ginger) and Natalie Schafer (Lovey)—both Jews. Is this television show an instance of Jews making fun of *goyishe* stereotypes? Is it an example of Jews attempting to show how disparate people create community? Is my first question anti-Jewish? Is the second apologetic? Larry and Anthony encourage the questions.

Anthony notes that many Christians have never met a Jew. On the other hand, it's likely that these Christians have *seen* Jews, a lot. We could start with pictures of Jesus (okay, most of the time he doesn't "look Jewish"—a cliché that requires some parsing of its own), and work down (up?) to Bob Saget, Bernie Sanders, Adam Sandler, David Schwimmer, Jerry Seinfeld, William Shatner, Sarah Silverman, Gene Simmons, Steven Spielberg, Ben Stiller, Howard Stern, John Stewart, Barbara Streisand . . . and those are just under "S." I also note that Phil Silvers did appear on *Gilligan's Island*. How do Christians engage in dialogue, let alone schmoozing, when there are no Jews in the neighborhood, or the county, or pretty much the state? Larry and Anthony give a sense of what this conversation would sound like.

Anthony and Larry not only explain but also show *why* such conversation, taking place today when the fastest growing religious group is the "nones," is necessary. Knowledge of the other produces better knowledge of the self: learning about Judaism makes Anthony a better Christian; learning about Christianity makes Larry a better Jew. They ponder, with difficulty, the analogy of the Shoah to Jesus' Crucifixion (note the capitalization of both terms); they ask questions of Christian complicity and Christian denial, even as they question the problematic typecasting of Jews as victims and Christians as perpetrators.

These conversations extend to other areas that require the same honest, rigorous interrogations: LGBTQI interests, American racism, Martin Buber and Émile Durkheim, Richard Rubenstein and Heinrich Gruber, Elie Wiesel and Martin Luther, Jacob and Esau, and more. In their schmoozing, they challenge each other, they challenge themselves, and by allowing us to listen in on their conversations, they challenge us as well. As I read this volume, I continually wanted to respond: *No, that's not how I understand Paul of Tarsus; no, that's not a necessary conclusion; yes, you should have said more about* . . .

Larry and Anthony open the conversation, they invite us—they even compel us—to join in. Let the schmoozing continue.

Preface

The book before you was not the book we set out to write. The initial idea was to write a "how to" or "and you can too" guide. In such a book, one might expect distilled wisdom and pro-tips that skim the surface for beginners. While such books are beneficial and necessary, we discovered that we had waded into the deep end. Moreover, we enjoyed the experience far too much to keep the conversation safe.

These pages are the product of nearly four years of conversations between the two of us, the coauthors of this book. There are risks in taking so long to write a book. One such risk is that things change. Anthony references Larry's rabbi, Laura Geller, in his introductory chapter. Rabbi Geller has since retired. Another risk of taking so long to write is that our views on certain topics may have changed. You, the reader, may sometimes see one of us say something in one chapter that differs from (even contradicts) what is said in a later chapter. The greater risk, of course, is that we'll repeat ourselves. This is natural in any ongoing dialogue. You will see certain topics come up repeatedly in this book, and sometimes we will discuss these topics without recognizing or remembering we've discussed them before!

One topic you may not find discussed here to your satisfaction is the modern State of Israel. Full disclosure: Anthony initially proposed that this book include discussion of Israel, and Larry vetoed the idea. Larry felt that as an American Jew, he was not equipped to represent the thoughts of Israeli Jews. Also, Larry felt that Israel is an advanced topic in Jewish-Christian dialogue, best tackled after the dialogue has addressed introductory (and perhaps, less difficult) topics. It's not that you won't find Israel mentioned in these pages. You will. But you're not going to find this topic addressed in the depth it deserves. This was by design.

Our process in writing this book was as follows: we picked five different conversation topics. For each topic, we each independently wrote a chapter. We did not read the other's chapter as we wrote our own. When the chapters were complete, we shared them and then recorded a conversation discussing them. Four of these five conversations are included here (we did not include a dialogue on the final set of chapters, as we thought these paired chapters served better as the book's conclusion). You may notice that our chapters on a given topic may recite identical facts, or reach different conclusions, in either case without apparent recognition of the duplication or contradiction.

The four conversations included herein have been lightly edited to eliminate pauses, sneezes, and subconversations about baseball and where to go for lunch. We removed some of the more boring parts of our discussions, and occasionally reordered pieces for greater sense and clarity. We mostly resisted the impulse to make changes to what we said to make ourselves sound smarter.

We have used a minimum of conventions in this book. One convention is how we've spelled the name of the Divine Being worshipped by both Christians and Jews: we've spelled this name "G-d" or "L-rd." When these names are contained in quoted material or in book or article titles, and the name was originally spelled with the "o," we added editorial brackets (thus, "G[-]d" and "L[-]rd"). We've omitted this "o" in recognition of a custom in certain parts of the Orthodox Jewish world that avoids printing material containing a sacred name of G-d. There are some Jews who consider the name "G-d" when spelled with the "o" to be such a sacred name. While Jews *do* of course purchase books containing the sacred name, some Orthodox Jews dispose of such books by burying them ceremonially, and it is courtesy to create written text that can be disposed of without triggering this requirement. To be clear, many Jews do not follow this practice of burying books, and many other Jews do not think that the English language contains a sacred name for G-d. Given that only a minority of Jews see a need to spell "G-d" without the "o," we debated whether we should accommodate this practice here. Ultimately, we decided that respect for the name of G-d is pretty much universal. We note that the Lord's Prayer recited by Christians is addressed to G-d, "Hallowed be Thy Name," and that many Christians recently took offense at a college classroom exercise where students wrote the name of Jesus on a piece of paper and then stepped on it. While the vast majority of our readers would have no problem if we used the conventional spelling for "G-d," our decision to spell this name differently led us both to think in new ways about sacred names and words.

We have both used the name "Old Testament" to refer to the books of the Bible that Jews consider to be sacred scripture. As Anthony discusses in his final chapter in this book, there are some who object to the label "Old," as if "old" connotes no longer good, or outmoded, or replaced with something better. There are other expressions we might have used in place of Old Testa-

ment. Jews often refer to these books as the "Tanakh." We might have used
"First Testament" to refer to these books, and "Second Testament" to refer
to what's more commonly referred to as the "New Testament." Ultimately,
we decided that "Old Testament" and "New Testament" would be the most
familiar terms for a Jewish-Christian audience, though Anthony sometimes
refers to the Old Testament books as the "Hebrew Bible." For the record, as
Larry is pushing toward Social Security age, he's inclined to think of "old"
as a good thing.

Rules of the Road: An Invitation to Dialogue

> There are three things I have learned never to discuss with people . . .
> Religion, Politics, and The Great Pumpkin.
>
> —Linus van Pelt[1]

What was it that made you pick up this book? Perhaps you're a Jew living among Christians, or a Christian living among Jews, and you'd like meaningful informal conversations with members of the other religion. Perhaps you're a college student who grew up in a religiously homogenous community, but now your dorm-mates include peoples of all faiths (and no faith) eager to talk about *your* faith. Or perhaps, you've been asked to participate in a more intentional interreligious conversation. Perhaps your synagogue has invited a group of Christians for an evening presentation followed by small group discussions. Or perhaps your church has invited a prominent rabbi to participate in a conversation with members of your congregation. So you thought: There's a "how to" guide for everything else. Shouldn't there be a guide for Christians who want to talk to Jews, and vice versa?

The coauthors of this book (Larry and Anthony) have spent much of their lives trying to figure out what leads to good dialogue between Christians and Jews. When we've asked our elders and teachers for their advice, we've sometimes been told: Just follow the rules you'd follow in any sort of polite conversation. Be nice. If you're hosting the conversation, be hospitable. Serve cake. If you're guests of another house of worship, be a good guest. *Bring* cake. But if the goal is to conduct an authentic conversation among peoples like Jews and Christians with a history of misunderstanding, conflict, and worse, the usual social norms for hosts and guests might not be

---

1. This quote is from *It's the Great Pumpkin, Charlie Brown* (1966), an animated television special based on the comic strip *Peanuts* by Charles M. Schulz. See "It's the Great Pumpkin, Charlie Brown," Wikiquote; https://en.wikiquote.org/wiki /It's_the_Great_Pumpkin,_Charlie_Brown.

enough. Mary Boys, a veteran of such dialogues, suggests that we practice "communicative virtues."[2]

> They include tolerance, patience, an openness to give and receive criticism, a readiness to admit that one may be mistaken, the desire to reinterpret or translate one's own concerns so that they will be comprehensible to others, the self-imposition of restraint in order that others may speak, and the willingness to listen thoughtfully and attentively.[3]

Larry and Anthony want to affirm this wise word: virtue is a good guide for civil conversation. But we shouldn't misread Boys's rule as a call to mere civility. If all we wanted was civility, we'd follow the advice of Charlie Brown's friend Linus and avoid discussing religion altogether. If we value civility above everything else in interfaith dialogue, then we risk dulling the authenticity of the conversation. Let us not make the mistake of skipping over this key phrase in Boys's rule: "an openness to give and receive criticism." Anthony and Larry have found that this sort of openness is hard earned and risky. We admit that learning to live by this rule is an ongoing process of two steps forward, one step back.

Our guess is that most present-day settings for Jewish-Christian dialogue are more civil than they are open. There are reasons for this: after nearly two thousand years of open conflict, it feels like an accomplishment to exit dialogue with a modicum of good feeling. But we pay a price for valuing good feeling above anything else.

A friend recently told us, "Nothing is more boring than Jewish-Christian dialogue." Perhaps this is true for many who have experienced dialogue featuring civility, good feelings, and nothing else. But we are convinced that Jewish-Christian dialogue can and should be more than this. Indeed, in these pages you will find that "openness to give and receive criticism" results in heartbreak, laughter, raised voices, and interruptions. In the process of writing this book, we have needed to apologize often. We have found that dialogue after a heated argument takes on a different shape than it did before. We have each (though not at the same time) wanted to walk away from this project, concluding that it was too taxing, that we'd put too much at stake here, and that (following Linus) our friendship meant too much to risk it

---

2. Boys credits Nicholas Burbules for this phrase. Suzanne Rice and Nicholas C. Burbules, "Communicative virtues and educational relations," in H. A. Alexander, ed. *Philosophy of Education 1992* (Urbana: Philosophy of Education Society, 1993), 33–44.

3. Mary C. Boys and Sara S. Lee, *Christians and Jews in Dialogue: Learning in the Presence of the Other* (Woodstock, VT: Skylight Paths, 2006), 55.

by talking about religion. We have also discovered that authentic dialogue has produced virtues in us that we never would have been able to bring to the table on our own.

Your mileage, of course, may vary. With this in mind we've each written rules that we've learned in Jewish-Christian dialogue. Perhaps some of these might produce or reveal some virtue you find helpful. Anthony wrote his rules first, and Larry responded with his own. As you will see, Anthony's rules differ from Larry's in both tone and audience. We write these in the first person.

Rules of the Road (Anthony)

Before the State of California issued me a driver's license, I was required to take a class on driving. I was then required to take a written test. I practiced for miles alongside an experienced driver, then I took another test. Even so, I hadn't mastered all of the road signs I would encounter along the way. My experience with Jewish-Christian dialogue has been a bit like this.[4]

I read dozens of books about Jewish-Christian dialogue. I read books by Jews and Christians. I read broad surveys and focused discourses about the Holocaust. I read introductions, course packets, and dictionaries. I also sat in the passenger seat next to experienced theologians, pastors, and rabbis. I even coauthored a book on the topic. Still, there are new road signs I will encounter along the way. And hopefully I will learn a great deal more about myself in the process.

The following is a list of nine things I've gleaned from my experience with Jewish dialogue partners along the way. To keep with the metaphor, I would imagine the "rules for the road" differ from country to country and state to state. These are just a few road signs that I've encountered. Some of these will be new to Jewish ears and common knowledge among Christians. Others will be new to Christian ears and common knowledge among Jews. I'm sure that some of these will prompt disagreement among my readers. I offer these only as points of learning opportunity within my own experience.

---

4. In this introduction and throughout this book, the authors mixed metaphors. For example, sometimes we talk about interreligious dialogue as a "conversation table," or a "room" of mixed company. Here we refer to dialogue as journey that requires "rules for the road." The varieties of metaphors you'll find in these pages are (we think) necessary. Dialogue can take on various forms of formality, hospitality, intentionality, etc. It is therefore not helpful to think of dialogue as any single thing.

1. *Conversion is off the table.* The Christian drive to seek converts has no place in Jewish-Christian dialogue. At least most of the time. This will exclude many Christians from the conversation from the outset, but so it must be. Larry may have a more nuanced view on this, but his webpage for Jewish-Christian dialogue calls this "rule number one."[5] There are few things more likely to push Jews away from meaningful interchange than the drive to "win souls" for Christ. This has never been an aspiration of mine, but I know several Christians who have been perplexed by this. What Christians must understand is that the vast majority of Jews consider conversion to Christianity to be an abandonment of Judaism. In a recent e-mail on this topic, Larry explains a common Jewish perspective: "We regard conversion as loss of Jewishness, and ergo conversion efforts appear to us as seeking our destruction as a people." From this vantage point, to seek the conversion of Jews is tantamount to seeking the destruction of Jewish identity, and even of the Jewish people. It's my experience that Jews are averse to conversion efforts of all kinds, no matter who it is that might be seeking converts, Jew or non-Jew. My Jewish friends are quite happy that I am not seeking to convert, myself, to Judaism. They (although they've never said it in these words) respect that I am secure in my religious identity. In dialogue, we seek to understand and be understood. We do not seek the conversion of the other.

2. *It might be "interfaith" dialogue and it might not.* Christians tend to think of religion in terms of belief and faith. From a Christian perspective, to be a "person of faith" is to identify with a particular belief system. Many Jews think in terms of faith and belief too, but this is not a given. Jewish identity does not hinge on faith or belief. Most Jews did not become Jewish by personal faith or belief. Rather, most Jews were born Jews and will consider themselves Jewish, whether devout or secular. As a case in point: most Christians would consider atheism a non-Christian position. In other words, if a Christian were to become an atheist, she would give up Christianity. We might say that such a person "lost her faith." This topic is approached differently in Jewish experience. Some Jews will also identify as agnostic or atheist. I have heard this phrase often from Jews in dialogue: "We didn't *get in* by belief; we can't *get out* by disbelief." So "interfaith dialogue" might be a misnomer at times. Judaism isn't—strictly speaking—just a faith. At least, it isn't *just* faith that makes a Jew.

---

5. Larry Behrendt, "No Proselytizing," Jewish-Christian Intersections, March 25, 2012, http://jewishchristianintersections.com/?page_id=11.

3. *Christians generally like Jews.* It seems a bit odd (bordering conde-scension, perhaps) to write that line. I will take the risk anyway because it must be said. This is a point I must risk because we Christians have a two-thousand-year history of anti-Judaism punctuated by violence, forced conversions, and mass murder. Much has changed (although much change is still needed). Most Christians I've met are quite interested in what Jews think, how they worship, and what insights they might lend on spiritual matters. We are largely ignorant (see points 4 and 5 below) of Judaism, but we are generally interested. We have our skinheads and hatemongers, but they do not represent Christianity at large.

4. *Most Christians have never met a Jew and never will.* There are roughly 2.7 billion Christians in the world, making over 30 percent of the world's population Christian. There are 14 million Jews, making only .2 percent of the world's population Jewish.[6] There are more Christians in Angola (17 million) than there are Jews in the entire world. The same claim could be made of thirty-plus other countries including Chile, Madagascar, and South Korea. Christianity is truly global. By contrast, over 80 percent of all Jews live in either the United States or Israel.[7] There are just too many Christians spread over too many different places; the vast majority of Christians will never cross paths with a Jew.

5. *Many Christians have anti-Jewish tendencies.* This point might seem to contradict my claim that *Christians generally like Jews.* But these two state-ments are equally true. We Christians often demonstrate such tendencies unwittingly. This is to say that many Christians think and speak in ways that are "not good for the Jews" and do so without knowing it. The Christians who are surprised to learn of "rule number one" above concerning conver-sion provide a great example. By and large, Christians do not know how most Jews feel about proselytizing. Another example of our anti-Judaism is demonstrated in our storytelling. I have witnessed countless defamations of "the Pharisees" in church, including stories designed for children. The *vast majority* of Christians have no idea that this is an anti-Jewish tendency. Ironically, I see a great many of my peace-loving, progressive friends leaning toward a belief that the violence of the Old Testament is replaced by a way

---

6. "The Global Religious Landscape," Pew Research Center, December 18, 2012, www.pewforum.org/2012/12/18/global-religious-landscape-exec.

7. "Israel and the U.S. are Home to More Than Four-Fifths of the World's Jews," Pew Research Center, March 20, 2013, www.pewforum.org/2013/03/20/israel-and-the-us-are-home-to-more-than-fourfifths-of-the-worlds-jews/.

of peace in the New Testament. Their hope—a noble one—is to emphasize peace and justice in the modern world. Again, they are unaware that such a stance might contribute to an anti-Jewish climate. Indeed, the Christian title "Old Testament" for Hebrew Scripture is another example. In these cases and dozens more, Christians act in ways that are contrary to their general affection for the Jewish people.

6. *It is generally bad form to assume that all Christians have any one thing in common. It is bad form to assume that all Jews have any one thing in common.* Christianity is the most culturally diverse religion in the world. While *most* Christians have a few things in common, we must continue to use qualified language wherever we can. It is important that we speak in terms of *some* Christians, *most* Christians, or even *the vast majority of* Christians. The same goes for statements about what Jews have in common. I know very few American Jews who feel comfortable speaking on behalf of Israelis or Eastern European Jews. Moreover, as Larry has said to me often, we must not confuse Jews with Judaism. Just because Judaism has traditionally taught A, B, or C, it doesn't mean all (or even most) Jews believe A, B, or C. Stereotyping must be avoided. Therefore we ought to choose our words a bit more carefully. I will offer one more comment along this line: "insiders" are often just as guilty of stereotyping as "outsiders." I have heard Jews (in dialogue with Christians) say blithely, "Jews do not believe in hell." While this might be true of *many* or even *most Jews*, it cannot represent all Jews. We must be careful when we represent ourselves. Even something like "I've never met a Jew who believes in hell" would be more beneficial and less likely to create a stereotype.

7. *For some Jews, the titles "Christ," "Jesus," and "New Testament" are jarring.* These words represent a long history of persecution and anti-Semitism. These are words that are associated (rightly or wrongly) with the murder of six million relatives in very recent history. A Jewish friend once told me, "I've been seeking spiritual truth alongside Christians for years now, but there will always be something about the name 'Jesus' that will stick in my throat." My friend is not consciously anti-Christian; he is just aware that he still has a few knee-jerk reactions that he grew up with. Christians cannot sit down at the conversation table with a blank slate. The label "Christianity" has the capacity to taint the conversation from the outset. The name "Jesus" means something entirely different for Jews than it does for Christians.

8. *Our differences are just as important as our commonalities.* Christianity and Judaism have much in common. But any Jewish-Christian dialogue worth having does not overlook the important distinctives. The notion that

all religions are basically the same with only superficial differences is both in-correct and insulting. There will always be some folk who enter interreligious dialogue hoping to find out that we're all the same, so we can all get along just fine. The premise here is faulty. *We are not all the same.* Furthermore, we must learn to get along without seeking sameness. As cliché as it has become, the mantra "celebrate diversity" has virtue. In order to celebrate diversity, we must first acknowledge diversity. This, in part, explains the idea of "dissonance" in the title of this book. Larry and I will not always be singing the same tune at the same time.

9. *Stendahl's Rules are generally helpful.* Krister Stendahl (1921–2008) was a Catholic theologian and Harvard professor who wrote insightfully about Christian-Jewish relations. He is also admired greatly by my dialogue partner in this book. Larry summarizes Stendahl's "three rules of religious understanding" on his webpage.[8] I will conclude my "road signs" with Larry's summary. Besides, I like the idea of a Trinitarian conclusion. (1) If you want to understand another religion, ask its adherents, not its enemies. (2) Don't compare your best to their worst. (3) Leave room for "holy envy"—that is, room for discovering some aspect of another religion you admire, while at the same time accepting that this aspect belongs not to you but to a separate faith community.

Rules of the Road (Larry)

I like Anthony's rules for the road. I like them so much, I thought I should add a handful of my own. These rules are directed primarily toward Jews. They're not intended to be complete.

---

8. While Stendahl may be best known for his "Three Rules of Religious Under-standing" (rule 3 being to leave room for "holy envy"), it does not appear he ever wrote them down. Instead, these rules were stated by Stendahl in some form in a press conference he held at the dedication of the Mormon Temple in Stockholm in 1985. These rules have been widely printed. See, for example, "Krister Stendahl," Wikipedia, https://en.wikipedia.org/wiki/Krister_Stendahl. The idea that "holy envy" precludes incorporation of another's religious ideas is not found in every formulation of Stendahl's "Three Rules of Religious Understanding," but it was stated clearly by Stendahl. See Stendahl's lecture "From G[-]d's Perspective We Are All Minorities," delivered on February 27, 1992, at Harvard University's Center for the Study of World Religions; see Jim Burklo, "Krister Stendahl on Religious Plural-ism," *Pluralism*, July 23, 2008, https://pluralismsunday.wordpress.com/2008/07/23/krister-stendahl-on-religious-pluralism.

1. *They're Christians, not Christianity.* I came to dialogue wanting to learn about Christianity. But dialogue doesn't work that way. In dialogue, you meet people, not religions. Many of the best Christians I meet make it a point to tell me they're not typically Christian. Other Christians take the opposite tack and swear that theirs is the only way to be a Christian. But if you decide to speak only to Christians who are accepted as Christian by all other Christians, then you'll never speak to anybody! If you're hoping for a picture of Christianity, your best hope is that such a picture emerges gradually over the course of many conversations.

2. *We're talking beliefs, not truths.* It's not uncommon to be approached in dialogue by someone who argues (a) there is one G-d, (b) one G-d can have but one truth, and (c) it is our goal in dialogue to identify that truth. There is no more deadly starting point for interfaith dialogue than this, as it leaves each faith present for dialogue struggling for that single truth-token of legitimacy. Respond to this "one truth" point of view by speaking in terms of belief. There *is* room in dialogue for more than one belief.

3. *Be sensitive to asymmetries.* The problem of interreligious asymmetry probably deserves its own book. But in a nutshell, this is a problem of apples and oranges. More accurately (as I've written elsewhere),[9] religious asymmetry is a problem of apples and baseballs. From the perspective of the apple, a baseball tastes terrible. From the perspective of the baseball, an apple performs badly when thrown from a pitcher's mound and hit by a slugger's bat. The problem is that each perspective understands the "foreign" object in terms of the ideal characteristics of the "known" object. If the two objects are asymmetric, then these ideal characteristics do not match up.

If we understand a new religion solely in terms of our own, we'll have an apples and baseballs problem. And, indeed, this is how many newbies approach the study of another's religion. So, it's common in my experience for Christians to understand Judaism first and foremost as a religion lacking Jesus. But you can't understand a religion by identifying what you find missing there, any more than you can understand a baseball as a sphere lacking seeds and a stem. Nor will it work to understand Judaism by trying to find a Jewish counterpart to Jesus (Moses, say, or Abraham). Judaism simply is not built around any single person in a way that's comparable to Christianity's focus on Jesus.

---

9. Larry Behrendt, "Apples and Oranges," *Jewish-Christian Intersections*, September 10, 2012, jewishchristianintersections.com/?p=163.

Another Jewish-Christian asymmetry is how the two religions see each other. Christianity sees itself as emerging from (and sometimes even as replacing) Judaism. Catholic philosopher Michael Novak writes that in order to understand their own faith, "Christians must also accept as true nearly the whole of the Jewish faith," including a belief in the validity of the Old Testament covenants between G-d and the Jewish people.[10] But Judaism's self-understanding does not rely on Christianity or the New Testament. Judaism does not promote or enforce any particular view of Christianity, nor do Jews define themselves in any theological way in relation to Christianity.

Participants in Jewish-Christian dialogue need to be sensitive to the problem of asymmetry. We must try to understand another's religion on that religion's own terms.

4. *They've come further than you think to join you in conversation.* I've described how Jews can feel threatened among Christians. The reverse is also true, but in an asymmetrical way. For Jews, religion is something you're born or convert into, and once you're in, you're in. If I'm persuaded that Santa Claus flies through the skies on Christmas Eve, my fellow Jews will still regard me as Jewish. Meshuggah,[11] but Jewish. But Christian identity is a question of having the right beliefs. If a Christian questions the virgin birth, or the resurrection, or the Trinity, that Christian's status *as* a Christian may be in jeopardy. We place our beliefs at risk in dialogue with an "other"; Jews need to respect the risks Christians take in entering into dialogue with us.

5. *Walking on eggshells.* I'm frequently told in dialogue to relax and be myself. "We're not walking on eggshells here." That's wrong. We are very much walking on eggshells. We're talking *religion* here, people, and the possibilities for causing and taking offense are just about limitless. So when you speak, do so honestly, but also carefully, politely, and respectfully. And rest assured that you're sometimes going to break eggshells no matter how carefully you tread, so be ready to join your dialogue partner in cleaning up the mess that follows.

6. *Still crazy after all these (2000+) years.* From a Jewish perspective, some fundamental Christian beliefs can sound a little strange, even irrational. Virgins giving birth? G-d being in three persons, yet there being only one G-d? ($1 + 1 + 1 = 1$?) But religion is not supposed to make mathematical

---

10. Michael Novak: "Jews, Christians, and the One True G[-]d," *Crisis Maga-* zine, September 1, 2006, www.crisismagazine.com/2006/the-two-novaks-jews- christians-and-the-one-true-god.

11. Yiddish for "crazy."

sense. We Jews proclaim that we're free to choose good or evil, even though many Jews believe that G-d knows in advance everything we're going to do. That's not logical, either. Face it: there are secrets and mysteries at the heart of every religion. You can't embrace religion without tolerance for mystery.

Our Goal

In writing this book, we are inviting you into a conversation. It is not a conversation we began. Jews and Christians have been dialoguing with varying degrees of success for a very long time. You are joining a program already in progress. Nor is the program likely to end—not as long as there are Christians and Jews who continue to provide new and interesting voices to guide us. With this in mind, we invite you into this sacred and sometimes dissonant encounter. We hope that you begin to experience interreligious dialogue as a process of maturation, reevaluation, and transformation. Welcome to the table.

Part One

How We Got Here

How I Got Here

Larry Behrendt

Christianity will go. It will vanish and shrink. I needn't argue about that. I'm right and I will be proved right. We're more popular than Jesus now. I don't know which will go first—rock 'n' roll or Christianity. Jesus was all right, but his disciples were thick and ordinary. It's them twisting it that ruins it for me.

—John Lennon[1]

How did I become interested in Jewish-Christian dialogue? Here's the briefest dialogue-oriented biography I can manage. In three sentences:

1. I became interested in Christianity before I became interested in dialogue with Christians.

2. Before that, for most of my life, I was not interested in Christianity or dialogue with Christians.

3. In my lack of interest in things Christian, I was more typically Jewish than I am now.

To explain further, I need to tell my story, grounded as it is in a different place and time.

I grew up in the 1960s in a New York suburb that was mostly Jewish but also had small populations of Catholics and African-Americans. We Jewish kids went to public school with the African-American kids, and the Catholic kids mostly went to "parochial school." While the two schools were across the street from each other, they might as well have been on different

---

1. John Lennon, speaking of Jesus, religion, and the Beatles in an interview with Maureen Cleves, published in "How does a Beatle live?" *London Evening Standard*, March 4, 1966.

planets. For a time, I thought that all Christians were Catholics, and I don't remember thinking about the religion of my African-American schoolmates. That someone might be of no religion never occurred to me. Religion was something you were born into, like race.

I learned next to nothing about Christianity growing up. My parents owned a copy of *The Passover Plot*,[2] but not a New Testament. About all I knew about Christians was that they celebrated Easter and Christmas. I was a fan of the *Peanuts* comic strip, so I watched *A Charlie Brown Christmas* on TV most Decembers. On earth peace, good will toward men. "That's what Christmas is all about, Charlie Brown." I liked that just fine, but it wasn't much to go on. We sang Christmas carols every December at our mostly Jewish public school (the church-state separation thing really hadn't kicked in yet), and I didn't like them as much as Charlie Brown. "Round young virgin"? Why would she be round?

I felt no need to know more about Christianity. We Jews might be the world's oldest persecuted minority, but within the boundaries of my world, we were a comfortable majority. My neighborhood was Jewish, our parents belonged to Jewish clubs, and most of the fathers in our neighborhood worked for Jewish businesses. The Jewish doctors practiced in Jewish hospitals, and the Jewish lawyers practiced in Jewish law firms. Looking back, it might seem like I grew up in a Jewish bubble. Maybe I did . . . but that's not how it felt at the time.

Back then, I felt I was living in changing times. My family—German Jews on my father's side, Eastern European on my mother's side—was becoming less Jewish from generation to generation. We thought this was a good thing. Growing up, nearly everyone I knew was a hybrid: if not a Jewish-American, then an Italian-American, a Polish-American, or an African-American. But I assumed that the goal for all good hyphenated Americans was to stress the "American" part and eventually drop the label in front of the hyphen. Being American meant baseball, backyard barbecue, rock 'n' roll and everything else associated with the "good life." More importantly, it meant freedom, and so long as America meant freedom, there was no contest. The American life was more precious to me than the Jewish life, and I was happy to downplay the latter in order to enjoy the former. I think all my Jewish friends felt this

---

2. Hugh J. Schonfield, *The Passover Plot: New Light on the History of Jesus* (New York: Bernard Geis Associates, 1965). *The Passover Plot* was a best-selling book arguing that Jesus faked and staged his own death to inspire his fellow Jews to greater religious devotion. This book is regarded as nonsense today, and I don't remember my parents taking it seriously.

same way. We prayed not too often, and when we did pray, we did so in English and with a minimum of G-d-talk. Like ourselves, our G-d kept a low profile and was not ostentatiously religious.

It seemed like Christians were also becoming less Christian. That's the way it looked on TV and in the movies, where just about everyone I saw was Christian. At least I assumed they were Christian; they certainly weren't Jewish. But they never built a church on *Gilligan's Island*, and if *Father Knows Best* knew about Jesus, he didn't share what he knew with me. There *were* Christians on TV and in the movies who took their Christianity seriously, but outside of a Christmas special, these Christians were mostly caricatures, like the missionaries in *Guys and Dolls* who opposed people having fun. Or they were ethnic American hybrids, showing their ties to the Old World by crossing themselves or having sad-looking portraits of Jesus on their walls. Or they were the bad guys, like the fundamentalists in the movie *Inherit the Wind*, who opposed science and freedom of thought. The few good Christians I saw on TV, like Sally Field's *Flying Nun* were simply good people, perhaps more naive than most, and we knew they were good people because (like the prospective nun Maria in *The Sound of Music*) they didn't fit into a Christian world much better than we did. There was a message in this, that Christians were good when they weren't being too Christian, just as the Jews I knew all seemed to be trying to be less Jewish.

I saw a retreat from religion everywhere I looked, and it looked good to me. I knew that my American Jewish life was a whole lot better than the lives of Jews nearly everywhere else, and at just about any other time in our history. If I'd been born thirty years earlier, I could have been my dad, living in Berlin and surrounded by Nazis. If I lived in Israel, I would be confronted by hostile Arab countries all seeking my destruction. If I lived in the Soviet Union, I would have found it close to impossible to practice my religion. I may have been intent on backing away from religion, but I wanted that to be *my* choice.

I lived in good times, knowing that bad times were never far away. My family's identity began with what we had fled from. My mother's side of the family was Russian-Polish, and their escape occurred in the late nineteenth century. Their stories were about immigrant struggles and successes, but also pogroms.[3] My dad escaped Berlin with his family in 1936, barely in time

---

3. A "pogrom" is a violent riot aimed at massacre or persecution of a particular group. The term is most commonly used to refer to attacks on Jewish communities in Russia and Poland in the late nineteenth and early twentieth centuries. These particular pogroms led to mass Jewish immigration to the United States and other countries.

to avoid Kristallnacht and the death camps. This was part of my lesson of growing up Jewish, that beneath the genial surface of my ordinary suburban life lay the memory of murder. The German Jews had thought they were safe before Hitler arrived. You could never be certain. Your mother might tuck you in at night, but there could be monsters under the bed.

True story. In 1963, my family moved to Los Angeles for a year, and my mother placed my three-year-old sister in a nursery school run by a local church. My mother was told that the church's nursery school was not religious, but she had her doubts, and at the first opportunity she had my five-year-old sister attend the school as well, to check it out. Evidently the five-year-old took this responsibility seriously, because at the end of the school day she ran out the church screaming, "They sang Jesus loves me! They sang Jesus loves me!" This story became one of my mother's favorites; she'd describe how she stood there, red-faced in front of an uncomprehending group of Gentile mothers, while my sister pointed accusingly at the church doors. My mother told the story to poke fun at herself, at her own unfounded suspicion that a little church preschool might be trying to steal Jewish souls. But as I remember it, my mother found another nursery school for my youngest sister to attend.

It's an exaggeration to say so, but Christianity was something like a monster under my childhood bed. It was something to fear, even if I wasn't sure the fearsome thing was really there. Then again, it could be that the monsters were real, and the good, safe, American Jewish life was the illusion. We Jews had felt safe before, and the safety had never lasted. *The German Jews had thought they were safe, too.* Yet religious difference was unavoidable—*religion was something you were born into.* The hope was to be religiously different in a place like America, where religion seemed to grow less important by the minute. Gradually, the threat posed by Christianity might disappear, as religion receded further into the background, eventually to "go . . . vanish and shrink," just like John Lennon had said.

In the meantime, the Jewish goal was to live separate from and unnoticed by Christianity.

⌗

I figured that religion would decline nationwide as I got older, and I could not have been more right . . . if I had lived in a different nation. Study after study shows precipitous declines in religious observance throughout the industrialized world, with the United States being the only exception. The respected Pew Research Center stated it succinctly in the following 2002 headline: "Among Wealthy Nations, U.S. Stands Alone In Its Embrace of Religion." According to that study, 59 percent of people in the U.S. say religion plays a very important role in their lives, compared to just 30 percent in neighboring Canada, 27 percent in Italy, 21 percent in Germany, 12 percent in Japan, and 11 percent in France.[4]

As I reached adulthood and grew older, the presence of Christianity in my larger world seemed to be growing, not shrinking. Conservative Christians began to shape American politics, even insisting that biblical creation be taught alongside evolution in some school districts. It made me wonder whether the Christian "villains" I'd once identified in *Inherit The Wind* were trying to rewrite the movie's ending. It began to dawn on me . . . if I was going to live in America as even a halfway intelligent person, I would eventually have to learn something about Christianity.

My attitude toward Judaism was also changing. I married a lapsed Protestant, and seemingly out of nowhere I insisted that our children be raised Jewish. *Religion was something you were born into.* I could not have my children born into someone else's religion. My wife relented and later converted to Judaism. I had talked the talk, and as a result found myself with a Jewish wife and daughter, both of whom expected me to walk the walk.

We chose a synagogue. In 2004, the synagogue chose to give a presentation on the issues surrounding Mel Gibson's movie *The Passion of the Christ*. And I was hooked.

It's been thirteen years since Gibson's movie was released, but the movie remains controversial. Sister Rose Pacatte penned an article marking the tenth anniversary of the film's release, and the article's title says it all: "A decade later, 'The Passion' still raises questions of anti-Semitism."[5] Gibson's movie focuses on the last twelve hours of Jesus' life, and Gibson chose to portray Jesus' torture and crucifixion with a bloody realism that made the

---

4. "Among Wealthy Nations U.S. Stands Alone in Its Embrace of Religion," Pew Research Center, December 19, 2002, www.pewglobal.org/2002/12/19/among-wealthy-nations/. See also "Unfavorable Views of Jews and Muslims on the Increase in Europe," The Pew Global Attitudes Project, September 17, 2008, www.pewglobal. org/files/2008/09/Pew-2008-Pew-Global-Attitudes-Report-3-September-17-2pm. pdf.

5. Sr. Rose Pacatte, "A decade later, 'The Passion' still raises questions of anti-Semitism," *National Catholic Reporter*, February 22, 2014, https://www.ncronline. org/news/art-media/decade-later-passion-still-raises-questions-anti-semitism.

movie difficult for many to watch (full disclosure: I've never watched it). One famous review called the film "a two-hour-and-six-minute snuff movie—The Jesus Chainsaw Massacre—that thinks it's an act of faith."[6] Other reviews were strongly positive. Deacon Keith Fournier wrote for Catholic Online that the movie "evoked more deep reflection, sorrow and emotional reaction within me than anything since my wedding, my ordination or the birth of my children."[7]

The movie was controversial in the Jewish community for other reasons. According to scholar Adele Reinhartz, Gibson's movie "identifies the Jews as the instruments of Satan, the material agents . . . who initiate the events that led to Jesus' death."[8] We Jews can be sensitive about how we are portrayed in the Passion story. So-called passion plays were popular in medieval and early Renaissance Europe, and frequently, Christians were so inflamed by these plays that they'd leave the performance to attack local Jewish communities. The Oberammergau Passion Play continues to be performed to this day, and continues to be controversial. "It is vital that the Passion play be continued at Oberammergau," Adolf Hitler said in 1934. "For never has the menace of Jewry been so convincingly portrayed as in this presentation of what happened in the time of the Romans."[9] "The Passion narratives have been a lethal weapon against Jews," according to Sister Mary Boys, and she said so in an NPR piece about Gibson's film.[10]

So, the question of Gibson's *Passion* was of keen interest to Jews. At our synagogue's discussion of *The Passion of the Christ*, I remember the sense

---

6. David Edelstein, "Jesus H. Christ: The Passion, Mel Gibson's bloody mess" Slate, February 24, 2004, http://www.slate.com/articles/arts/movies/2004/02/jesus_h_christ.html. A "snuff movie" is a film showing an actual murder—someone is actually killed on screen. Of course, Gibson didn't actually kill anyone in the making of his movie. Edelstein is utilizing a metaphor here.

7. Deacon Keith Fournier, "Film Review: The Passion of Christ," Catholic Online, August 11, 2008, https://www.catholic.org/news/national/story.php?id=28863.

8. Adele Reinhartz, "Jesus of Hollywood," in *On The Passion of the Christ: Exploring the Issues Raised by the Controversial Movie*, ed. Paula Fredriksen (Berkeley: University of California Press, 2006), 178.

9. See James Shapiro, *Oberammergau: The Troubling Story of the World's Most Famous Passion Play* (New York: Vintage Books, 2001), 28.

10. Sr. Mary Boys, "History of Passion Plays and Why Jews are Concerned about Renewed Anti-Semitism Resulting from Mel Gibson's Film 'The Passion of The Christ,'" *NPR*, February 22, 2003, www.npr.org/programs/wesun/transcripts/2004/feb/040222.passion.html. Boys is a scholar and long-time participant in Jewish-Christian dialogue.

of fear. It is key to Jewish survival to know when you're no longer safe. *The German Jews had thought they were safe, too.* We know we're not safe when a passion play is being performed nearby. What would happen when a passion play was performed simultaneously at thousands of movie theaters worldwide?

Another question still sticks with me: How could the making of such a movie possibly be more important to Christians than the risk (however small) that Jews might be hurt in the process?

But one other question from our synagogue discussion also sticks with me. The speaker argued that Matthew 27:25 should not have been included in Gibson's film.[11] In Matthew 27:25, Matthew has Pilate claim that he is innocent of Jesus' blood, and the Jewish people "as a whole" answer, "His blood be on us and on our children!" Matthew 27:25 is probably the most historically lethal phrase in the New Testament. It has been interpreted by Christians throughout most of Christian history as an admission of Jewish guilt *for all time* for the death of Jesus, effectively justifying whatever calamities might be visited on Jews from any source and in any age.

I well knew the calamities that followed from Christian anti-Judaism, but thirteen years ago I did not understand the nature of Christian Scripture. Was it really true that so much hatred could flow from a single passage in a single Gospel? I thought at first, since Matthew 27:25 is in the Christian Bible, how can we Jews possibly expect Gibson to omit it from his Bible movie? As much as I might like Gibson to express his Christianity in a Jewish-friendly way, how could Jews claim the right to tell Christians how to tell their sacred story? But as I learned during the lecture, the scene in Matthew 27:25 is *only* in Matthew. The Jews "as a whole" do *not* curse themselves throughout eternity in the Gospels of Mark, Luke, or John. If this curse is omitted from three Gospels out of four, it could also be omitted from Gibson's movie.

What I realized during that lecture was simple: *Jesus' story could be told biblically in different ways.* Moreover, the consequences of *how* this story are told are immense. The story could be told in a way that pleased Hitler. It could be told in a way that fit into an animated *Peanuts* Christmas special. *Jewish* lives depend on the telling of the Christian story. It dawned on me that Jews should be active in how this story is told.

---

11. Gibson's film is performed mostly in Aramaic, with subtitles. While the text of Matthew 27:25 is spoken in the film in Aramaic, Gibson did respond to Jewish and other protests by removing the subtitle translating the Aramaic.

Silly me. At the time, Jews *were* active in reforming the telling of this story. Some of the top scholars in the field of Gospel study are Jewish, including at least three that are superstars: Paula Fredriksen, Amy-Jill Levine, and Adele Reinhartz. Of course, if I'd *known* this thirteen years ago, I would probably have concluded that we Jews had the situation well in hand, and I would have gone on to study ancient pottery. But unimpeded by the knowledge that my fellow Jews were already on the case, I decided to learn what a twenty-first-century Jew ought to know about Jesus and the Gospels. I decided to buy a book. I figured one book ought to satisfy my curiosity. It didn't. I decided to buy another. And another. Thirteen years later, my curiosity remains unsatisfied.

Most of the Jews I encounter think that my fascination with early Christianity is . . . odd. More than a few think that I've gone off the deep end. In turn, I don't get why they don't get it. Christianity is the largest and most powerful religion in the world. Moreover, if you take the story of how Christianity got to be what it is and look at it with Jewish eyes, the story becomes the greatest mystery ever told. Through Jewish eyes, Jesus is just an ordinary Jew with some extraordinary abilities, and Christianity arises without any special assistance from the Holy Spirit. How, then, did Christianity manage to get off the ground? How did someone like the apostle Paul persuade Gentiles that something special had happened in a backwater of the empire among a group (the Jews) not particularly loved by Greeks or Romans? Amid the greater mysteries are a host of smaller ones. Why did Paul scarcely mention the events of Jesus' life in his letters? Did he not know about them? How did the Gospels (four anonymous and confusingly interrelated reports of the life of Jesus) come to be written in the first place, and why did it take so long (according to scholars, roughly forty years) after the death of Jesus for the first Gospel to be written? Why did the early Christians largely abandon writing in scrolls and adopt the codex (book) for their early writings, nearly three hundred years in advance of the rest of the world? I figure that all the smaller mysteries add up to a big mystery just aching to be solved, but the solution remains tantalizingly out of reach; it's a cliffhanger that never gets old. Not for me, anyway.

As much as I enjoy studying Christianity, I've never lost the sense that there's a danger in it. I feel a greater sympathy now for how my mother must have felt fifty years ago, sending her youngest daughter to a church preschool. There is a nagging sense that I don't belong here, that with the New Testament I am reading a forbidden book, and one that has been forbidden for good reason. Here's an example of what I mean. About eight years ago I started to read every book in the New Testament, not in the order they appear in the Christian Bible, but chronologically, in the order scholars think they were written. I figured, *this* would give me a sense of how Christianity developed! I started with what I thought was the earliest of these books, Paul's First Epistle to the Thessalonians.[12] I could not proceed two pages into this earliest of Christian books without confronting the following:

> For you, brothers and sisters, became imitators of the churches of G[-]d in Christ Jesus that are in Judea, for you suffered the same things from your own compatriots as they did from the Jews, who killed both the L[-]rd Jesus and the prophets, and drove us out; they displease G[-]d and oppose everyone by hindering us from speaking to the Gentiles so that they may be saved. Thus they have constantly been filling up the measure of their sins; but G[-]d's wrath has overtaken them at last. (1 Thess. 2:14–16)

It is there, from the very beginning of the very first Christian writing: a "succinct summary of classical Christian anti-Judaism"[13]—we Jews are Christ-killers, rejected by G-d. It is heartbreaking. There is anti-Judaism in the very first pages of Christianity, shortly after the first mention of peace and love, and before any mention of repentance, forgiveness, and grace. It is as if the Christian tradition is saying to me, forget about searching for an essence of Christianity apart from hatred of Jews; it is not there. It has taken me years to learn that I need to see Christianity through the eyes of my Christian friends, that the true essence of Christianity is love of neighbor, even if this true essence has been frequently forgotten over the years, particularly when the neighbor of the Christian was Jewish.

Why, then, do I persist in this effort? Why engage in Jewish-Christian dialogue? The best answer is the simplest: Christianity is interesting to me, and I'd like to talk about it. If there were Jews interested in the discussion, I suppose I'd engage in intra-faith dialogue. But as it turned out, nearly everyone who cares to discuss these matters with me is Christian.

---

12. Many scholars argue that Galatians is older than 1 Thessalonians. I relied on the dating of Paul's letters in Raymond E. Brown, *An Introduction to the New Testament* (New York: Doubleday, 1997), 433.

13. *The Jewish Annotated New Testament*, ed Amy-Jill Levine and Marc Z. Brettler (New York: Oxford University Press, 2011), 374. This summary is by David Fox Sandmel, who notes that some scholars believe this passage is an interpolation that was not written by Paul. Sandmel himself concludes that the Pauline authorship of this passage should be presumed.

There's another reason. Some Jews approach the question of interfaith dialogue as if we have a choice. We do not. We live in a larger world, inside of a larger culture, and that world and its culture speak constantly to us, sometimes out loud and sometimes silently. We are influenced by this speech, even if the core of who we are remains quintessentially and characteristically Jewish. Since this speech exists, we should engage it consciously. We should say our piece.

I'll mention one last reason, the primary reason that's driven me to co-write this book. I believe in the dialogue of possibility. By this I mean not that we should talk about what is possible, but instead we should talk in a way that opens the widest possibility for things to say and ways to say it. In this, I go back to how I was taught to conduct an interview. I was taught to leave "yes or no" questions to a minimum. *Ask open-ended questions.* Take your interviewee (nicely, gently) to unfamiliar places. Ask things they've never been asked before. Ask in a way where the answer might go in any direction, or many directions.

Please understand: my best dialogue with my fellow Jews is a dialogue of expansive possibility. But there are possibilities in dialogue with an "other" that simply are not present in a discussion between like types. With Anthony, dialogue turns in directions I've never gone, into territory I'm not sure of. In the process, I change.

Let the conversation begin.

My G-d Had a Jewish Mother

Anthony Le Donne

I conclude that if someone had followed Jesus out of a restaurant and asked him who he was, he would have answered that he was a Jew. If pressed, he might say that he was a Jewish Jew, and if pressed further, he would say that he was Mr. Jewish Jewy McJew Jew.

—Larry Behrendt

How did I become interested in Jewish-Christian dialogue? For me—to quote *Cool Hand Luke* out of context—it was about getting my mind right. Or to misquote Yoda, I had to unlearn what I had learned.

The reasons that Christians might want to engage in Jewish-Christian dialogue are several, manifold, and complex. Some of us are trying to live out Jesus' commandment to love our neighbors in this particular way. Perhaps we've realized our role in the countless sins of anti-Semitism in history. Some of us might be attempting a penance of some kind. Perhaps trying to understand and be understood is an attempt at "kingdom come" and "peace on earth."

Some Christians are attracted to dialogue for other reasons. I know that I have felt some degree of "holy envy" from time to time.[1] There is a sense among many Christians that Jews occupy unique spiritual real estate. Some Christians are simply curious. I would imagine that other Christians have the secret hope that their Jewish friends will convert (although, I believe and hope that this is decreasing and will continue to decrease as we learn more about our Jewish neighbors). According to a 2013 Pew study, an important component of Jewish self-identity is a "good sense of humor." Could be that many Christians find Jewish-Christian dialogue invigorating because of the

---

1. We discuss the term "holy envy" in the introduction to this book.

laughter involved. I know this continues to be a factor in my involvement. But none of the above represents my primary attraction to Jewish-Christian dialogue.

When Larry and I first met, we were both well along the path of dialogue. For my part, I had been academically invested in Judaism for almost two decades, my fascination and admiration ever increasing. I took my first Hebrew Bible class in 1994. I took my first Hebrew language class in 1999. But I think that my journey toward Jewish-Christian dialogue began long before I knew what would come of my interests.

In the Christian Sunday school of my childhood, Jews were Israelites and Israelites were ancient peoples in stories alongside rivers of blood, angelic hosts, giants, and talking animals. They were the central characters in G-d's Story. The late Rich Mullins (a Christian musician from my youth) was right to say that such stories make boys grow bold and men walk straight. I think this was true in my case. I learned from the boy-king David to be brave. I learned from the prophet Daniel to be righteous. And to the extent that I am a good man now, my parents and pastors are to be thanked for inviting me into those magical stories about Israelites. *Who would I be without those stories?*

Sacred stories possess transformative power. For good and ill, my masculinity, my politics, my religious outlook, and my vocation were shaped by the ancient Israelites. Or, at least, these identity markers were shaped by Israelites in their storied form, as seen through a particular ideological lens. And this is where *Cool Hand Luke* and Yoda become necessary teachers. Because, you see, my perception of Jews was quite narrow and distorted. Jews were characters in stories. Even in my adolescent awareness of the Holocaust, Jews were European victims of World War II. Jewish life was something that I studied in history books. I knew that there were Jews in the modern world in the same way that I knew that there were Amish communities or Eskimos. I never had the opportunity to humanize or complicate my picture-book imagination.

I grew up evangelical in the 1970s and '80s. We evangelicals loved Jesus, had a very high regard for the Bible, hoped for eternity in heaven, and yearned to make the world a better place. At least these were the markers of evangelical Christianity when I was young. Allow me to point out that the first two of these markers anchored us in the historic past. Our spirituality and well-being in the present rooted us to an ancient figure and an ancient text. The right understandings of Jesus and the Bible were crucial to us—to me. I've been devoted to reading the Bible and relating to Jesus for as long as I can remember.

Somewhere along the way I realized that both the Bible and Jesus were Jewish. It may seem strange that this had not always been obvious to me. After all, Israelites of all kinds colored my imagination. I suppose that it was the category "Jewish" that gave me pause.

As I learned more and more about Jesus, I found that—in word, deed, and theological impact—he was a Jew deeply invested in the Jews and Jewish worship. As Jesus emerged from my study of history, I realized that Jesus wasn't just ethnically Jewish. Spiritually, religiously, politically, Jesus was a Jew and remained a Jew for his whole life. Or as Larry once quipped, Jesus was a "Jewy Jew."

Reinforcing this revelation was a statement that was almost a mantra among Bible professors at the Christian University I attended: *You simply cannot understand the New Testament unless you understand how Jews were interpreting the Hebrew Scriptures in the first century.* During these years, Judaism had become more than an interesting neighbor; it had become essential and central. After extensive study of the Dead Sea Scrolls, Philo, Josephus, and so on, I concluded that the New Testament could only be understood when read alongside other Jewish texts from the same period. It is, in large part, a collection of Jewish texts, composed by Jews, on the topic of Jewish theology. I don't think that any of the authors of the Hebrew Bible or the New Testament ever considered that their words might be read by millions of non-Jewish worshippers who might never meet a Jew.

Most Christians throughout the ages have believed that Jesus was the unique expression of G-d in human form. In other words, if the Creator were to become created, we'd get Jesus. In the words of Jesus provided by John's Gospel, "Whoever has seen me has seen the Father" (John 14:9). If believed, when G-d became human, G-d became Jewish. Of course, this makes sense with what I read in Hebrew Scripture. When the Creator spoke to Moses, it was in Hebrew. When the "Father" chose to adopt children, they were the children of Israel. Jesus' mother was Jewish. Jesus was a Jew.

I'm not.

If I'd have witnessed whatever Moses witnessed, I'd have been an intruder. If I'd have witnessed Jesus preach the "Sermon on the Mount," I wouldn't have understood a word. The Torah was not shipped to my doorstep via Amazon Prime. I am removed in time, place, culture, and language from these special revelations. St. Paul asks, "Is G[-]d the G[-]d of Jews only? Is he not the G[-]d of Gentiles also?" Paul (himself Jewish) then answers his own question, "Yes, of Gentiles" (Rom. 3:29). This would seem to include me. Even so, it is difficult to skip past the thoroughgoing

Jewishness of the G-d we meet in the Bible. Indeed, this was Paul's difficulty long before it was mine.

Paul is just one among hundreds of Jewish voices who contributes to the various theologies, debates, and narratives that comprise my Bible. I benefit from these voices, but they very seldom represent me as a Gentile. And somehow, my identity—*the core of who I am*—is tied to the religious experiences of these ancient Jewish theologians.

It didn't take long for me to recognize that many of the scholars who were best prepared to provide insight along these lines were Jews. They were Jews, or they were Christians who were deeply invested in Jewish scholarship and Jewish well-being. This began in friendship with a Christian friend of mine, Joel Lohr. Joel is a very careful reader. Joel appreciates sacred texts in and of themselves, not for how they might be leveraged toward an agenda. He is also the kind of person who always has his hands on really interesting books. It was Joel who first introduced me to Jewish authors such as Leonard Greenspoon, Joel Kaminsky, and Jon Levenson. In New Testament studies, I've appreciated the insights of Michael Cook, Amy-Jill Levine, Adele Reinhartz, and many others. These scholarly voices have been nothing short of life-changing. This is how I came to be interested in Jewish-Christian dialogue. My path toward a better understanding of Jesus and the authors of the Bible brought me here.

But while my study of Judaism (ancient and modern) occupied much of my time, and while I was interested in dialogue, I was still not engaged in face-to-face encounter. I had matured beyond my picture-book imagination. My media resources for the study of modern Jews and Judaism had changed. But even with a more academic approach, my ability to humanize and complicate my understanding of Jews and Judaism was woefully untrained. I had unlearned some of what I had learned, but I hadn't yet gotten my mind right.

One of the lessons that I learned in face-to-face Jewish-Christian dialogue, friendship, and collaboration is twofold: (1) the academic study of Jewish history had not prepared me for real-world intercultural encounter; and (2) those picture-book images of ancient Israelites became obstacles that I needed to overcome. It wasn't until I learned this that I realized that Jewish-Christian dialogue was a requirement for my maturity as a Christian. While the ancient Israelites helped to shape my childhood Christianity, my Jewish friends and mentors have shaped my adult Christianity. I imagine that many Christians actively engaged in interreligious dialogue feel the same way.

But while I may have come to the table seeking better conversation partners toward a better understanding of Jesus and the Bible, my years of dialogue have had numerous, unexpected, and delightful by-products. Some of these by-products have kept me interested and invested in ways I couldn't have previously imagined.

Chief among these unexpected benefits is this: I believe that I have matured as a Christian in ways I would not have without Jewish conversation partners. One of these ways relates to my experience of reading sacred texts.

I have come to love reading the Bible alongside Jewish readers. Reading the Bible in conversation with Jewish scholarship continues to expand my literary palette. Imagine that you've only ever eaten Hershey's chocolate. Then one day you're given a dark chocolate truffle handmade in Belgium. This analogy conveys something of my experience in reading Jon Levenson's *The Death and Resurrection of the Beloved Son*. It could be the best book ever written in biblical studies, yet few Christians have ever heard of it.

A conversation I recently had with Larry illustrates my point from another angle. Larry invited me to his synagogue a few months ago where I experienced no little degree of "holy envy." After hearing the teaching of Rabbi Laura Geller, I expressed my appreciation to Larry. Larry agreed, saying, "She's a talented teacher; my Bible is bigger after synagogue than it was before."

Allow me to reiterate in italics: *My Bible is bigger after synagogue than it was before.* This does *not* describe my experience in most Christian worship services. Indeed, Larry's words might describe the opposite of most of Christian preaching. Much of Christian preaching takes a passage of the Bible and distills it to a simple nugget of applicable advice. Christians tend to reduce the Bible toward simplicity. The rabbis I've had the pleasure of learning from teach by questioning, problematizing, and expanding possible interpretations. Very often a "best reading" emerges, but the process is one that expands rather than reduces.

In my upbringing, a large part of being a good Christian was being a good Bible reader. By this measurement, the Jewish voices in my life have made me a better Christian.

In addition to my academic interests, I've also appreciated Jewish friendship along a more "pastoral" line. I have experienced years of G-d's silence. I have experienced G-d's hiddenness profoundly. In these respects and others, I have found companionship with biblical authors. The theologians who wrote lament psalms, Ecclesiastes, and Jonah have created sacred space for my disappointments, doubts, and dark humor. These are, as Christians believe, elements of Holy Scripture. Even so, most Christians are not comfortable with overt expressions of disappointment with G-d, doubt, and dark humor.

We tend to express these dispositions in hushed tones and almost never in the company of the more happy-clappy churchgoers among us. I have had good Christian friends who have understood me and worshipped with me despite my dispositions. But, for whatever reason, my Jewish friends have been invaluable conversation partners on these topics. For one thing, my experience of G-d's silence is not seen as shortcoming among my Jewish friends.

Perhaps most importantly, my Jewish friends have fortified my identity as a Christian. They do so by reminding me that my faith does not hinge on my own beliefs and inclinations. In my Jewish conversation partners, I have found examples of authentic belonging without concern for personal merit. It could be that I have become a better Calvinist by dialoguing with Jews.

At times I've found that my Jewish mentors have coaxed me toward a more Christian mind-set. A few years ago I was e-mailing Rabbi Michael Cook, a New Testament specialist at Hebrew Union College. In an e-mail exchange, I used the expression "oh geez!" I would normally use stronger language, but Michael is sort of a grandfather figure—maybe I was channeling my inner Eddie Haskell. Michael corrected me, writing, "You're a Christian. You shouldn't say 'geez' as it is a shortened curse for Jesus." I've never asked Michael if this was a serious concern or if he was just joking. *But does it matter?* Either way—either by holiness or humor—it enhanced my well-being as a Christian. Not because it made me more pious, but because I internalized his compassion for my faith. This too is part of getting my mind right: my Christian identity is enhanced by external reinforcement.

But as my friend Leonard Greenspoon reminds me, there is a danger in having too high an opinion of any particular people, and the same goes for Jewish folk. Leonard acknowledges that there are brilliant and deeply spiritual mature Jews out there. You also might encounter rowdy and raucous folks who defy easy characterization and organization. This is what I mean when I say that my early impressions of Jews required humanization and complication.

I am still trying to get my mind right.

How We Got Here

Dialogue

Anthony: One of the things that you said in your chapter, and it's something that I've heard from other Jewish friends as well—is that, for many Jews, Christianity is something to be feared.

Larry: Yes. I wanted to bring out this "fear factor" in my chapter.

Anthony: It's more than a truism to say that we generally fear what we don't understand. But as far as a self-identifying Jew goes, you know a lot more about Christianity than most.

Larry: Yes, that's right.

Anthony: And the fear has not gone away.

Larry: No. It's diminished. But this has not been a smooth process. Part of learning about Christianity was discovering things to fear that I hadn't known were there. The story of Christian anti-Judaism does not get prettier when you look at it closely. On the other hand, if there's one thorough-going positive in this journey for me, it's been my encounter with Christians.

Anthony: And I'm guessing that a lot of these Christians have not tried to convert you.

Larry: I've had very little of that, personally.

Anthony: I can point you in the direction of four churches around here where that would happen.

Larry: It would be an interesting experiment! And we might try it.

Anthony: [*Laughs*] Let's not try it.

Larry: I'm not going to try it today! But the Christians who encounter me, who may be very . . . can I say very "evangelical" in this sense, would that be the right word?

Anthony: "Evangelical" is a vague term, but I think that when you say it, most people have the image of a Billy Graham to Jerry Falwell range—Billy Graham being the best possible example and Jerry Falwell being the worst possible example. And those people who don't like Billy Graham just think that being evangelical is bad. So if you use that term, you have to understand that a lot of people are just going to think that's a bad thing.[1]

Larry: I was looking for a better term. How do I refer to a Christian who is seeking converts?

Anthony: Evangelical.

Larry: Then let's stick with that term, knowing what we mean by it. I've had remarkably meaningful encounters with Christians, even Christians who are evangelical, even Christians who may have come to the encounter with the hope of converting me. And I think at a certain point it will dawn on these people that if they want to be evangelical with me, the best way to do it is by witness, by personal example. It should also be relatively clear to anyone who encounters me that I'm not a big fan of overt proselytization. I find it an unattractive quality.

---

1. Elsewhere in the dialogue, Anthony gave Larry the following definition of "evangelical," using four criteria: "(1) Evangelicals love G-d, specifically through Jesus . . . not to say that they don't love G-d in other ways. (2) They are missional in orientation, in other words, they feel like they are on a mission. The mission could be about opposing human trafficking, it could be about seeking converts, it could be environmental, but they've got a mission; they think G-d wants them to do something in the world. (3) They are eschatalogically oriented; that's a fancy way of saying that they have a hope of heaven. They have an idea about an eventual future reality whereby they will experience G-d more fully. (4) This may be the most important: they have a high view of scripture, Genesis through Revelation. It's almost a supernatural book; it communicates the very mind of G-d to us. There may be other moving parts, but these four points are central to who evangelicals are, and how they view themselves."

Anthony: Well yeah, but one thing I would like to emphasize is that a lot of Christians you meet would not know that you find proselytization to be unattractive.

Larry: I understand that Christians do not proselytize out of a desire to destroy me, but they do it out of love.

Anthony: [*Groans*]

Larry: I truly believe that. I can go even further and say that even the evangelical desire for Jews to all return to Israel, to bring the last days to the fore, where only a remnant of us are going to survive . . . even that's done out of love.

Anthony: I don't know about the second part of that. [*Laughs*] I think it may be done out of a sense of triumph.

Larry: Those things aren't incompatible.

Anthony: Ah . . . but they don't coexist very well!

Larry: I've tried to indicate that just because I don't like proselytization, this doesn't prevent me from seeing that a person who proselytizes might still be a fine person.

Anthony: And you're an interesting case, because in a very bizarre kind of way, you might actually enjoy the experience of someone trying to convert you to Christianity, simply so you can see how the person ticks.

Larry: When my doorbell rings on a Saturday (it's invariably on a Saturday), and there are two young Christian missionaries on my doorstep who want to give me a pamphlet and invite me to a lecture, or see a film . . . am I tempted to invite them in for coffee and talk to them because I want to find out what makes them tick? I have never done it, because what I'm afraid of is that they'll walk out of my house with their faith shaken . . .

Anthony: That's funny, because when I encounter missionaries, I worry about the same thing. We were using the word *evangelical* earlier. Those two young people knocking on your door? Chances are that evangelicals would not consider them co-religionists. Rightly or wrongly, most evangelicals would not consider a Mormon or a Jehovah's Witness to be a Christian. Like

I said, rightly or wrongly. But those are probably the people knocking on your door. From your eyes, they are Christian, but it's an ugly part of our projection of otherness: we've got a lot of venom for people who look very Christian but who we don't consider Christian.

Larry: I do try to identify people denominationally when they come to the door, but often they don't like to be identified that way.

Anthony: That's exactly right.

Larry: But to answer your question—the idea that a Christian might encounter me with some evangelical purpose in mind, and then leave the encounter with doubts—well, maybe it would be good for them. But I wouldn't sleep well. I want my Christian friends to be good Christians. It's not that I'm afraid of being proselytized. I don't find it a pleasant experience . . .

Anthony: And that makes you typically Jewish, because I don't think there are a lot of Jews I've met in my life who are worried that at some point they might accidentally convert against their better judgment. It's just an offensive thing. They find proselytization offensive.

Larry: You know a highly self-confident population of Jews, because most of the Jews you know are in academics.

Anthony: That's true.

Larry: I think there is always a fear of the unknown. How do you account for the negative attitude most Jews have toward the New Testament? One factor is the feeling that the New Testament can lead you away from Judaism. I think there is a general fear about associating with the wrong people, reading the wrong books . . . It is like raising your children, you know that your kids are good kids, you know they want to do the right thing, but you worry about the kids they hang around with after school. You worry about the parents of those kids. The company you keep is important, and there's a Jewish feeling that the New Testament is not good company. Now, I have spent enough time in the New Testament to know that there is no danger for me in the New Testament.

Anthony: Then where *is* the danger? You said in your chapter, even with this last decade of experience of the Christian encounter, you still feel a sense of danger, however moderate.

Larry: The fear is not just about the New Testament. There is a perceived danger in the Jewish-Christian encounter. As a whole, we Jews would rather not deal with you Christians. The Jewish fantasy is to be left alone.

Anthony: So, this brings us to the next thing: the Jewish fantasy is to be left alone. Which *is* a fantasy.

Larry: Yes.

Anthony: Jews have always had to negotiate a larger cultural matrix. The Egyptians, the Canaanites, the Babylonians, the Romans, you name it. The Christians.

Larry: The Greeks. Possibly the biggest negotiation we ever had was with the Greeks.

Anthony: You're living in New York, in Israel—these are very multicultural places. Your life is about negotiating non-Jewish presences, peoples, neighbors. So, this fantasy is not helpful!

Larry: No, it's not. But is this fantasy purely Jewish? I see plenty of Christians who seem to prefer life in a Christian bubble. Here's one example. You wrote in your chapter about the realization that Jesus and the New Testament are thoroughly Jewish. You had this realization most profoundly when you attended a Christian liberal arts university. I went online to see who teaches at this institution, and I couldn't find a Jew on the faculty. There are no Jewish professors of Christian thought at your alma mater?

Anthony: Can a Jew believe that Jesus Christ is his L-rd and Savior?

Larry: That's not a Jewish belief.

Anthony: Well, that's why. You have to sign a Christian confessional statement to teach at my alma mater.

Larry: I cannot resist this: How can a Christian get a Christian education about the Jewish Jesus and the Jewish New Testament without an exposure to a Jewish teacher?

Anthony: [*In an embarrassed voice*] We had Jewish scholars come and lecture.

Larry: Well, that's something, that's good.

Anthony: [*Laughs*]

Larry: That's better than nothing.

Anthony: No, it's a real issue. And probably common practice at most evangelical colleges with a required faith statement.

Larry: You are talking about the Jewishness of Jesus being taught at an institution that will not allow a Jew on the faculty. That's weird.

Anthony: That is weird.

Larry: The only role for a Jew at your alma mater is as the Savior. That's weird.

Anthony: The rule is not aimed at Jews. It's about not being Christian. Not only that, certain kinds of Christians could not sign off on that faith statement. I could not sign that faith statement. I couldn't teach at my alma mater.

Larry: I can't let this irony go.

Anthony: You want to know how an administrator might answer this question?

Larry: Yes.

Anthony: "Yeah, we will hire a Jew. As long as he or she signs our faith statement."

Larry: The question that pops into my mind is, could *Jesus* sign this faith statement? I think it's obvious, that even if he could have signed, he would have refused to do so as a matter of principle. It would have meant that no one who had ever taught him, any of his teachers, no one in the entire world that he grew up with could be included in the faculty!

Anthony: [*Laughs*]

Larry: You're laughing, but that's what you are saying here. You said in your chapter that you realized "Jesus was Jewish. I'm not." It sounds to me like you are describing a moment of alienation.

Anthony: Yes, but in a context. For example: if you were to transport me into the story, the narrative of Moses, then as a Gentile I would not have belonged in that story.

Larry: Why not?

Anthony: Gentiles have a bad time in that story.

Larry: You're not an Egyptian.

Anthony: I'm not, you're right. I'm kind of a Roman, though.

Larry: [*Laughs*] Now, you are really getting anachronistic!

Anthony: Well, this is an anachronistic realization. The Christian position is to read ourselves into every story, but after realizing that my holy scripture was Jewish, I could not read it in the same way. Here's another example. I went up to one of my professors early on in my educational experience and asked, "What kind of evidence can you give me from the Gospels that Jesus was G-d?" And he said, "Whoa! I think that there's good evidence in the Gospels to suggest that Jesus was the Messiah. Let's stick with that." So, this *is* a certain moment of alienation for me, to come to this realization that not everything attributed to Jesus in the year 300, or the year 600, or whatever, all these creeds, can be supported when you read the texts of the New Testament very closely.

Larry: In your chapter, you did a very interesting thing: you linked your discussion about coming into closer contact with Judaism, with a discussion about your "disappointment with G-d."

Anthony: Okay, let me say more about that. I don't view Scripture like I did before. I don't view mission like I did before; my view of heaven is different. In all of these ways, I might be unrecognizable to my nineteen-year-old self. And as I changed, there's a certain alienation that went along with it, feeling like, "I don't think I could worship in the denomination I grew up in," because I probably would not be accepted there if I honestly described the ways I have changed. But for Jews, this kind of change and honesty about it is less of an issue. I can go to your synagogue, Larry, and find a handful of members in good standing who are atheists! So my evolving belief in the biblical G-d wouldn't be all that scandalous.

Larry: More than a handful.

Anthony: Yeah, sure. It would not be an issue, and those people are not kicked out! [*Laughs*] They are not made to feel ostracized, and there's something comforting about that kind of worshiping community, where you can be honest and say, "My faith looks different now than it did when I was 10 years old." And I don't feel I can find that in most evangelical churches.

Larry: My synagogue might be more that way than, say, an Orthodox synagogue. I understand what you're saying, but the way you phrased it, what you describe sounds less like "disappointment with G-d," and more like disappointment with Christianity.

Anthony: Well, these two things are connected. There are certain Christian avenues in place by which we recognize G-d, experience G-d, and believe in G-d, and those avenues are all interconnected. When the avenues no longer work, there is a sense of feeling alienated from G-d.

Larry: And alienation is disappointment?

Anthony: Well, disappointment is part of it for sure. For me, I feel that my theological education has led me to redefine lots of categories in my life. It's inevitable, you know? But there's not a whole lot of room in the evangelical world for your mind to change on these particular issues. If your mind does change, you have to find solace elsewhere. "I used to be an evangelical, and now I'm a mainliner." "I used to be an evangelical, and now I'm an agnostic." But I realized somewhere along the line: "Look, I'm not going to be something other than evangelical." Ultimately, these are the cards I was dealt. In this realization, I was encouraged by Jewish friends who view their Judaism in this way. "Judaism is something I was born into; it's not something I'm going to get out of by believing the wrong thing; this is part of the core of who I am." That was comforting to me, to think that this is a legitimate way to view one's heritage. You might change in significant ways, but you don't just get to jump ship. Who I am always stands in some relationship to who I was.

Larry: That's interesting. I've been thinking about something during this conversation. You've heard me say that Jewish-Christian dialogue makes me a better Jew, but I struggle to express how this works. But listening to you, I'm thinking my contact with Christians makes me feel more comfortable about my discomfort with Judaism.

Anthony: [*Laughs*] You don't envy us nearly as much!

Larry: [*Laughs*] Something like that!

Anthony: Let's get back to *your* path to dialogue. You wrote that your entry point into the Christian encounter was this fascination with the various interpretations of *The Passion of the Christ*, the Mel Gibson film.

Larry: It wasn't so much fascination; it was more like a fear. Here is a movie designed, we think, to provoke the biggest possible audience response, the biggest possible outrage, to the torture and death of Jesus . . . and to boot, the movie portrays the Jews as the villains in the story.

Anthony: So, fear drew you to the synagogue to hear this particular lecture on this particular film. What this tells me, and correct me if I'm wrong, Jews must engage Christianity at certain times, for the purpose of damage control.

Larry: Yes, but that's a particular kind of engagement. It's sort of like . . . a tornado watch. Are we being threatened? Where is the threat coming from? Where do we hide? If a tornado comes, you go into the basement and lock the door until the tornado passes and it's safe to come out. So what we needed to know was, when were you coming, and when were you leaving? And while we're down in the cellar, were we talking about Jesus? It's possible. We like to talk. In any event, what got me to attend that lecture was fear, but what drew me into the study was the idea that the Christian story could be told in different ways, legitimately. Not spun. Not something motivated by the desire to tell the story in a nice, polite way that we could all feel good about.

Anthony: But there's some of that out there.

Larry: I don't have a problem with political correctness, but in this case I wasn't trying to smooth the rough edges and make the story more palatable to Jews, Christians, and everybody else. What got me interested was learning that the gospel story can be told *biblically* in different ways. There are four

Gospels, and they each tell the story slightly differently, so Gibson's decision to include Matthew 27:25 is a deliberate decision. That passage does not have to be in his story of Jesus.

Anthony: That's a good point. And this is what the speaker at your synagogue said?

Larry: Yes.

Anthony: The point I'm trying to make is this: it's not that Jews refuse to engage Christians; it's that there are times and places for it, and like you said, it's like a tornado watch. But dialogue is not going to work well if the only time you have a Jewish-Christian encounter is when you have a film like *The Passion of the Christ*, where damage control is required. A better way is to have a conversational mechanism in place, so that when a movie like that is produced, it enters into a dialogue that's already underway.

Larry: Well, arguably, that's what happened.

Anthony: My point is this: in your chapter, you mentioned Adele Reinhartz's clear indictment of the film and the way the Jews were portrayed in the film, and her indictment was extremely helpful. But I wonder if that isn't more helpful to Christians than it is to Jews. You also mentioned that Mary Boys made a very similar indictment of the film, as a Catholic nun who is a scholar of early Christianity and someone who is well-versed in Jewish-Christian dialogue. My feeling is that it's more helpful when Boys makes the indictment than when Reinhartz makes the indictment. From a Jewish perspective, don't you want a thoughtful, intelligent Christian to come out and say, "That's inappropriate, because that leads to this"?

Larry: Yes.

Anthony: But Mary Boys does not become the person she is unless there are at least a couple of Jews who are willing to talk with her.

Larry: Yes. Of course, we have organizations like the Anti-Defamation League. It's not that we're unwilling to pay a few of our smartest rabbis and scholars to do interfaith damage control. But the argument, as I hear you making it, is that you cannot produce a Mary Boys if the only reason you're talking to Mary Boys is with the hope that she'll take on Mel Gibson when the time comes.

Anthony: Or that she's eventually going to leave you alone.

Larry: I agree with you. Mary Boys does not get to be Mary Boys unless we talk to her about things that *she* cares about. We have to be willing to talk about issues of faith, spirituality, G-d, Scripture, canon . . . something more than the threat to Judaism posed by Christianity.

Anthony: Right. That's a discussion that needs to happen.

Larry: This is one reason why I'm trying to get beyond the fear factor in terms of my own development as a Jew. The great and holy surprise of Jewish-Christian dialogue for me is that it has come to mean much more than self-protection. But self-protection is still in the mix for me. I wish it were otherwise. I don't think that I have personally experienced anything remotely close to the threat I feel.

Anthony: Well, the threats are still out there. You've mentioned to me your running into anti-Semitic websites.[2] We know that there are still threats out there.

Larry: Yes. But there's another problem with dialogue based on the fear factor that needs to be mentioned. If our primary motivation to speak with Christians is the fear factor, we are going to lose interest in the dialogue as the objective reasons for fear subside.

Anthony: That's interesting.

Larry: I think this has already started to happen. Even when the Mel Gibson movie came out, and we had what was in effect a German passion play about to be broadcast simultaneously in four thousand theaters, the kind of passion play that once routinely incited medieval Christian mobs to attack Jews . . . even with the fear that inspired, I also felt a certain confidence that this is "not going to happen in America." Are American Christians really going to come to Jewish neighborhoods and, I don't know, burn crosses on our lawns, throw rocks through our windows? It just didn't seem like a real

---

2. Since the recording of this dialogue, the uptick in anti-Semitic incidences (including neo-Nazi marches and the burning of synagogues) has increased. Larry and Anthony both connect this development with the larger political realities of 2016–17.

possibility. So, the reasons I would like to articulate for dialogue are reasons that don't go to the fear factor, because at least in America, we don't have as much to be afraid of.

Anthony: Well, here's where the fear might be healthy. My point so far is that the "tornado watch" mentality is not a good entry point into the Jewish-Christian encounter. That's me speaking from my limited perspective to my Jewish friends. But if I were just going to address the Christians in the room, I would say that there are a dozen things Christians do and think, and they do it unknowingly, that are not good for the Jews. They will walk into Mel Gibson's movie, and it will be completely lost on them that someone could be offended by it. For most Christians who saw the movie and liked the movie, their intentions are good, but they don't know that the mentality that leads to anti-Semitism is in place in most churches. In other words, there are seeds still planted, theological, political, ways of being in the world—the seeds are there that might lead to bad things. I would say that most Christians don't know what the consequences of certain beliefs might be.

Larry: I wrote in the chapter that it astounds me that Christians would make a movie like *The Passion of the Christ* that had a potential, no matter how small, to create anti-Jewish feeling. What could possibly have been the benefit that could have outweighed that danger? In my mind, I cannot imagine one. Now, it can be argued that Jews looked at this movie purely through Jewish eyes, and that it never dawned on us that our Christian neighbors would not see anything anti-Jewish in this movie at all! Which seems by far to be the dominant reaction.

Anthony: If you surveyed one hundred Christians who saw this movie, ninety-five of them would say, "Oh, there was anti-Semitism? I didn't see it."

Larry: I'm not saying this is what I think, but let's suppose that Mel Gibson set out to make an anti-Semitic movie about Jesus. If 99 percent of the Christians who went to this movie didn't get it, wonderful!

Anthony: How many Christians are there in the world?

Larry: 2.2 billion is the number I've heard.[3]

---

3. The current number is roughly 2.7 billion and will be closer to 2.8 billion by the time this book is published.

Anthony: Even if only 1 percent of that number dons a white hood from time to time . . .

Larry: That's 22 million.

Anthony: That's a lot of anti-Semitism.

Larry: That 1 percent is larger than the entire worldwide Jewish population.

Anthony: This is what most Christians don't get. They'll watch a movie like *The Passion of the Christ*, and the question of anti-Semitism won't cross their minds; it will be brought up by someone on *NPR*, and they'll immediately think, "I've never burned a cross on someone's lawn; I've never wanted to burn a cross on anyone's lawn; no one I know would ever burn a cross on anyone's lawn, so what's the problem here?" The problem is, I met someone who had a cross on their lawn that was on fire. He was a Jewish guy, living in a certain part of the United States; this was his experience. So it's not inconceivable that this might be a consequence to a movie like Mel Gibson's.

Larry: But if your point is that our only hope to stop a Mel Gibson movie is to make as many friends as we possibly can in the Christian community long before somebody gets the idea of making that movie . . . Let me put it another way. I think that Mel Gibson and a lot of other people reacted to Jewish and certain Christian opposition to the movie by saying, "We want to make the most authentic gospel movie possible. And you're not trying to be helpful; you're throwing other concerns at us." If we had better Jewish-Christian dialogue and better Jewish-Christian relations, the idea of what makes for the best possible gospel movie would change. People would have a different view of Jews who do not accept Jesus as their Savior and Messiah.

Anthony: I can go in two directions on this. Part of me feels like, yeah, you're making my point for me, because we need more people like Mary Boys. We should have more thoughtful Christians aspiring to be like her. The other part of me says, yeah, I think we may be underestimating how important every single verse of the Bible is to many Christians. The verse in Matthew that we continue to discuss . . .

Larry: 27:25. Pilate stands before the Jewish crowd, and the crowd shouts for Jesus' crucifixion. Pilate declares himself innocent of Jesus' blood. And then, in Matthew 27:25, "the people as a whole" answer Pilate: "His blood be on us and on our children!"

Anthony: I can wish all I want that this verse was not included in my Bible, because I know the history it begat. But I think that most evangelicals you'll talk to, the Biblicists you'll talk to, would say, "I'd rather tear off my right arm than scalpel out one verse of the Bible." I mean, I sat across the room from a Christian a while ago who said, and these were the exact words, "I would rather die than to say the Bible is wrong about anything." If that's the mentality, that someone would rather die than distance himself from Matthew 27:25, this is a huge barrier for Jewish-Christian dialogue.

Larry: But I'm arguing *from* the Bible. Let's just look at Luke for a moment. You can't get more Bible than Luke. Luke tells the story of Jesus' passion without resorting to the material in Matthew 27:25. And if Luke could tell Jesus' story without this tradition, then so can you and I. No one need include that passage in their personal narrative.

Anthony: Well, if I am going to do my own personal *Passion of the Christ* reboot . . .

Larry: And I would pay $15 to see this.

Anthony: Let's say I do that, and I don't include this verse. But when I go home at the end of the day, at the end of the movie, this passage is still there in Holy Scripture. And as a Christian, that's an identity marker for me, my holy text is part of who I am, and part of how I encounter G-d; the passage is still there, and it is still a problem.

Larry: Yes. It's a huge problem for me that Matthew 27:25 is in someone's canon. Historically, this is one of the most damaging texts that has ever been penned. It has cost perhaps millions of lives. Millions of Jewish lives. My family members. This text is not in my canon, but it is in yours. I get that. But I don't think it's unrealistic to say that every Christian must form their own Christian narrative, their own narrative of the life and death of Jesus. Christians have four Gospels; they each tell the story slightly differently, and I'm not trying to exaggerate those differences and say that Christians can make up whatever story of Jesus they might prefer. There are limits on the story you can biblically tell about Jesus, but excluding Matthew 27:25 from the story is well within biblical limits. *Because Luke didn't use this text.*

Anthony: I want to rephrase your point so that it won't be heard as asking to revise the canon. My Bible has footnotes—even my most stripped down threadbare Bible has footnotes. These footnotes tell me that Mark's ending is not in the earliest manuscripts.[4]

Larry: Yes, I was thinking about that very example.

Anthony: These footnotes tell me that some translations say this and others say that. This is not unheard of. So, rather than revise the canon, we might suggest something along the lines of a footnote.

Larry: But few people read footnotes, except people like you and me!

Anthony: There are *very few* footnotes. Any evangelical who picks up Mark's Gospel and reads to the end cannot avoid this footnote. So, what if there's a footnote for Matthew 27:25, a few sentences explaining that Christian anti-Semitism and murder are tragic results of this particular passage?

Larry: I'm hoping for better than that.

Anthony: Well, you may ask for more, but you are not going to get more.

Larry: No, I think I can get more.

Anthony: What do you think you can get?

Larry: I think I can get a footnote that says that this passage is only in Matthew. It could be news to some people that Matthew 27:25 is not in Luke, or Mark, or John, or Paul.

Anthony: It very well could be . . . that would be an important point to make.

Larry: Let's go further. The text says, "The people as a whole answered, 'His blood be on us and on our children!'" The people as a whole, meaning that Jesus says it too. Because Jesus is certainly a person in the story. But wait a second, Jesus could not have said that, no one thinks Jesus said that. So, we're

---

4. In the earliest manuscripts, Mark ends with 16:8, with Mary Magdalene and Salome fleeing the tomb. There is no appearance in these earliest manuscripts of the risen Jesus.

already reading, "all of the people except Jesus." So, Peter said that? No, no, Peter could not have said that. Peter is the rock on which the church is built.

Anthony: No, he's pretty wishy-washy, he could have said that!

Larry: Ah . . . no. And, how about Mary? The mother of Jesus, she could not have said that. So, who said it? Do we add a footnote that says . . .

Anthony: "The people as a whole" could not have said this.

Larry: All the people—much less all the Jews—could not have said this. This is somehow a poetic exaggeration.

Anthony: Yeah.

Larry: Do we put that in?

Anthony: Yes. And by the way, we should clarify: it could be that this is just not there, in any early tradition. That the reason why this is not said in Mark is that no one knew about this until Matthew. It would be better to say that Mark doesn't include it because Mark doesn't know about it.

Larry: Luke doesn't include it because . . .

Anthony: . . . Luke doesn't know about it.

Larry: John doesn't include it because . . .

Anthony: . . . Well, if *John* knew about it, he would have included it!

Larry: [*Laughs*]

Anthony: All I'm saying is, if you have a bunch of New Testament scholars in the room, they would explain that verse to you in this way: this is part of Matthew's literary agenda, and this does not tell us anything about what anyone was thinking during Jesus' trial.

Larry: But I'm talking about your canon.

Anthony: I think that most Christians would be happy to read in their footnotes, first, this passage is only in Matthew, and it's possible to tell the story without including this passage. Second, this passage cannot be indicative of all Jews, because we could not imagine that Jesus or Mary said this. So it doesn't make sense to say that all the people—much less all the Jews—said this. And third, this passage has led to all kinds of violence, including the most horrific kinds of violence. I think that most Christians would be happy to learn these things about the verse.

Larry: I want a fourth thing.

Anthony: I think three is a good Trinitarian number; I think we should stop at three.

Larry: There are four Gospels. Let's go for four.

Anthony: Okay.

Larry: I want Christian pastors to preach from the pulpit that Matthew 27:25 did not happen. It's part of the tradition, and I don't want it excised, but it didn't happen and Christians should not include it in their personal narrative.

Anthony: You're not going to get that. I mean, you'll get that from very few pastors. And it's lamentable that you're not going to get it more, but part of dialogue is about . . .

Larry: Then why have the footnote? What's the footnote for, if it's not there to change belief? Is it just there to appease our consciences? To say to our Jewish friends, "Look, we included this footnote to be nice to you, but not to challenge anyone thinking that this actually happened"? Why the first three steps, if the fourth step is impossible?

Anthony: Look, I'm with you. In a lot of ways, I take my Christianity from Paul. And Paul is willing to redefine some really core elements of Judaism to be inclusive. He's willing to give me a version of monotheism that seems altogether different from a lot of other Jews of the time. He's willing to give me a version of Halacha, food purity, circumcision, these things that are central markers of Jewish identity, he's willing to give me an interpretation of these things that spiritualizes them. So these are core tenets of his religious identity that he's willing to reinterpret for the sake of inclusion. I wish that modern Christians would be able to do the same thing, but it's very difficult for us. It feels like you're demoting our sacred text, and I'm speaking collectively, because, honestly, I wish that pastors would do that from the pulpit. I wish they would problematize the text. If a pastor stood up and said, "Here's the footnote, here's A, B, and C, and also D, you should not believe that Matthew 27:25 ever happened," that pastor would be fired from many, many churches. That is a bridge too far, it's taking something core about most Christians' central identity, and it is creating an immense insecurity. As an honest dialogue partner, I'm telling you that point number four is not going to fly.

Larry: In dialogue, you've said that you want honesty from us? You want from us, true engagement that goes beyond tornado watching?

Anthony: Yeah.

Larry: Be careful what you wish for.

Anthony: Well, you can ask for it! I'm glad you're asking for it.

Larry: I get that it's a big ask. But how can I enter into dialogue with somebody who thinks I have the blood of Jesus on my hands?

Anthony: I am fairly confident that most Christians do not believe that you've got blood on your hands.

Larry: You're right that I've never encountered a Christian who has said any such thing to me. I don't go into dialogue with Christians worried that they're thinking this about me. But I have to wonder what I'm doing in dialogue if what you're telling me is that most Christians would still insist that Matthew 27:25 tells the story as it really happened.

Anthony: I see what you mean. It's got to be very hard to sit down with someone who holds a text like that as historical fact. I . . . I would hope . . .

Larry: This is fundamental to dialogue! How can we talk to people who insist on their right to remember us in this way?

Anthony: You have every right to ask for what you are asking, and you *should* ask for it.

Larry: And I have no problem if what you're saying is that what I am asking for is next to impossible, that what I am asking for might take ten million years to achieve. I don't care how difficult you want to tell me this is. But if you tell me it's impossible, then please stop giving me such a hard time about our supposed reluctance to talk to you.

Anthony: What I'm saying is this: I'm not telling you not to ask for it. I'm telling you that we—most of us—can't give it. In fact, I'm telling you that you *should* ask for it. But there are certain things that have to be said in Jewish-Christian dialogue that will not bring about any other result than the fact that they were said. Not every point of dialogue will be translated into appropriate action. Some things we are going to disagree on. Sometimes the dialogue is important even if there's no tangible result that comes at the end of it, aside from mutual understanding. But let me be clear: I teach pastors for a living. In my classrooms, Matthew 27:25 is not presented as a historical fact. It's part of Matthew's literary agenda. The Romans killed Jesus! And I could—I haven't—but I could teach my students to preach from the pulpit that Matthew 27:25 never happened. But those pastors just are not going to do it.

Larry: I've said to you in the past something that possibly sounded innocuous to you: that Christianity has to become a Jewish-friendly religion. Your initial reaction, I believe, was along the lines of "How nice!"

Anthony: Yeah, I'm happy with that.

Larry: What did you think I meant? Did you think I was going to define Christianity as a Jewish-friendly religion if Matthew 27:25 is part of the narrative? I get that you're not going to take a razor and cut this text out of your canon. I'm saying that I don't want it in your narrative. That's a different thing. Luke didn't have it in his narrative.

Anthony: Look, part of the Christian narrative, and this is absolutely central, we teach it to our kids at a very early age, is Noah's Ark.

Larry: I was going to bring up Noah's Ark.

Anthony: No Christian that I know of includes Genesis 6:1–4 in the story of Noah's Ark. Christians do not believe that G-d had progeny, sons of G-d, and this progeny, these demi-gods, had sex with daughters of men. But that's what my sacred text says! Right?

Larry: Right.

Anthony: That's not going to come out of the canon. You are not going to get a pastor to stand up on the pulpit and say that this did not really happen—or that pastor is getting fired. But that pastor can say, "Look, there are a lot of ways to interpret this, and here are some helpful ways to think about it, and here are some unhelpful ways to think about it. Lots of folks will say that this is just mythology. As your pastor, I really don't know what I'm supposed to tell you about this passage." That pastor probably keeps his job. But the pastor who says what you are asking the pastor to say, from the pulpit, doesn't have a job for very long. But that pastor can come to Jewish-Christian dialogue with a group of other Christians, his parishioners in the room, and he can say, "I get it; this is offensive to me; I wish it was never put in my Bible." I think this is the best you are going to get. I guess what I'm saying, as the Jew in the room, you should continue to ask us to get rid of Matthew 27:25, knowing all the while that it is not going to be excised from the Bible, the New Testament. That's what I'm saying.

Larry: Right. What I have asked for—I never asked for any text to be excised, because otherwise, how would we explain our shared history?

Anthony: But that's what we hear, when you tell me to say that "this never happened." What is heard in most congregations is that he has just removed an element of Holy Scripture. That's how it's heard.

Larry: I understand. Let's take a step back for a moment. I think we both agree that a Jewish-friendly version of Christianity has difficult questions to address. I've seen in my lifetime what I think are remarkable efforts to address some of these questions. For example: I've seen Christianity begin to address the question of supersessionism.[5] A lot of Christians are saying, supersessionism is inappropriate. A lot of other Christians are saying, it's problematic. Many Christians seem to be saying, G-d doesn't break G-d's covenant, so G-d's covenant with the Jews remains in place.

Anthony: Yeah, but I think this discussion deserves more than a sidebar. You might find quite a number of Christians, intelligent Christians, who

---

5. Supersessionism is the Christian doctrine that the New Testament nullifies or replaces the promises made by G-d to the Jewish people in the Old Testament, and that the Christian Church has taken the place of Israel in G-d's plan.

would defend supersessionism by saying, "That's our theology! That's what it says in Hebrews, that's what it says in Matthew, that's what it says in Paul, and we're not getting rid of that."

Larry: I hear intelligent *Jews* say that they cannot imagine Christianity without supersessionism. But that's not my point; my point is that number one, it's now a discussion point.

Anthony: Hmm.

Larry: I don't know of any Christian who would say, "I am offended that you would even bring up supersessionism as something to talk to me about."

Anthony: Right. Okay.

Larry: And just to get to this point is an enormous move on the part of Christianity, and I acknowledge and appreciate the difficulty of that move. I'm not saying that Christians have not been willing to examine, maybe I shouldn't use the word *fundamental*, but that's how it feels to me, fundamental aspects of the Christian faith.

Anthony: Yeah, and that is very fundamental, you're right. So, we are happy to reexamine, most of us are happy to reexamine. The next step is the hardest step.

Larry: I don't know how many "next steps" there are. The reexamination of Christianity is, to me, essential to the kind of dialogue you're asking for.

Anthony: My hope is that any Christian who would want to enter into Jewish-Christian dialogue would do so because they think they might be changed in some way by the process. Not necessarily to become more Jewish, but to become more Christian in the process.

Larry: What I hear you telling me, and I think you've been saying this in so many words for as long as I've known you, and not so much "telling me" as "asking me," is that you would like us to *ask* you to be better Christians.

Anthony: Yeah! Please ask us to be better Christians! And I think it needs to be described in detail, the ways you would like to see us change. Something like, "Look, there are some really offensive things in your sacred texts, and you should know about it." I think this is a conversation that has to happen.

Larry: Yes. The idea is that Christian change is something I should desire from the heart; this is part of Jewish-Christian friendship. This would take a series of developmental steps, and I don't know if I'll ever get there: to truly desire you to be a better Christian, in the way I want anything that I want, to believe that your becoming a better Christian is going to be good for me. To believe that in this process, I become a better Jew. And to believe that there is something reciprocal you can offer me, in terms of your wishing for me to be a better Jew.

Anthony: Well, that's where I need your help. I need to know where you want to go, because I can be an honest and hopefully interesting partner in this. But you know, I'm not in a position of authority to tell you what's good for the Jews and what's not . . .

Larry: Anthony, our preference, if you are talking about where we want to go, is to be left alone. I've already told you that. But you have said, and you are right, that is not a practical policy.

Anthony: Yes.

Larry: And it's probably not a spiritually sound policy either.

Anthony: That's a part of it I would not know anything about.

Larry: Yes you do. Yes you do.

Anthony: No, I really don't! Honestly, I wouldn't presume . . . Look, I've got all kinds of personal issues that I need to attend to before I give anyone else advice on how they can seek to become better . . .

Larry: Anthony, we're opening a door here to a different kind of dialogue, one that's not limited to your talking about what I say I want to talk about, and vice versa. I've already said that Jews want to talk to Christians about damage control, and then be left alone. You said, no, that's a fantasy, you have to talk to us about big issues like G-d and canon. You've said, we have to challenge you about your sacred texts. We don't get to ask you which texts you would like us to challenge. You see, we are opening a door.

Anthony: Yeah.

Larry: This is a Pandora's Box of a door. Open this door, and things are going to start pouring out. The desire to be left alone may be a fantasy, I've already granted you that, but it's a fantasy based on some fairly sound ideas, and one of them is that I don't have any business telling you how to live your life spiritually. We are opening a door here. I don't know what's on the other side of that door, but there will be things on the other side of that door that are unexpected. You are asking me, as part of opening this door, to talk to you not just about things that matter to me, but about things that matter because I care about you. You want me to value you as someone who won't leave me alone, even if that's what I say I want.

Anthony: Well, we do this together, right? I mean, there are certain things that can be accomplished, if there is listening and talking being done, that you can't accomplish if you simply put up a monument and walk away. This is the issue: sometimes, you don't have the right questions to ask. But as the door opens, and we don't know what's on the other side, if we walk through it together, the possibilities open up before us, and I would hope there are a hundred more questions, and hopefully the questions get more intelligent as we go.

Larry: It has to be an interactive process.

Part Two

Borders

A Pilgrimage of Many Borders

Anthony Le Donne

Love recognizes no barriers. It jumps hurdles, leaps fences, penetrates walls to arrive at its destination full of hope.

—Maya Angelou[1]

There once was a Christian theologian in conversation with a chief from the Tsawwassen tribe of British Columbia. The chief, hoping to learn something worth knowing about the Christian, probed: "Tell me about your place." To the dismay of both, the Christian replied, "We don't have places; we have careers."

I first heard this story from a seminary professor. He meant to critique "the West"—that vague empire of freeways, fast food, and house flips. But I think there is a deeper truth to be mined here. It is certainly true that the Western world is perpetually transient. But doesn't this proverb also teach us something about Christianity? Isn't the Christian story that of an outward-focused mission? We are a people ever on the move, expanding, crossing borders, redefining boundaries as we go. Even when we do settle in a place, the architecture of our cathedrals points heavenward. Christians (in my experience) tend to have an onward-and-upward mentality. Maybe tweaking the proverb just slightly strikes closer to the heart of the matter: "We don't have a place; we have a mission."

Concerning Pilgrims

Jesus left home. Some say he was homeless. He banded together "followers" who lived on the hospitality of strangers. They began from Israel and

---

1. Maya Angelou's Facebook page, January 11, 2013, https://www.facebook.com/MayaAngelou/posts/10151418853254796.

were sent to the far reaches of the known world. The story of early Christianity is that a stone dropped in Galilee rippled throughout the Mediterranean.

Stories about pilgrimage were important for the early church. Paul boasts about his travels, including his hardship. A popular second-century fiction called *The Shepherd of Hermas* uses pilgrimage as a metaphor for the Christian life. The pilgrim in this story experiences spiritual adversity and temptation along the road. A Christian letter from the same period preserves these words:

> [Christians] live each in their native land but as though they were not really at home there. They share in all duties as citizens and suffer all hardships as strangers. Every foreign country is a fatherland to them, and every fatherland a foreign land. . . . They dwell on earth but they are citizens of heaven. (*Letter to Diognetus*, 5)

Gregory of Nyssa—a Christian bishop of the fourth century—said that the most important pilgrimage is the interior one to G-d. Augustine of Hippo advises his readers to "witness the prayer of the whole city of G[-]d in its pilgrim state" (*City of G[-]d* XIX.27). Here Augustine preaches that the Christian community exists in a "pilgrim state." According to St. Augustine, there is no earthly "Christian city," there is just a Christian way in the world. This ought to include prayer, repentance, and harmonious relationships with our neighbors.

The theme of pilgrimage was among the most important for medieval Christian authors. It influenced their views of the "Holy Land," missions, heaven, and hell. Indeed the theme is integral to Dante's *Divine Comedy*.[2] John Bunyan's *The Pilgrim's Progress* follows a similar path. We see the theme again in the 1800s with the multiauthored Russian work, *The Way of a Pilgrim*. Christian authors throughout the centuries teach us that we are a people without any single holy place. We sing that we're "just passing through." Our true home is heaven.

Christians are pilgrims. It's engrained in us.

So allow me to expand and explain the theologian's proverb: "We don't have places; we have careers." We do, in fact, have places. We occupy many places. Some Christians have occupied places for several generations. But even when we put down roots, we tend to describe our spiritual lives in terms of a journey. For the Christian, being a pilgrim is the journey that results from the simple call: "Come, follow me."

---

2. For more on this theme, see Julia Bolton Holloway, *The Pilgrim and the Book: A Study of Dante, Langland, and Chaucer* (New York: Peter Lang, 1992).

We all interpret this call differently. Some Christians understand this as a general call to make the world a better place. Indeed, I have met more Christian environmentalists than I have evangelists. That said, Jesus' call "Follow me" (Matt. 4:19) has been traditionally understood as a call to seek Christian converts. Christian pilgrims tend to have an impact on the people they meet and the places they occupy.

Concerning Strangers

Recently Larry invited me to his synagogue. I'd been in synagogues before but never this one. Larry navigated us through the mean streets of Beverly Hills in his blue Prius. There was nothing particularly sacred or strange about the journey. It really didn't feel like much of a pilgrimage. But as we crossed the border from sidewalk to synagogue, an unmistakable boundary marker caught my attention.

Adjacent to the synagogue was a beautiful little chapel, but I was distracted. Standing at the front door was a guard. Shaved head, blue uniform, expressionless. *Was that a sidearm I saw?* I was somewhat disturbed by the display, but for the moment I said nothing.

I don't know if this is a Beverly Hills thing or not, but my first experience at Larry's synagogue was a Buddhist-styled session of meditation. The rabbi encouraged us to be present and observant within ourselves. But the security guard just beyond that threshold was on my mind. Rather than being "present in the moment," the image of a sidearm dominated my meditation. Then I wondered how my fellow meditators felt about the guard. *Did the show of force provide them comfort, or distract them?*

As Larry and I left the chapel, I broached the subject, "What's up with him?"

Larry is usually direct, but he played coy. "Who?"

"The armed guard."

Larry's eyes twinkled as he answered, "He's here to protect us from our enemies."

Clearly he had more to say but settled in this moment for a quip. I didn't say much more as we turned the corner and walked into the foyer. Here was another guard with a similar uniform and posture. Worship was beginning and our "borders" dialogue would require much more time to unpack. I placed the guest *kippah* on my head and entered.

I take no pleasure in saying this, but a great many people have been trampled over in the name of Christian pilgrimage. Countless Jews have encountered Christians who are on some crusade, quest, or adventure. Even when we have good intentions—and this cannot be assumed—we Christians leave a heavy footprint when we travel. Peter Bellini is my colleague here at United Theological Seminary; he teaches missiology to aspiring Christian leaders. Peter puts it like this, "For the last 500 or so years evangelization has often coattailed on colonial exploration and exploitation. We spent the better part of those years making a mess; I think it might be better to move a bit more slowly." I would echo this assessment and add that Christianity's traditional hostility toward our Jewish neighbors is older still. Augustine's hope for a "City of G-d" by way of contrition and harmonious relations has proved false in Jewish witness.

I do take pleasure, however, in saying that most Christians hold no ill will toward Jews. I would like to think that most of us are not intentionally anti-Semitic. As one Christian friend told me, "All those stories I learned about Israel in church have stuck with me. I really do have a special place in my heart for Judaism." I don't doubt that many Christians feel the same.

But consider again the numbers. There are 2.7 billion Christians worldwide as I write this (there will be 2.8 billion by the time this book is published). Contrast this with a total of 14 million Jews worldwide. So we measure Jews in millions and Christians in billions. Even if only one out of every hundred Christians were anti-Semitic (1 percent of 2.7 billion), this would make for 27 million anti-Semitic Christians in the world. Even if my absurdly low estimate is close to the mark—and this doesn't even include non-Christian anti-Semites—*there are far more anti-Semites in the world than there are Jews.*

So Larry says, ". . . to protect us from our enemies."

It will be almost banal to point this out, but one of the differences between Jews and Christians is religious. By this I mean that we are different both in how we relate to our own religions and how we relate to the religions of others. My Jewish friends tend to respond differently to religious borders as compared to my Christians friends. Jews have a history of living in proximity of dangerous religious borders. Many Jews live near neighbors who curse them or have family members who have. And when religious neighbors outnumber you on all sides, such curses become unsafe. History—even recent history—teaches us that many of these neighbors wish expulsion or extinction for the Jews. This, I imagine, is why armed guards are employed outside some synagogues.

Extinction is not a real-world concern for Christianity. We may have unhealthy denominations and we may be declining in North America. But there is no real danger of Christianity's imminent demise. In contrast, Jewish extinction is a real-world concern for many Jews. There are several factors that fuel this concern. Israel's political instability and intermarriage with non-Jews are both factors. The Holocaust—which is both part of Western history and an identity-shaping family memory—is a major factor. Too many family members were lost and too much culture was destroyed. It is therefore understandable that many Jews would worry about the longevity of the Jewish people. Related to this worry—this might be hard for Christians to hear—is the problem of Christian evangelism. For many Jews, the Christian drive to seek converts (especially of children) is a threat. It may not be the only factor, but it is related to the worry nonetheless. So Jews tend to relate to religious borders differently than do Christians.

After worship we moved to a room adjacent to the synagogue for a meal. Larry and I talked about my experience at his synagogue. I was humbled by the hospitality shown me. My worship at Temple Emanuel was, without a doubt, a sacred experience for me, a gift. But I said none of this to Larry. Perhaps another time.

We passed the guards again. We repositioned ourselves in Larry's Prius. The streets of Los Angeles served as my reentry into the "Christian" world. I saw no immediate danger lurking. This wasn't 1933 Berlin; it was just Southern California. I continued to puzzle over the security guards. Larry and I picked up our previous dialogue.

"Is the guard necessary?" I asked.

"I would love it if you'd ask my rabbi that question! She's convinced that the guard is necessary. I think it sends the wrong message."

Larry's reply illustrates another problem. Not every Jew will relate to religious borders in the same way. I happen to know that Larry and his rabbi respect each other and like each other. But they seem to disagree on this point.

Despite Larry's misgivings and my discomfort, it is not uncommon in urban settings to employ security guards, some of them armed. Perhaps I just never noticed them before. Larry asked, "Don't 'megachurches' do the same?" I don't rightly know the answer to his question, but I told him that I've never in my life been in church with an armed guard.[3]

Judaism has a long history of pilgrimage. But in the Jewish story, pilgrimage takes the form of forced displacement and attempts to flee persecution.

---

3. I have since become a member of an urban Presbyterian Church in Dayton that employs uniformed guards. But they are not armed.

Jews throughout the centuries (from Canaan, to Babylon, to Brazil, to twentieth-century Europe) live in a world of borders that most Christians can hardly imagine.

Our conversation about the necessity of the armed guard was left open-ended. But a few days later my Facebook feed introduced a new and horrifying development to this topic. A strange man shouting "Heil Hitler!" trespassed onto a Jewish Community Center in Kansas.[4] The shooter murdered three people. I immediately e-mailed the link to Larry. He replied: "It is wildly inappropriate for me to think this, but . . . this ties into so many different things we've talked about." I confessed: "I was thinking the same thing."

These two memories are now connected in my mind: the intimidating armed guards outside the Beverly Hills synagogue and those Kansas victims. The border between synagogue and sidewalk is more complicated than I'd previously imagined.

And so I arrive at my point. The difference between a dangerous border and a sacred pilgrimage depends on the perspectives and intentions of the people guarding and crossing the border. Indeed, the Latin word *Pereginus* can mean both "pilgrim" and "stranger."

Strangers

I have occupied many borders in my life. Allow me to explore one of them: I am a dark-skinned Italian with other dark-skinned ethnicities in my genealogy. I am asked every so often if I am black, or "mulatto," or "point 5." I am most often asked this by African-Americans. Sometimes these moments are quite direct, "Are you black?" Sometimes an assumption is made that must be clarified later. This makes me think that many white folk also perceive me as black, but are too shy to ask (although some have). In Zimbabwe I was called "colored" a few times. This is a word that Zimbabweans use to label someone with both black and white parentage. I've never considered myself black; my family has always identified as Italian-American. But I would be naive to think that the way others perceive me doesn't have some impact on my social interactions. It is an odd and sometimes awkward border to occupy. It has, however, caused me to think of the complicated topics of race and ethnicity more carefully.

---

4. "Suspect in Kansas shootings a longtime anti-Semite, group says," *Chicago Tribune*, April 14, 2014, www.chicagotribune.com/news/chi-kansas-jewish-community-shootings-20140413-story.html.

My daughter once wrote in a third-grade assignment that her daddy was "a black." After learning about the Civil Rights Movement, she was required to write a letter to Martin Luther King, Jr. She wrote, "Dear Dr. King, thank you for helping the black people, because if you hadn't I would never have been born because my daddy is a black." My wife and I have saved this letter. It is particularly precious to me. It reminds me of when my daughter was smart enough to connect the dots between the Civil Rights Movement and interracial marriage, and still innocent enough to think that dark skin is the key factor in the determination of race. (Any serious student of ethnicity will tell you that skin color is only one factor among many in the construct of race.)

At the time, however, her letter presented a problem for me. I was confronted with the opportunity to teach my daughter about American racial borders. Or I could say nothing. I had to ask myself: *Do I really want my eight-year-old daughter to know that I don't think I'm black?* Isn't there something beautiful in the fact that my daughter's border between "black" and "Italian" is fuzzy? Isn't it great that she simply assumed this about me but never thought to mention it before? And what will I teach her by saying, "*I* am not *them*"? On the other hand, the fact is that I don't think of myself as black. Don't I do her an ultimate disservice by withholding this key bit of information?

After a great deal of struggle within the borderland between black and white, I decided to be definitively gray. I told her that some people see me and think that I'm black, but most people look at me and think that I'm not black. In all honesty, I don't know that this is true. But it is what I came up with in the gray borderland. I decided that race is too important a border in America to pretend it's not there. The border may be of our own making, but we cannot "unmake" it by wishing it away. Moreover, if I had not found myself on this particular border, my education on the topic would have been weak.

This experience leaves me with a simple impression: the world is simply too complicated to avoid certain borders. It is almost impossible to avoid crossing one or two unwittingly, even if you're not on a pilgrimage. How much more, then, should we as Christians be aware of the cultural borders around us?

I was once told that that the best educations are acquired in proximity to a border. When one lives on a border—especially one that is marked by cultural differences—there is a greater possibility of seeing how your neighbor lives and thinks. Of course, it takes more than a border to provide an education. It is possible to live near a border and learn nothing of significance about one's neighbor. This observation is one of possibility. Living in a borderland affords you the *possibility* of education. Becoming truly cosmopolitan involves adopting a curious and receptive posture.

If Christians are pilgrims by nature, then we ought be among the most religiously literate people in the world. Yet we repeatedly stumble from one sojourn to the next, repeating our mistakes. These mistakes are too many and varied to detail here. But one observation is relevant: *When Christians cross into new territory, we tend to impose new borders onto that territory.* When it comes to cultural markers and sacred practices, this tendency can be especially troubling.

Along its most elegant contours, Christianity is universal in acceptance. Our better angels see the image of G-d in every face. We are commanded to welcome every stranger as if that stranger represented Christ himself. There is something breathtaking about this sort of impossible hope. To be a single community without borders is noble from the Christian perspective—like Doctors Without Borders is noble; like Albert Schweitzer was noble. Theologians Willimon and Hauerwas write, "Christianity is an invitation to be part of an alien people."[5] They explain, "We serve the world by showing it something that it is not, namely a place where G[-]d is forming a family out of strangers."[6]

But here it must be said that this impossible hope seems all the more problematic. Because to speak of "forming a family" suggests that we are "drawing a new border." Families create borders. These borders are not necessarily bad. Consider these stock parental phrases:

In this family, we share.

I don't care what your friends are allowed to do.

Will you please pull the shade? I'm in my nightgown.

. . . because she's your grandmother, that's why!

The concept of family implies intimacy and mutual sacrifice, among other things. Appropriately placed borders allow me to create a culture that works for my family. The trouble comes when the borders that seem appropriate to me and my family infringe on the borders of others. Christians may

---

5. Stanley Hauerwas and William H. Willimon, *Resident Aliens: Life in the Christian Colony* (Nashville: Abingdon, 1989), 24.
6. Hauerwas and Willimon, *Resident Aliens*, 83.

aspire to create a family out of strangers, but we have often disrespected the borders of others in the process.

In a previous career, I worked with emotionally disturbed and "at risk" youth. Most of these kids were in foster care, in "boys' homes," or between homes. I've met a great many wounded children along the way. Perhaps too many because I was guilty—at one point in my life—of "helping" in situations wherein my help wasn't wanted.

When I was twenty-two my teenaged sister was dating a boy who claimed to be from an abusive home. My sister came to me for help. For a short while, our family took this boy in. This seemed the most natural thing to do. I probably learned this at a young age as my father had a habit of welcoming strangers in need. From my perspective, it seemed best for the boy to find some sort of safe haven. After welcoming him in, I called his mother to tell her where her son was and to hear what she might have to say. She was livid. She accused me of helping her son run away and quoted me Bible passages about "sparing rods" and "spoiling children." In my attempt to extend the family culture taught to me by my father, I had transgressed another family's border. After a great deal of conflict, the boy returned home. His father promised him and me that he wouldn't use corporal punishment with his son anymore.

To this day, I'm not certain that I did the right thing. Perhaps I shouldn't have allowed the boy to "run away" in the first place—he very well could have been conning me. Perhaps I shouldn't have allowed his parents to sway me from my initial suspicions. In retrospect, whether in error or not, I think I would probably take the same course of action.

This is what makes the sins of Christianity so repugnant to outsiders: we continue to see ourselves as the heroes even when we are the perpetrators. Worse, and I hope that my story illustrates this, we are convinced that we can "do it better" the next time. Convinced as we are that we are without borders, we have repeatedly crossed borders where we are not wanted. Still, having now repeated this indictment several times, I'll confess that I still find the ideal attractive. Pilgrimage born of zeal may be monstrous, but a pilgrimage born of pain may be humane. Allow me to clarify.

The Christian notion that we are strangers in a strange land *can*—I will not say *does*—coax us toward a posture of social justice. I will confess that I cringe when I hear "just pass'n through" theology. But recognizing that we too are "strangers" can help, especially if we must negotiate borders from time to time. If we are aliens *not heroes*, then perhaps we can better identify with the alienated. Peruvian, Catholic theologian Gustavo Gutiérrez teaches that Christianity should be good news for strangers. But this is only true, he argues, if Christianity casts off institutional power rather than accumulates and defends it. If so, it can indeed be good news for strangers.[7] In his view, Christians must forsake places of power, erase the borders that promise false security, and themselves identify with the oppressed.

James Hal Cone makes a similar suggestion concerning American race-relations. Cone suggests that, in order to be Christians, white Christians must *become* black. Not surprisingly this perplexed many of his readers. It seemed that such a border was impossible to cross. So Cone's program was met with resistance. Many liberal, white Christians were eager to offer help. But it seemed as though Cone was making "blackness" a necessary require-ment for Christianity. Cone explained:

> Being black in America has very little to do with skin color. To be black means that your heart, your soul, your mind, and your body are where the dispos-sessed are. . . . Therefore, being reconciled to G[-]d does not mean that one's skin is physically black. It essentially depends on the color of your heart, soul, and mind.[8]

Gutiérrez and Cone are attempting to reclaim something good about Christian pilgrimage. They are inviting Christians to cross borders but with the aim to eschew entitlement and power. To do so is to find a deeper and richer goodness within the good news. Christian pilgrims do not act heroically; they simply take the path born of pain because that is the path Jesus took.

Finally, Frances Young suggest a different and compelling twist. After and during years of struggling with G-d over her son's physical disability,

---

7. Gutiérrez writes: "The unqualified affirmation of the universal will of salva-tion has radically changed the way of conceiving the mission of the Church in the world. It seems clear today that the purpose of the Church is not to save in the sense of 'guaranteeing heaven.' The work of salvation is a reality which occurs in history. . . . the Church must cease considering itself as the exclusive place of salvation and orient itself toward a new and radical service of people. Indeed, the Church of the first centuries lived spontaneously in this way. Its minority status in society and the consequent pressure that the proximity of the non-Christian world exercised on it made it quite sensitive to the action of Christ beyond its frontiers, that is, to the totality of his redemptive work." *A Theology of Liberation: History, Politics, and Salvation*, trans. Caridad Inda and John Eagleson (Maryknoll: Orbis, 1988), 143–44.

8. Quoted from Gayraud S. Wilmore, *Black Religion and Black Radicalism: An Interpretation of the Religious History of African Americans*, 3rd ed. (Maryknoll: Orbis, 2002), 249.

she writes, "Through my son I have been brought to a very different place." Young continues, "I stand alongside him as a vulnerable creature, disabled and mortal, knowing my creaturely limitations and my lack of knowledge, especially of G[-]d."[9] Here Young goes further than Gutiérrez. Not only does she acknowledge her powerlessness—she cannot save her son from his pain—Young becomes herself disabled. She is a pilgrim navigating with mapped pain.

In these ways, traditional Christian borders are renegotiated and redefined as motivated by empathy and suffering. Spiritual pilgrimage in these cases is not motivated by zeal, heroism, or sentimentalized calls to adventure. But perhaps they strike closer to the heart of Jesus' way. Paul teaches us that while we were still strangers, while we were still enemies, G-d suffered. This might seem old hat to Christian ears. It must be heard, however, in a different way. I would suggest that Christians must cede power—especially religious power—to our less powerful neighbors. But—and this is easier said than done—we must know our neighbors well enough to respect their borders. Otherwise the Christian pilgrimage becomes roughshod.

I do not think that Christians should be asked to become something other than pilgrims. It is too ingrained in us to imagine an isolationist Christianity. Christians can, I hope, be challenged to reconsider our motives, assumptions, and practices as pilgrims.

---

9. Frances M. Young, *Brokenness and Blessing: Towards a Biblical Spirituality* (Grand Rapids: Baker, 2007), 59.

Bordering Possibility

Larry Behrendt

Therefore it was called Babel, because there the L[-]RD confused the language of all the earth; and from there the L[-]RD scattered them abroad over the face of all the earth.

—Genesis 11:9

It was 2011. My wife and I were on Whidbey Island, Washington, for our summer vacation. A friend on the island invited us to her church's "Bring a Friend to Church" Sunday. The fact that we are Jewish troubled my friend not at all. The charge was to "Bring a Friend." We were friends. Nothing said the friends couldn't be Jewish. Did we want to come?

My wife answered before I could equivocate. "What is the dress code?" It was casual. She could dress casual. "Fine. We'd love to be there."

I knew what my friend was thinking. "Larry is interested in Christianity." Even my most casual acquaintances know this. My wife likes to introduce me as a nice Jewish boy from New York who writes a blog about Jesus— and when she gets to that last word, she channels her inner Billy Graham, and pronounces the name "Geeeee-zuz," in a way that can frighten people, particularly Jewish people.

Since I'm a nice Jewish boy who is interested in Jesus, it made sense for my friend to invite us to church. Isn't church the place to go when you're interested in Jesus? But I did not want to go. To this day, I feel weird about going to church when Christians are praying there. I have no problem going to church as a tourist, say, to admire its art and architecture. I go to churches for weddings and funerals, not to mention public lectures and concerts. I attended Mass once at the magnificent cathedral in Chartres outside of Paris, an anonymous American tourist among many.

But there was something ominous about "Bring a Friend to Church" day. The event felt suspiciously like proselytizing to me, and like a lot of Jews, I am allergic to proselytizing. I don't know how successful Christianity is at converting Jews, but I'm visited at home about once a month by unsuspecting Christian missionaries who are attracted (I think) by the mezuzah on our doorpost. In most cases, these missionaries are so young and naive that I worry about the effect I might have on *their* faith. But I also worry about what happens when these missionaries ring the doorbells of other Jews. By one source, roughly 2.7 million people convert every year to Christianity[1]—2.7 million converts a year? There are only 14 million of us Jews worldwide, which makes it seem like just a few good seasons of Christian evangelicalism could cause Judaism to disappear altogether.

It is one thing to encounter evangelism-minded Christians in my doorway, and quite another to visit them in church on a day they'd designated for evangelism.

Did I need to be concerned about "Bring a Friend to Church" day? It seems like a silly question, but maybe it isn't so silly. Scholar Daniel Boyarin writes that "the borders between Christianity and Judaism are as constructed and imposed, as artificial and political as any of the borders on earth."[2] My friend had asked me to cross this border, and even a brief border crossing requires preparation—passports must be in order, goods must be declared, luggage inspected. Citizens departing are treated differently than foreigners entering. Few border crossings are casual. In the days of the "Iron Curtain" separating Communist Eastern Europe from the capitalists to the west, I once crossed the border from Austria into Hungary, and a Hungarian officer entered my train compartment to check my passport and ask me where I was going—he wore a military uniform and carried an automatic weapon. He was friendly and tried to engage me in conversation. But his dress and his equipment said all I needed to know about the nature of the border I was crossing.

I was certain there'd be no automatic weapons on display at "Bring a Friend to Church" day. But sometimes, we don't know the nature of a border until we try to cross it.

---

1. Here, I am relying on Wikipedia's citation of figures found in the World Christian Encyclopedia. "Growth of Religion," Wikipedia; https://en.wikipedia.org/wiki/Growth_of_religion#Christianity.

2. Daniel Boyarin, *Border Lines: The Partition of Judaeo-Christianity* (Philadelphia: University of Pennsylvania Press, 2004), 1.

⚜

Let's consult the works of two Jewish authors—Daniel Boyarin and Rachel Adler—to better understand the nature of the Jewish-Christian border. Boyarin begins his book *Border Lines* by describing the religious climate in first-century Palestine following the death of Jesus. At this time, the early Christians were Jews who continued to live as Jews, even (according to the New Testament) worshiping in the Jewish Temple in Jerusalem. Like many scholars, Boyarin thinks that these early Christians were regarded as Jews by their fellow Jews, or more precisely, that the early Christians were seen as a Jewish sect, just as the Pharisees, the Sadducees, and the Dead Sea Scrolls community were all Jewish sects. But Boyarin may be a bit unusual in the way he imagines how these sects got along. He sees the Jewish-Christian space as contentious, but he also sees a degree of mutual tolerance, so that a person residing in this space could be regarded as Jewish while spending time both in church and synagogue, and while believing that Jesus was the Jewish Messiah.[3]

This Judeo-Christian space did not last; eventually, there was a "parting of the ways" that made it impossible to be Christian and Jewish at the same time. Like many present-day scholars, Boyarin believes that this "parting of the ways" took place gradually, over the space of hundreds of years. Scholars identify critical moments in this early history that eventually separated these two religions, such as the success of the apostle Paul's mission to the Gentiles, and the devastation that followed the Jewish rebellions against Rome. For Boyarin, the most critical of these moments took place in the mid-second century, with the rise of the Christian concept of *heresy*. Boyarin's view is that the Christians of this period began to view themselves in terms of what they did *not* believe, in order to clarify what it was they *did* believe. And the thing that Christians did not believe came to be described in terms of Judaism.[4] "If we still live after the manner of Judaism, we avow that we have not received grace," wrote Ignatius of Antioch near the beginning of the second century. "It is monstrous to name the name of Christ and to follow Judaism."[5]

---

3. Boyarin, *Border Lines*, ch. 1.

4. Boyarin, *Border Lines*, 12.

5. "The Epistle of Ignatius to the Magnesians," chapters 8 and 10, from translation in J. B. Lightfoot, *The Apostolic Fathers* (London: MacMillan and Co., 1885), 124, 133. For a more modern translation, see "The Epistle of Ignatius to the Magnesians," NewAdvent, http://www.newadvent.org/fathers/0105.htm.

According to Boyarin, at around this same time the rabbis, who were then emerging as the Jewish leadership, created a Jewish orthodoxy to mirror that of the Christians. "If you do not believe such and such or practice so and so, you are not a Jew," is the message Boyarin finds in the Jewish texts of the period.[6] It was as if Jewish and Christian leaders were working together to create a religious border each could use to define their respective faiths. Christians who crossed the border in the wrong direction were labeled by the church fathers as *Judaizers*, and Jews who crossed this border in the other direction were labeled by the rabbis as *minim*, but the result in either case was the same: the border crosser was branded as "out of bounds," a heretic, anathema.[7]

Boyarin's view of religious borders is essentially a negative one. He describes religious borders in political/geographical terms, as forming territories "constructed out of acts of discursive (and too often actual) violence."[8] In contrast, the view of Rachel Adler is more nuanced. In her article "To Live Outside the Law, You Must Be Honest," Adler argues that religious borders are necessary.[9] It is through the establishment and regulation of its border that a group maintains "its distinctiveness and its integrity."[10] Adler believes that Jews in particular need borders. Without a Jewish border, "we would be inundated; Jews and Judaism would become indistinguishable from the external environment."[11]

Adler thinks of religious borders in terms of biology instead of politics. Adler notes that the cells of the human body are bounded by "a membrane that keeps the inside and outside from merging and governs exchanges between the two environments."[12] Like a cell, a religion needs to regulate what comes in and goes out. If a religion's boundaries are too porous, it ceases to be unique or distinguishable from the outside—it loses its identity—or it runs the risk of external invasion. But if a religion's boundaries are too rigid, its contents are shut off from needed light and nutrition, and the religion calcifies and dies. The survival of a religion depends on its ability to govern

---

6. Boyarin, *Border Lines*, 10.

7. Boyarin, *Border Lines*, 2.

8. Boyarin, *Border Lines*, xiv.

9. Rachel Adler, "To Live Outside the Law, You Must Be Honest: Boundaries, Borderlands and the Ethics of Cultural Negotiation," *The Reconstructionist* (Spring 2004): 4.

10. Adler, "Boundaries," 4.

11. Adler, "Boundaries," 10.

12. Adler, "Boundaries," 10.

its borders to maintain the requisite separation from the outside world while permitting the optimal level of border crossing.

Adler points out that Jews have had a difficult time maintaining boundaries. The promised Jewish land of Israel was located on one of the busiest intersections in antiquity, a "narrow strip of land between the desert and the sea that offered the only access between great rival empires north and south of it."[13] Not only did foreign armies frequently cross Israel's borders, but so did foreign ways of thought and worship. The potential for outside incursion only increased as Jews lost political independence, Temple, and land. The instability of Jewish boundaries created something of a paradox: Jews became naturally anxious about the integrity of the Jewish border, but the thing we call Judaism is itself partially a product of these border incursions. In Adler's words, "There never was a time when ancient Israelite religion or the Judaism that succeeded it were not being influenced by the cultures and religions they encountered."[14]

But even before Jews had borders we needed to protect, we were busy crossing other people's borders, beginning with Abraham's crossing into the promised land and continuing through the Exodus, the Babylonian exile, the Diaspora, and the founding of the modern State of Israel. There is something Jewish in the possibility of crossing over, the possibility that (in Adler's words) "a slave can become free, a Moabite can become an Israelite, and an Assyrian city doomed to destruction can turn in repentance and be saved."[15] Adler is in effect arguing that while Judaism needs borders, these borders must be open to crossing in order to be "Jewish" in character.

Clearly, Boyarin and Adler see religious borders in different ways. But both teach that religious borders raise moral questions. From Boyarin we learn that people can be hurt by the imposition of religious borders, and that any religious border causing injury is a border begging to be reconceived. Adler teaches that it is sometimes right to "guard" the border, other times to "cross" it, still other times to "resituate" it, and sometimes the border must be eliminated altogether.[16] The challenge we face is in figuring out which of these border actions to take and when to take them.

---

13. Adler, "Boundaries," 5.
14. Adler, "Boundaries," 5–6.
15. Adler, "Boundaries," 6.
16. Adler, "Boundaries," 14.

※

As "Bring a Friend to Church" Sunday approached, I felt less and less inclined to face the moral challenge posed by Boyarin and Adler. My alternative plan was to sleep in. I figured that my wife would cooperate, unable to resist a typical Sunday morning spent over coffee, brunch, and the arts section of the local newspaper. But instead, the idea of taking me to church grew on her, in reaction (and in proportion) to my nervous anticipation of the event.

So I found myself doing what many good Christians do on good Sunday mornings: driving to church. Church in this case being Coupeville's Christ the King Church, which holds services in a building located on a local nature preserve. Driving into the preserve's parking lot, it was easy to figure out which of the preserve's buildings housed the church: it was the building dominated by the pastor standing in its doorway. Humans come in all sizes, and some of the larger humans are long or leggy, while others are towering or lofty. Pastor Todd King is just big: big in a goofy kind of way, like the biggest kid in your elementary school class who just wants to fit in with the other kids and can never quite manage that.

With Todd dominating the doorway, we weren't about to pass inside the church anonymously. That turned out to be a good thing. Todd is nothing if not a good greeter. He welcomed us. He had been told we might be there. He was happy we had come. But he didn't go overboard. He didn't act like he'd never seen a Jew in church before. He didn't make us feel exotic. It's a gift, to be able to make a stranger feel welcome, and at the same time not strange. Todd has that gift.

Entering the church, the first experience was of quiet. At the back of the pulpit were two teenage boys, setting up drums and an amp for electric guitar. Off to one side was a life-sized wood carving of Jesus on the cross. The wood carving was mounted on a wheeled platform, so that poor Jesus could be moved into a closet for secular occasions.

Perhaps a dozen congregants had already arrived; most talked in low tones in the back of the church, by the coffee urn. Our friends had not arrived yet. We were early.

I looked around for the prayer books. But there were no prayer books, and this unsettled me. Prayer in synagogue means a book, or more often, books: not just a *siddur* (prayer book), but also a prayer supplement special to that synagogue, plus announcements, study materials, and sometimes a copy of the Torah and Haftorah. Learning to juggle all these materials without allowing any of them to hit the floor is a part of growing up Jewish. Todd's church encourages folks to bring their Bibles with them, but most of his congregants sat down to pray with nothing but coffee cups in their hands. It was as if they were about to watch a movie! Almost by instinct, I grabbed a church membership brochure from the back of the room. Something to read, *anything*, felt better in hand than nothing.

Next question: where to sit? Sitting in the back row would have felt most comfortable, but it also felt too noncommittal, like I couldn't wait to get out of there. I could not sit in the front row, because Jesus had complained about Pharisees who took "the best seats in the synagogue," and I didn't want to appear like that kind of Jew (Matt. 23:6). We settled on seats away from the aisles, equidistant from the front and back rows. There would be plenty of room on either side for our friends to join us.

We waited. The church filled in. The seats to each side of us were taken by people we did not know. A girl joined the two boys at the pulpit; she was the singer, dressed in rock 'n' roll black. The band began to play, in a soft electric style with the beat pulled back so we could understand the lyrics. Not that there was any problem understanding the lyrics, which were displayed, PowerPoint-style, on a screen above the band.

I tried to sing along. I figured it was okay for a Jew to sing in church, so long as the Jew stuck to Jewish topics like receiving daily bread. I meant to avoid any nonkosher lyrics, such as G-d being in three persons. I figured I could edit out the non-Jewish stuff on the fly.

But the lyrics didn't work like I'd expected. Instead, the songs were all about how Jesus had suffered and died. Actually, the songs went beyond suffering and dying. Jesus had been crushed, smashed to bits. The imagery was both violent and immediate. It was as if Jesus had been crucified just a few minutes earlier. Moreover, in these songs Jesus had died not just for "you" or for "us," but for "me," the "me" in this case being each individual person in the room who felt that suffering and believed in its power of salvation.

The band's lead singer appeared to be suffering also. She sang with eyes half-closed, her focus deep within. She sang of the misery she'd known before she'd known Jesus. While Jesus had suffered, so she no longer had to, she sang as if she acutely remembered the terrible place from which she'd been delivered by Jesus, as if that place would remain uncomfortably close to her forever. Or perhaps, it was her remembered suffering that gave her a path to Jesus, as if suffering is the thing we most share in common with G-d.

For me, this was the most surprising and palpable experience of this particular morning: that of pain. It was like walking through the corridors of a hospital, not being sure whether the polite thing to do was to notice the suffering of the sick and dying in the rooms to my left and right, or pretend not to notice.

The music ended after thirty minutes of angst, and Todd took over. Standing at the pulpit, Todd looked larger than before. He wore a t-shirt, blue jeans, and sandals. Sandals! My friend wasn't kidding about the casual dress code.

If I remember correctly, Todd's sermon began with Matthew 22:34–46, where the Pharisees test Jesus by asking him which command of Torah is the greatest. Jesus answers with Deuteronomy 6:5, from the Shema, the basic prayer of Jewish belief ("You shall love the L[-]RD your G[-]d with all your heart, and with all your soul and with all your might"), and Leviticus 19:18, possibly the basic tenet of Jewish ethics ("You shall love your neighbor as yourself"). Good Jewish answers! I wondered if Todd chose this sermon to make me feel at ease. Todd said that nearly every Jew in first-century Palestine knew their Holy Scriptures backwards and forwards (a gross exaggeration I'm sure, but I didn't mind a little flattery of my ancient relatives), and that the Pharisees were the acknowledged masters of scripture. The problem with the Pharisees, according to Todd, was that in their mastery they lost sight of the great simplicity of the greatest of the commandments. It was a forest-and-trees kind of problem. While I hated to admit it, Todd had a point. I too feel that something can be lost in too much attention to detail.

But Todd wasn't preaching about Jews and Judaism. He was talking about people he regards as "Pharisees" within present-day Christianity. These "Pharisees" preach things in addition to the Christian basics and try to make those additions fundamental to the faith. These Christians preach of loving G-d and neighbor . . . but they also preach that Christians must vote the right way, and believe that the Bible is inerrant, and believe that Creation took six days, and believe that there was a historical Adam . . . or else risk being drummed out of the church for lack of faith. Todd called this approach "Christianity Plus": the Christianity of what Jesus taught, plus a bunch of other stuff that's not supposed to be there.

Then Todd did something unexpected. He apologized. He said that he was a representative of *the* Church, the Church at large, and not just his church. He said that *the* Church had hurt many people, by distorting the teaching of Jesus, and by effectively excluding Christians who loved G-d and neighbor but couldn't hack the extras demanded by Christianity Plus. He apologized for the pain this had caused.

Todd was close to tears. So were many in the room. So was I, even though I knew Todd was not apologizing to me. The pain inflicted by Christians on Jews could be addressed another day. Today, I had witnessed a private moment within the Christian border.

The worship service was over. We spotted our friend, who had arrived late for services with her new boyfriend. They were late for their next appointment, so we set a time to meet for dinner in the next few days. The remainder of the congregation departed as they had arrived: quietly and seriously. No one lingered to chat up the pastor, or share news, or ask us what it all meant to us.

We exited the church, recrossing whatever border we had traversed earlier that morning, without incident.

✳

What did it mean, to cross the Jewish-Christian border that Sunday morning in Coupeville? These border crossings mean something different to Jews than they do to Christians. To understand, think of this border as Boyarin does, like a border that separates neighboring countries. But keep in mind that today there are nearly 3 billion Christians in the world, and fewer than 15 million Jews. It won't do to consider the border between countries of roughly equal size, such as Canada and the United States. Instead, think of the Jewish-Christian border as separating a large country from one that is very, very small. A good example is the border lying between Germany and the Grand Duchy of Luxembourg. You say you've never heard of Luxembourg? It's no wonder. The little nation of Luxembourg is smaller than the smallest of the states in the United States. It is only two-thirds the size of Rhode Island.

(If you're like me and your knowledge of geography is weak, just imagine anything bordering on something 150 times bigger.)

The nature of the German-Luxembourg border depends on which side of the border you're standing on. A German might be forgiven for not noticing this border at all. But as Germany has invaded Luxembourg twice in the past hundred years, this border is of great consequence to Luxembourg. The invasions make it clear: despite international law, the border between Germany and Luxembourg is effectively controlled by Germany.

The Germans can close this border, or force it open, or move it, or (as they have done) wipe it off the map. The only power Luxembourg can exercise on its own (without German cooperation) is to control the passage of its citizens into Germany.

Here, the analogy to Judaism and Christianity is apt. For most of our shared history, Christians have crossed the Jewish-Christian border with impunity and without Jewish permission.[17] Some of these crossings took the form of full-fledged invasions, whether organized as crusades, inquisitions, pogroms, or other acts of violence. Other crossings were more subtle. For example, there were times when Jews were routinely and periodically forced to listen to Christian sermons aimed at their conversion.[18] Christians controlled the Christian-Jewish border in other ways: sometimes preventing Jews from crossing the border,[19] sometimes redrawing the border to further confine Jews, and sometimes expelling Jews outside of national borders.[20] For most of this history, Jews had no comparable power; it being a crime in most places and times to convert to Judaism or seek such conversion.[21]

---

17. It is impossible to write a book about Jewish-Christian relations without referring to the history of Christian anti-Semitism and anti-Judaism. Good short summaries of this history can be found on the websites of the Anti-Defamation League, "A Brief History of Anti-Semitism," Anti-Defamation League, 2013, https://www.adl.org/sites/default/files/documents/assets/pdf/education-outreach/Brief-History-on-Anti-Semitism-A.pdf; and the United States Holocaust Memorial Museum, beginning at "Antisemitism in History: From the Early Church to 1400," https://www.ushmm.org/wlc/en/article.php?ModuleId=10007170. There are good book-length treatments of this topic, including Phyllis Goldstein, *A Convenient Hatred: The History of Antisemitism* (Brookline, MA: Facing History and Ourselves, 2012).

18. Harvey Hames, "Discourse in the Synagogue: Ramon Llull and his Dialogue with the Jews," September 17, 1994, www.ramonllull.net/sw_studies/studies_original/hhames.html.

19. Some of the earliest anti-Jewish actions of Christendom were designed to keep Jews "in their place" on their side of the Jewish-Christian border. Jews were forbidden to marry Christians in 399 CE, were prohibited from holding positions in Roman government in 439 CE, and were prevented from appearing as witnesses against Christians in court in 531 CE. See "A Brief History of Anti-Semitism," Anti-Defamation League, 2013, https://www.adl.org/sites/default/files/documents/assets/pdf/education-outreach/Brief-History-on-Anti-Semitism-A.pdf.

20. Gerhard Falk, "History of the Ghetto," Jewish Buffalo on the Web, jbuff.com/c032307.htm; Joshua Levy, "Expulsion and Readmission," My Jewish Learning, www.myjewishlearning.com/article/expulsion-and-readmission/.

21. Magda Teter, "Conversion," *The YIVO Encyclopedia of Jews in Eastern Europe*, www.yivoencyclopedia.org/article.aspx/Conversion#idoeslai.

Of course, the Jewish-Christian border is today a much safer place, but the Jewish fear of this border has not disappeared, nor is this fear completely unjustified. There are Christians today who target Jews with aggressive and well-funded missionary efforts.[22] I hope it's obvious that these continued efforts are an obstacle to Jewish-Christian dialogue. It is not possible to engage Jews in dialogue and simultaneously seek to transform us into something else. At the same time, Jews who wish to participate in this dialogue need to accept that Christian evangelism is fundamental to the Christian faith, and is not intrinsically anti-Semitic. We can also appreciate recent debate, particularly within the Catholic Church, to determine whether Christians should stop seeking the conversion of Jews.[23]

But there's no way around it: the Christian evangelistic impulse creates a problem for Jewish-Christian dialogue. This impulse creates an *asymmetry*, as there is no corresponding desire within Judaism to seek the religious conversion of non-Jews. We Jews approach Jewish-Christian dialogue with the reasonable request that we be accepted in this dialogue for who we are, *as Jews*, and not as potential Christians. But to reciprocate, we must in turn accept our Christian dialogue partners as Christians, and not as some Jewish-idealized version of what we wish Christians to be. So long as the evangelistic impulse remains at the heart of Christianity, we Jews must somehow learn to live with this impulse.

In turn, Christians must understand that we Jews perceive Christian evangelism as a threat. Despite whatever Christians might hear about the possibility of being a "Jewish Christian," the vast majority of Jews worldwide reject this possibility. A Jew who adopts a "belief" in Jesus will be regarded

---

22. The organization Jews for Judaism claims on their website that there are over 1,000 Christian missionary groups spending over $300 million annually on programs targeting Jews for conversion to Christianity, http://www.jewsforjudaism. ca/home. From the website of the Evangelical Council for Financial Accountability, http://www.ecfa.org/, the five largest organizations I could find devoted to evangelism aimed at Jews have a combined annual budget of over $85 million. These organizations are Jews for Jesus, Jewish Voice Ministries International, Messianic Vision, Chosen People Ministries, and The Friends of Israel Gospel Ministry (search performed on May 23, 2017). Other large organizations (in particular, the Southern Baptist Convention and the Assemblies of God) are reputed to fund substantial efforts targeted at converting Jews to Christianity. Additional efforts at proselytization are funded by "Messianic Jewish" groups.

23. See, for example, John L. Allen, Jr., "Church should not pursue conversion of Jews, pope says," *National Catholic Reporter*, March 10, 2011, https://www.ncr online.org/blogs/ncr-today/church-should-not-pursue-conversion-jews-pope-says.

by nearly all Jews (except, of course, by "Messianic Jews") as having left Judaism behind to join a Christian community.[24]

If there's a danger for Jews in Jewish-Christian dialogue, then why engage in this dialogue? For me, the answer to this question begins with "holy envy."[25] In my experience, there are insights that come from holy envy that cannot be realized in any other way. These insights can arise from our experience of the Jewish-Christian border, and the *intention* we bring to this border. Again, it's useful to think of the way we behave when we cross an international border to spend time elsewhere. True, some of us behave badly in foreign lands, making no effort to learn the local language or appreciate the local culture. But some of us behave like amateur ambassadors, trying to give others the best possible impression of who we are and where we come from. When I write my blog and when I talk to Christians, I try to make such an impression, so that they come away with a positive feeling about Judaism.

And it's true . . . in order to do my best to reflect Judaism . . . I change. I try to be more Jewish. I do things I would not normally do around my Jewish friends and neighbors. For example, I write a blog on Jewish-Christian interfaith topics, but I do not post to my blog on Shabbat. Normally, I have no qualms about using a computer on Shabbat—denominationally, I associate with Reform Judaism, and Reform Judaism does not bar the use of computers on Shabbat. But Orthodox Jews do not use computers on Shabbat, and it is part of Jewish practice in all denominations to keep Shabbat holy by abstaining from at least some activities that are workaday or mundane. My blog is in a Jewish-Christian space—how can I demonstrate to Christians the sanctity of Shabbat if I publicly post material to my blog on Shabbat?

---

24. In this book, I use the term "Messianic Judaism" to refer to present-day movements combining some features of Judaism with a Christology (the theological interpretation of the nature, person, and deeds of Jesus) adapted from Christian roots. I similarly use the term "Messianic Jew" to refer to those persons affiliated with or belonging to such movements. I have struggled with how to refer to these movements in this book, as the term "Messianic Judaism" consists exclusively of contested elements: (a) the vast majority of Jews consider "Messianic Judaism" to be part of Christianity, not Judaism, and (b) the coming of a future Messiah is a fundamental Jewish belief (not that all Jews hold this belief or hold it in the same way), and is not the exclusive property of those who think that Jesus is their Messiah. By placing "Messianic Jew" and "Messianic Judaism" within quotes, I mean to say (without intending disrespect) that this is the way this movement and its followers have chosen to identify themselves.

25. We discuss the concept of "holy envy" in the introduction to this book.

And if I'm not going to post to my blog on Shabbat, I certainly cannot post comments to *Anthony's* blog on Shabbat. Eventually, my practice spreads: I now try not to send e-mail on Shabbat. I try to use the computer on Shabbat only for private "religious" purposes. Orthodox I am not! But I am, in this small way, more self-consciously Jewish.

Here's another example: Recently, Anthony attended a conference in Orange County, which is about fifty miles from my home in Los Angeles. We wanted to get together after the conference was over. But the conference ended on a Friday night, when Shabbat begins. Jewish practice varies on the matter of driving on Shabbat—Orthodox Jews won't drive on Shabbat except in a life-and-death situation, but Jews like me drive on Shabbat without giving the matter a second thought. But I was reluctant to drive on Shabbat to pick up Anthony. *It didn't seem right to me.* With Anthony, I feel the need to represent Judaism—not just my Judaism, but the Judaism of all Jews. Yes, I understand that I cannot represent a diverse body of 14 million people. Yet it seemed wrong that Anthony might be the cause of my taking an action that some Jews believe is a violation of the sanctity of Shabbat. I not only want to represent Judaism well to non-Jews; I also want to represent *dialogue* well to those outside of the dialogue.

After debating the matter internally, I decided it would be okay to drive to Orange County to pick up Anthony, so long as we drove from there directly to my synagogue in Los Angeles for Shabbat services. Does this make any sense? Oddly enough, the decision I made coincides in certain respects with the rule adopted by Conservative Judaism, a denomination to which I do not belong. I'm not sure what my decision actually "represented" to Anthony, or to anyone else. But my point remains: in front of non-Jewish witnesses, I engage in new practices that feel more "Jewish" to me.

And some of these practices stick. I am a more observant and faithful Jew today than when I started my study of Christianity. I am changed when I cross the border into Christian territory, but I'm also changed by the return journey home. Think about what it's like to come home after a trip to another country. The trip causes the familiar things of home to become temporarily unfamiliar. When I return home, I find myself saying odd things, such as, "I'm looking forward to sleeping tonight in my own bed." I don't normally think it's special to sleep where I usually sleep. But returning home, the usual place isn't usual anymore, and I can experience the particular things I like about "my own bed": the configuration of pillows and blankets, the objects I like by my bedside, even the slight indentation my body has made over the years into the surface of the mattress. These are things I'll stop noticing after a few days home. But for a short time, I can truly appreciate that there's no place like home.

There are other things I notice on my return from a foreign land that I don't like. The cars, for example. They seem crazy-big, in comparison (say) to the cars in Europe. I'll find myself thinking aloud, "Why do you Americans have to drive such big cars?" This is another odd thing to say, for me to talk about "Americans" as if I were not an "American." And of course, taking a vacation overseas does not transform me into someone not American. Instead, my border crossing allows me to see things from a different perspective, almost from the outside looking in.

When I crossed the border into Todd's church, I saw much to appreciate. For example: I admire the easy way Christians talk of their experience with G-d. We Jews (or at least, those of us outside of Orthodox Judaism) aren't exactly comfortable with G-d talk. We're either too rational to feel right about the supernatural, or too "spiritual" to feel right about a rationally constructed G-d. We want to distance ourselves from language that makes G-d out to be a male when we'd like to eliminate male privilege, or as a father when we're suspicious of patriarchy. In our concern for what G-d is not, we have deep Jewish roots: the Jewish philosopher Maimonides wrote that "the description of G[-]d by means of negations is the correct description."[26] But our attempts at reforming G-d talk serve to make G-d more abstract—a "ruler" instead of a "king," the "Divine" instead of the "Almighty."

In contrast, the worshippers at Todd's church seemed to accept that Jesus was there with them—Jesus, a Jewish guy from two thousand years ago! This Jesus, who was perhaps supernatural, undoubtedly male, and a father only in a symbolic sense, also has a recognizable face. Moses wanted to see G-d in the face and could not (Exod. 33:18–20), but through faith in Jesus, Christians get to see G-d's face all the time. Does this cause me to feel holy envy? You bet it does.

But when I return home, to synagogue from church, I feel grateful for being able to "sleep in my own bed." There is a cost to seeing G-d in one particular face. In his article "Beyond the Personal G[-]d," Daniel Matt writes

---

26. Moses Maimonides, *The Guide of the Perplexed* (trans. Shlomo Pines; Chicago: University of Chicago Press, 1963), 58–59. I rely here on the discussion of Maimonides taken from Daniel C. Matt, "Beyond the Personal God," *The Reconstructionist* (1994): 38, available at http://www.therra.org/Reconstructionist/Spring1994.pdf.

that "as we define things, we confine them and confine our understanding."[27]
If I limited G-d's face to that of a single first-century Palestinian Jew, I move
further from the Jewish idea articulated by Arthur Green that "each person
is G[-]d's image."[28] Perhaps these Jewish ideas are less concrete than their
Christian counterparts, but they also strike me as more expansive, and I
think I prefer the expansive to the concrete.

Perhaps this is why I see a potential for good Jewish things in Jewish-
Christian dialogue. When the dialogue is working well, my dialogue partner
becomes something more than the religious "other" who defines who I am
not. Instead, my partner becomes a *possibility*, someone I might be and at
the same time know I cannot be. In dialogue with a Christian partner, I
know that two thousand years ago his spiritual ancestors and mine lived
together within a pluralistic Palestinian Jewish community, sharing (even
if contentiously) land, Temple, and Torah as fellow Jews. If I'd lived back
then, I might have known Jews who were followers of Jesus. I might have
been invited to join them. Probably, I would have declined the invitation.
But I would have considered the invitation differently than I would now.

When I look at Christianity today, I think I see things that were part
of Jewish life in the first century, even for Jews back then who did not follow Jesus. For example, the Christianity I encounter today often speaks of
heaven and hell, it being the goal to avoid the one and join the other. Without
knowing for certain, I imagine that many Jews in Jesus' day spoke in similar
ways, and that one aspect of "the parting of the ways" is that Jews came to
discuss the afterlife differently.[29] I'm simply not going to hear a rabbi today
threaten anyone with hellfire!

---

27. Daniel Matt, "Beyond the Personal G[-]d," *The Reconstructionist* 59, vol. 1
(Spring 1994): 38–47.

28. See Arthur Green, *Seek My Face: A Jewish Mystical Theology* (Woodstock,
VT: Jewish Lights Publishing, 2003), 79.

29. On this point, the apocryphal book of Judith talks about the wicked of the
earth being confined to a place that sounds to me a lot like the Christian concept of
hell: "Woe to the nations that rise against my people! The L[-]rd Almighty will re-
quite them; in the day of judgment he will punish them: He will send fire and worms
into their flesh; and they shall burn and suffer forever." See Judith 16:17; translation
from *The Catholic Study Bible* (Oxford: Oxford University Press, 1990). Granted,
the book of Judith does not appear in a Jewish Bible; it is a deuterocanonical book
included by the Catholic Church and other churches in their Bibles. I cannot state
for certain that this idea is Jewish, or that this text wasn't revised by the church to
make it more Christian.

I think that a present-day Jewish experience of Christianity carries with it this same tension between possibility and not-possibility. Take as an example the pain I observed in Todd's church. I reacted to this pain as something not Jewish, as being an example of what separates Judaism from Christianity. Yet during a recent trip to Israel's Shoah memorial at Yad Vashem, I found myself wearing a *kippah* as I wandered through the various exhibits and listened to the recorded testimony of those who survived the Nazi effort to murder world Jewry. When is pain a kosher religious experience? If the Christian experience of pain is an impossibility for me, does it nevertheless highlight a Jewish understanding of pain as a way to draw closer to G-d?

⁂

As planned, my wife and I had dinner with our Christian friend who had invited us to "Bring a Friend to Church" day, along with her boyfriend. They listened politely to our impression of their church. What was important to them was not what we'd thought, but the fact that we'd been there, to experience what they experience. They talked about their decision to bring Jesus into their lives, how it had changed them and made the world brighter and special. For my friend, the experience brought her closer to her teenage son, who had discovered the church first (and was one of the boys in the church band!).

As they talked, I thought I noticed a certain glow about them. It was not the kind of glow that can be objectively measured. But my impression was that here are two people who have recently entered sacred space and found there the presence of the Divine. For me, that was another moment of holy envy—or perhaps, it was a moment where I realized that I can encounter the Divine presence in church only with the help of a Christian intermediary. This, too, is a good thing, as it affirms yet another of Krister Stendahl's rules for religious understanding: When you are trying to understand another religion, ask the adherents of that religion and not its enemies.

Paul Tillich wrote that "the boundary is the best place for acquiring knowledge," but he also noted that boundary crossing "is difficult and dangerous in life, which again and again demands decisions and thus the exclusion of alternatives."[30] But Tillich's experience of borders included the

---

30. Paul Tillich, *On the Boundary: An Autobiographical Sketch* (New York: Charles Scribner's Sons, 1966), 13. This essay is a translation of Part I of Tillich's *The Interpretation of History*, written in 1936.

crossing of a national border maintained by Nazi Germany. In contrast, my boundary crossing during "Bring a Friend to Church Day" was not particularly difficult. As I wrote earlier, the character of a border depends on the intention of those who maintain it. The intention of the border I crossed that Sunday years ago was set by the church pastor in the church doorway: he took the role of host, making me his guest.

Perhaps we should revise Stendahl's rules for religious understanding: The best way to understand another's religion may be to score the right invitation to cross that religion's border.

Borders

Dialogue

Larry: Is the Christian ideal a world without boundaries?

Anthony: Yes, that is the Christian ideal. I mean, the ideal is to live without boundaries that create hostility or animosity.

Larry: But you can't make that distinction. Boundaries are by nature both good and bad. You can't say, I don't like the bad part of boundaries, but . . .

Anthony: But we do say that. We say we don't want the bad boundaries, but the good ones can stay.

Larry: Well then, what's a good boundary? What's a good, Christian boundary? Catholic and Protestant?

Anthony: Male and female.

Larry: That's interesting.

Anthony: There are certain boundaries we want to maintain. We know it is more complicated than that, but you asked about the ideal. At least this is the case with most conservative Christians.

Larry: Much of your chapter describes a Christian ideal of boundaries, and I think that is great. You describe an ideal Christian pilgrim fearlessly crossing boundaries, where in my chapter I wrote about the considerable fear I feel approaching very ordinary boundaries. I mean, why should I have felt any fear about going to a church, where I had friends, for "Take a Friend to Church Day," while in your chapter, you seem to recognize the boundaries you cross in your rearview mirror, as almost an afterthought!

Anthony: I was speaking in ideal terms in my chapter, thinking in terms of Christian beginnings. Several scholars of the apostle Paul have made this argument: Paul wanted to eliminate any boundary that would create distance between insiders and outsiders based on cultural markers.

Larry: That's Jimmy Dunn's argument, right?[1]

Anthony: Right. Paul wanted to keep a number of boundaries, but those boundaries we might consider to be culturally ethnic; if they got in the way of true unity within the early church, then for Paul they weren't worth keeping. That's an idealized vision. Whether it's Jimmy Dunn being idealistic, or whether this is Paul's idealism, it is an ideal. It's not something we Christians ever figured out. This is idealism in terms of this is the world we are trying to create; this is a good thing, we are on this pilgrimage together, we're trying to eliminate power structures that oppress, things like that. This is very idealistic.

Larry: Right. And at some point, when you get into questions of social justice, I think I'm reading in your chapter something that is particularly you.

Anthony: It's not necessarily *just* me.

Larry: I think when you talk about a borderless world, where the ideal Christian is a pilgrim of some type, that's a finger on the pulse of something sweeping.

Anthony: And maybe it's one of our biggest problems, as I'm trying to hint at in the chapter. If the dominant power structure, the folks who represent the system of power, view the world as borderless, but no one else does, then basically what you have is imperialism.

Larry: Yes. One thing that struck me in comparing our chapters is on this very question. If the ideal Christian world is borderless, then the ideal Jewish world has borders.

Anthony: Hmm.

---

1. James D. G. Dunn is an important Christian scholar. Larry informally refers to him here as "Jimmy" because this is how Anthony frequently refers to him in conversation.

Larry: Maybe in the messianic age, there will be no borders.

Anthony: No, it seems like even in Isaiah, there are borders. It just so happens that the border does not present a problem anymore. We can invite the Gentiles across the border to worship in the Temple, because they are no longer a threat. The people who are a threat are gone.

Larry: I struggle with that particular reading of Isaiah. I think your reading is fair, but I think there are other ways to read Isaiah that don't quite work that way.

Anthony: I think you're right. So yes, the Christian ideal would be a world like the one I just described in Isaiah, whether my reading is right or not—that there are borders, but they don't represent hostility. These borders are there to invite people to cross, in a way that is hospitable.

Larry: Yes. What you are describing now sounds more ideally Jewish to me. It sounds like the article from Rachel Adler that I described in my chapter. The ideal boundary has an ideal sort of permeability.

Anthony: Yeah.

Larry: It does serve to distinguish what's inside from what's outside, but you need a certain amount of travel, you need an open border.

Anthony: I wonder if I might get a different perspective from someone more conservative, who might say, "Look, the only way to preserve our identity as Jews is through a very well-defined border."

Larry: I don't think it's possible to maintain such a strict border. For example: something like half of American Jews are marrying outside of the faith.

Anthony: So that train has left the station.

Larry: In the United States at least, I don't think it is possible to get that train back. The Jews I know believe in the romantic ideal, same as Christians. We fall in love, and we want to marry the person we love. If the person you fall in love with is not Jewish, and that's my story, am I going to sacrifice my personal long-term happiness for the sake of preserving a more rigid religious border? Such a border would require not just a change in Jewish attitudes toward intermarriage, but a complete reorganization of Jewish life. Think of this in terms of generations. My mother and father never really imagined that they could marry outside of their faith, in part because Jews weren't perceived then as suitable marriage partners for non-Jews. But it was also the case that their social circle was exclusively or close to exclusively Jewish.

Anthony: And, vice versa, that works both ways. The social circle for a Christian was exclusively Christian.

Larry: Yes. In our discussions, you made something clear to me that I'd never carefully considered before—that many Christians have never met a Jew. Or the more scary thing you said is that the only Jew a Christian may have met is someone from Jews for Jesus who came to speak at their church.

Anthony: That's right. Cornel West talks about this in his book with Michael Lerner. West says that Judaism was an important concept for him, growing up in his Black Baptist church in Sacramento. But as far as meeting someone Jewish, this didn't really happen until he was at Harvard.

Larry: Half my family identifies as Orthodox. My younger sister and brother, the two youngest of my three siblings, are *ba'al tchuva*, which means that they were not brought up Orthodox, but they embraced Orthodoxy as young adults. They live in a nearly exclusively Jewish world. The kids go to Jewish day schools . . .

Anthony: Because only your brother lives in Israel, right?

Larry: Yes, but my sister and brother-in-law live in an Orthodox Jewish neighborhood in Queens, New York. The neighborhood is not exclusively Orthodox, it's maybe 50 percent, but their friends I believe are all Orthodox, their kids go to Orthodox schools, and there is not a great deal of "dialogue" in that world with non-Jews. I mean "dialogue" in the most informal sense. In this sense, it's much like the world my parents grew up in.

Anthony: Well, if you want it badly enough, you can create a personal community that reflects Old World ideas. It doesn't bespeak the culture at large.

Larry: The thing is, the Judaism I grew up with was eager to become part of the bigger world. We so wanted to contribute to that world. We wanted to attend secular universities. Jewish authors wanted to be read by non-Jews,

Jewish musicians want to play at Carnegie Hall. As kids, we wanted to be baseball players and, later, rock musicians! I can remember the generation that thought they were still breaking down barriers, and making it possible for Jews to do whatever Jews wanted to do, and be accepted at it. I don't think it's possible to go back to a life where Jews live predominantly in a Jewish world, and it's a whole other question whether it is desirable . . .

Anthony: Barry Schwartz would say that it is desirable, because you want your kids to be happy. You don't want to be strangers in a strange land. I know that this is a complicated position . . .

Larry: . . . and this raises the question of Israel, because Israel is a place where you can live a secular life, if you want to, and still travel in predominantly Jewish circles. I mean, a substantial minority of Israelis are not Jewish, but Judaism is the dominant culture in Israel. You don't have to live an Orthodox yeshiva kind of life to be part of that culture. There have been voices in Israel for a long time saying, "It's time for the Diaspora to end and for all Jews to return to Israel." There are a lot of Israelis who feel that you can't really be Jewish outside of Israel. And that's another answer to the question. Few American Jews think that way, but it's another answer.

Anthony: You talked about Boyarin in your chapter, so I want to bring René Girard into the conversation. One of Boyarin's premises is that the Jewish-Christian border is one of the most arbitrarily and socially constructed borders you could imagine.

Larry: Right.

Anthony: And that suggests it is an easy border to blur, if you want to think about it that way. Girard would say—and for the sake of disclosure, Girard is a Christian, although I don't think he's championed as such—but his main work relates to violence and the sacred.[2] His book of that title suggests that in a society, almost any society, there are acceptable and unacceptable forms of violence. Certain kinds of violence are viewed as not just acceptable but sacred, and there are other forms of violence that society views as unacceptable. All this takes place in a sort of well-defined culture. But if there's a breakdown in the cultural borders that defend the social function of the

---

2. René Girard, *Violence and the Sacred*, trans. Patrick Gregory (Baltimore: Johns Hopkins University Press, 1979).

group—if these borders become fuzzy, or they collapse—then you have
an explosion of unanticipated and unwanted violence. You can think of a
few examples of problematic borders that seem to engender more violence
than others. I think it's the case that for Christians and Jews, the borders
that create the most hostility are the ones that blur distinctions. Right now,
the most problematic border for Christians is the gender border. We don't
like the blurring of this border, and we are very hostile as an overall group
to a secular society that we see as an affront to our traditional views about
gender. And then there are many of us progressives who want to push back
on this; we want to have this conversation, we want to invite a reimagining
of some of these traditional systems. From the Jewish side, it seems like one
of the biggest problems, an obstacle to Jewish-Christian dialogue, is the
concept of a Jewish Christian. You can think of this in terms of Messianic
Judaism, whose insiders define themselves as Jewish, but most Jews would
not see them as Jewish.

Larry: That's right.

Anthony: They inhabit a problematic border state, and there's lots of hostility.

Larry: It feels almost as if they've crafted their identity to annoy us.

Anthony: They occupy that fuzzy state between Jewish and Christian. This
is one of those delicate topics we tend not to touch in Jewish-Christian dialogue. They are different kinds of border crossings, but they both occupy
that fuzzy state between Jewish and Christian.

Larry: Let's generalize. When you say that the ideal Christian state is borderless, we've already got a problem. "Neither Jew nor Greek" means no Jews.
When Paul says, "Neither Jew nor Greek," most Christians think, "What a
lovely thing to say; this is Paul at his best." But to Jewish ears it doesn't sound
like you want to have us around!

Anthony: But Paul continues to identify as a Jew.

Larry: Yes I know, but . . .

Anthony: [*Laughs*] You're right. It's a problematic ideal, very Christian, and
it doesn't consider Jewish well-being.

Larry: Well it does, but it considers it to be a temporary concern; because in an ideal state, this border falls away. It's like when East Germany and West Germany eliminated their border and called their land greater Germany, and presumably most everyone was happy about it on both sides. The Jewish-Christian border disappears, and the combined space ends up being called "Christian" in all likelihood, and that's the ideal long-term Christian solution. And on some level, I think Jewish partners in Jewish-Christian dialogue need to have a certain tolerance for the Christian ideal of a borderless Jewish-Christian space, so long as what Christians are talking about is some vague and general idea that at some future undefined point, something might happen that would eliminate the need for the border. We can leave it to our respective Jewish and Christian points of view to imagine this faraway time and place.

Anthony: This conversation has to look different post-Shoah. Because any self-reflective Christian has to say that the way we have thought of the Jewish-Christian border historically has been catastrophic.

Larry: Yes.

Anthony: And we need to think about this differently, we need to approach this border in a better way that respects the wishes of our neighbors.

Larry: There are certainly voices within post-Shoah Christianity that envision Judaism as a permanent neighbor, that proclaim that Christians need not imagine Jews as potential Christians in order to have a Jewish-Christian friendship. There is even an idea among some Christians that Judaism could represent an alternate path to salvation.

Anthony: We've had that thread in Christianity for some time, but it's not a prominent thread. And it's probably not going to be a prominent thread in the near future. We are still very particularist.

Larry: Some Christians say that Christianity is a universal religion, in contrast to Judaism's supposed particularism.

Anthony: This is part of the problem that Paul created for us. [*Laughs*] And maybe Isaiah before Paul, I don't know.

Larry: Maybe.

Anthony: Let me get at this in a different way. If I go to YouTube, and I punch in "priest and rabbi," I'll probably come up with an interesting conversation between a priest and a rabbi. It will be respectful, a lot of joking, it's like a lovefest. Not always, but most of the time. But if I go to YouTube and punch in "Jew and Messianic Jew," the tone is hostile. I can only make sense of that in Girardian terms. The border is too fuzzy, or some sort of border has collapsed that has made one or the other party feel uncomfortable and insecure. So a very different tenor happens with that conversation.

Larry: This is a complicated matter. My first reaction is that the border between Jew and Messianic Jew from a Jewish perspective is simply the border between Jew and Christian. Messianic Jews are Christians who poke holes in the Jewish-Christian border.[3]

Anthony: Let's just imagine for a moment that I'm a Messianic Jew who proclaims, "Paul says I'm grafted in." In other words, I'm not respecting the border very well, I'm not respecting the differences as my dialogue partner perceives those differences. I'm running roughshod over any perception of the border you might have, and this is a problem. For you to say that it's simply the same border doesn't work: it is a different border. For a Messianic Jew and a mainstream Jew to enter into dialogue, this is a much different border. Let me put it in a different way. I went to a lecture by Rodger Kamenetz, who was reflecting on his time visiting the Dalai Lama. There were a number of rabbis and other Jewish representatives visiting the Dalai Lama at the same time.

Larry: This is *The Jew in the Lotus* book? That's a great book.[4]

Anthony: Yes. And he acknowledged that there is no threat in that context. Jews are not a threat to Lotus Tibet.

Larry: And Tibet is no threat to Jews.

---

3. A clarifying note: To be certain, many Messianic Jews *are* Jews from birth, and others might be Jews as a result of a conversion to Judaism in accordance with rules respected by most Jews. Larry is stating here, somewhat inartfully, that Jews do not regard members of Messianic Jewish congregations to be Jewish solely by their membership in these congregations.

4. Rodger Kamenetz, *The Jew in the Lotus: A Poet's Rediscovery of Jewish Identity in Buddhist India* (New York: HarperOne, 2007).

Anthony: At least, not in the mid-1980s. While you might have had a few Orthodox folks saying, why are these Jews consorting with idol worshipers, or whatever, the border between Jew and Buddhist was so different from the one at the Jewish-Christian border, because there wasn't any history at the Jewish-Buddhist border: there was no animosity, both parties entered the discussion willingly, and with mutual respect. Kamenetz acknowledged this: There is less baggage for Jews to adopt Buddhist practices than more Christian practices. But at least in most settings of Jewish-Christian dialogue, there is some sort of border that provides security, and this border in some way seems disrespected by Messianic Jews. Is that fair to say?

Larry: Even talking about a border between, let's say, mainstream and Messianic Jews . . . If you remember my chapter, I have a long footnote because I'm not sure what to call Messianic Jews. But even talking about a border between these two groups is something that most Jews won't accept. There is no border. What there is, is a group of followers of Christianity who are attacking Judaism in ways that we recognize historically.

Anthony: So they act very similarly to the way Christians have always acted.

Larry: In modern times, with the rise of the nation-state, Christians could no longer employ the power of the state to compel Jews to convert to Christianity, so those Christians interested in continuing this effort had to find another way to do it. Some of these Christians—first in England and later in America—formed groups of "Hebrew Christians," where the goal was to make it easier for Jews to accept Christianity. These groups acknowledged that hundreds of years of Christian persecution had left Jews with negative feelings about Christianity, and their goal was to make Christianity look more acceptable to Jews. Do Jews have negative associations with crucifixes? Well, then let's put that symbol to the side for the moment. Do Jews feel that Jewish monotheism is violated by the Trinitarian idea of Jesus as G-d? Okay, then let's stress a more Jewish idea, that Jesus is the longed-for Jewish Messiah. Granted, this was a more humane effort than that of Christian crusaders who tried to convert us at sword point. Yet conversion was the Christian goal here, same as always. But my point here has to do with the border. These organizations were run by people located firmly on the Christian side of the Jewish-Christian border. They merely built outposts for their organizations as close to the Jewish-Christian border as they could, in order to entice Jews to cross. And Messianic Judaism today is a direct outgrowth of this earlier effort. Some organizations today, like Jews for Jesus, are very similar to the Hebrew Christian groups from a hundred years ago. They exist to bring Jews to conventional, mainstream evangelical Protestantism. For most Jews, Messianic Judaism *is* Jews for Jesus and groups like them. These are missionary groups, well funded by Christians.

Anthony: I think this is a very good description of Messianic Judaism from an outsider's perspective.

Larry: But today, there is something new on the scene that I think most Jews fail to recognize. There are many Messianic Jewish synagogues that don't function like a processing station for Jews emigrating to Christianity. These synagogues are intended as final destinations. It's not the goal of these institutions to get Jews into the Baptist Church or the Pentecostal Church. These institutions want Jews as permanent members, to persist in perpetuity as Jewish Christians. There is even a concept of post-missionary Messianic Judaism, whose members have abandoned the idea of seeking the conversion of non-Christian Jews.

Anthony: There's an analogue here that is going to make Christians just as uncomfortable. It's not a perfect analogue, but there is a similar insider-outsider problem in definition. In the church where I grew up, Mormons and Jehovah's Witnesses were not considered Christians. They were a "cult." I've also heard "Jews for Jesus" called a "cult." We weren't too sure about Catholics, and you could just go down the line. The borders are pretty rigid and narrow. And yet in Jewish-Christian dialogue, we repeatedly use these population numbers, 2.7 billion Christians worldwide, but these numbers would not work in the church where I grew up, because a lot of those Christians aren't really Christians.

Larry: Yes, your numbers get much smaller if you question the Christian status of Catholics.

Anthony: But in my old church, when it comes to Jehovah's Witnesses and Mormons, there wouldn't be "doubts." There would be outright denial. "They" are not "us." There would be an "us and them" distinction that, frankly, would be insulting to most Mormons and Jehovah's Witnesses.

Larry: Yes.

Anthony: So if you are in dialogue with someone like that, and a lot of evangelicals feel this way—like in your chapter when you talk about young Christian missionaries knocking on your door. Well, it could be, from an outsider's perspective, that many of those people are not Christians, but Jehovah's Witnesses and Mormons. Ninety percent of the people knocking on your door are probably Jehovah's Witnesses, even though they identify themselves to you as "Christian." But now we run into Krister Stendahl's rule: Do the insiders get to define themselves, or does the definition come from outsiders, those who are enemies of the insiders? In other words, when evangelicals say that Mormons and Jehovah's Witnesses are not Christians, this is a hostile statement: "You're not us; you think you're us, but you're not us." It's a delineation without agreement, a disputed border. This creates a problem for us. If these folks knocking on your door are Christian in your view but I don't think of them as such, then the Jewish-Christian border becomes problematic too. So here is the question: Who gets to decide whether they are Christians or not? My answer would be, to be safe, let the insiders decide, in which case I come to a position that would make people at my parents' church very uncomfortable. Because at that point I'm saying, if Mormons call themselves Christians, who am I to say that they're not? Well, in reverse, if Messianic Jews call themselves "Jews," who are you to say that they are not?

Larry: I think the Jewish response would be that we don't define who is a Jew in the same way that Christians define who is a Christian. If I go by the traditional definition of who is a Jew, it is either someone with a Jewish mother, or someone who converts to Judaism under the authority of a rabbi recognized by mainstream Judaism as having the authority to oversee a conversion. But I would think about this differently. You said this in your chapter, and I don't know how many Christians would agree with you, but you said that Christianity is under no threat of extinction.

Anthony: No, no, we're not. You'd have to get pretty apocalyptic to suggest otherwise.

Larry: The problem with Messianic Judaism is that it is perceived as a threat to our survival. If we cannot set up a firm boundary where this is not a Jewish thing, then the border erodes.

Anthony: Yes. But the problem is, and I don't have to name anyone, but someone might say that *you* are a threat to Jewish survival, because you married a Gentile.

Larry: I affiliate with Reform Judaism, and there are Orthodox rabbis in Israel who refer to Reform Jewish rabbis as "goyim."

Anthony: Right. So, you see, the border shifts depending on which "insider" is talking.

Larry: But this does not answer the problem I'm raising. Instead, it shows how serious the problem is, because Messianic Judaism undermines my ability to say that how I practice is "Jewish." Messianic Judaism is, in effect, proof within the Jewish world that not everyone who professes Judaism is within Judaism. It is proof I have to acknowledge that someone can call their practice Jewish yet do things and believe things that put them "beyond the pale." It potentially gives an Orthodox Jew a better ability to say that I, too, am located on the other side of that border, and I don't want to be on that other side.

Anthony: Or it defines the border in a way that is disorienting.

Larry: Let me put all my cards on the table. I acknowledge the need for dialogue between mainstream and Messianic Jews. I think it's a requirement. I don't know whether anyone is ready for it, but it's needed. On the mainstream Jewish side, I don't hear much desire for this dialogue. I think Messianic Jews seek this dialogue.

Anthony: Are they seeking dialogue, or an opportunity to convert?

Larry: I can't know until I try it. Certainly, traditionally, the dialogue was intended to convert. But I think I see among some Messianic Jews—and I don't have firsthand experience with this, just things that I'm reading—an increased identification with mainstream Judaism and a decreased identification with mainstream Protestantism. Perhaps from a practical, political point of view, I should seek to encourage this change in identification. But if you read about individual cases, there are kids growing up in Messianic Jewish congregations who consider themselves Jewish, but aren't being invited to bar or bat mitzvahs by their Jewish friends, and can't get their Jewish friends to come to their bar or bat mitzvahs. And this gets back to Boyarin. Boyarin says, any border that is being used to hurt people is a border that ought to be reconsidered. I think Adler says something similar. Perhaps we have to nuance this, because we can't throw out a border just because it hurts a few people.

Anthony: I guess my point is this: It's one thing for Boyarin to say this, but from a Girardian perspective, Boyarin is playing fast and loose with a border that, if deconstructed, will cause all sorts of trouble, hostility, even violence. I can't help but think that the Jewish-Christian border needs to be well defined. This is the best thing for both of our peoples; this is the way that promotes mutual respect and hopefully creates a context that will allow hospitality.

Larry: Ha! I'll drop a little something in the conversation. It's potentially a long discussion, but there is a question: Does Jesus belong in Jewish-Christian dialogue? I think many Jews would say "no," that the firm, well-defined border you describe places Jesus exclusively on the Christian side of the divide. And there are good reasons for Jesus to be positioned in this way. For one thing, while you and I frequently discuss the historical Jesus, I'm not in a position to discuss the Jesus of faith with a Christian.

Anthony: I'm not really comfortable with the distinction you're drawing between the historical Jesus and the Jesus of faith.

Larry: I know that, but I think it's a rough distinction that's useful for this conversation. To get back to what you said about Jesus: if we draw a border placing Jesus outside of the realm of Jewish-Christian dialogue, I think this limits dialogue in a significant way.

Anthony: I don't mind bracketing Jesus in some cases, because bringing Jesus to the conversation table sets ground rules in a way that favors Christians. And as you've stated, most Jews don't want to be defined in comparison to what Christians believe and don't believe. Jesus represents what Christians think about when we think about Jews, and perhaps we should bracket that out, so we can have a discussion table that works for both groups. Not that he should be bracketed out forever. You're talking to someone who thinks a lot about Jesus. But I don't mind taking this posture, at least initially.

Larry: I guess this becomes a question of what do we want to talk about—not so much you and me, but Jews and Christians. What are we doing in dialogue? The question becomes more important as the dialogue goes on. There were such obvious things for us to talk about following the Shoah. There was the need for Jews to feel safer in the world, and for Christians to understand that their faith was not intrinsically and inherently anti-Jewish. I think this drove the initial conversation. But I am talking to you with the idea that something more than a cessation of hostilities is possible in this conversation.

Anthony: Yeah.

Larry: We can go one step past that. If you can make yourself understood to me, and I can make myself understood to you, we will have accomplished something important. But I'm not primarily thinking about that. Maybe I should be. But this is something I tried to describe in my chapter: I find the process of dialogue to be transformative. I'm interested in that transformation. This requires me to be somewhat open to your religious experience.

Anthony: Let me stop you there. Let's just take for granted that dialogue is going to be transformative in some way. Whenever you learn something, you are changed by it. You are a different person than you were before. In your experience, in this dialogue, you may feel more connected to Judaism than you did before. You said this in your chapter. You had these church experiences, experiences among Christians, and you find yourself with a stronger Jewish identification. From a number of perspectives, you could say that Jewish-Christian dialogue has made you a better Jew.

Larry: I have said that.

Anthony: This is not always going to be the case! By talking to Christians, you feel a greater sense of solidarity with your Judaism. But we know that it happens in reverse sometimes. We know that sometimes when Jews talk to Christians, the border becomes fuzzy enough that they start wondering whether they want to jump ship. That kind of possibility should be acknowledged. If this is a dialogue of possibility, and transformation is one thing that could happen, you have to acknowledge that the transformation may happen sometimes in a way that seems bad to other insiders.

Larry: Yes.

Anthony: It's going to scare a few people off.

Larry: More than a few.

Anthony: More than a few, right. I don't know how many. But if this is a dialogue of possibility and transformation is inevitable, then we have a problem convincing people that this dialogue is necessary. You see what I'm saying?

Larry: Right. I'm uncertain enough about this process, that I'm not clear if anything we're doing *is* necessary for anyone else. It's necessary for me.

Anthony: All right.

Larry: I can't do my own personal pilgrimage without engaging in this dialogue. But I do think about what would happen if some twenty-two-year-old first-year rabbinical student asked me how to get involved in Jewish-Christian dialogue, because they wanted to be transformed. I'm not sure what I would recommend.

Anthony: That's funny, because I was thinking about a hypothetical on my end, where I was asked to arrange a lay dialogue between six folks on the Christian side and six folks on the Jewish side. What if one of the Christians came to me and said, "This is all fine and good, but if there's an opportunity for me to share the gospel, I'm going to do that." My response is going to be, "You don't get what we're doing. If that's the way you look at it, then you're not interested in dialogue." In other words, the border there is not sacred. You need the border to be sacred, so I'm not sure I want to be responsible for what that person might say if we visit the local synagogue. Yet a lot of Christians would probably think this exactly: "This is all very interesting, but if there comes a chance where I get to share the gospel, I'll feel the obligation to do so." This is a problem. There will always be Christians who will disrespect the border.

Larry: I think that Jews in dialogue with Christians have to have a certain tolerance for the impulse you describe, even if this tolerance is reluctant. Because we want to be accepted in dialogue for who we are. I mean, there's an irony here. The Christian that comes to dialogue and says, "I'm only interested in dialogue with a Jew I can change into a Christian . . ."

Anthony: That's different. That's a different posture, I think.

Larry: It's a more extreme version of the same posture.

Anthony: It could be. I want to nuance it a little, but you're right. It brings us to the same end, right?

Larry: Well, perhaps there is a distinction. Perhaps the person looking to share the gospel is thinking, "If I get the opportunity, I'm going to want to share the gospel with my Jewish dialogue partners, because this is who I am, and I need to be an honest dialogue partner. But I'm sharing this with you because we're sharing things that are important to us, and not because I have any desire in my heart to convert you, because I fully accept you as Jewish." If so, what is the problem? Unless, of course, we're saying that discussions of belief, of theology, are off the table. This is a point of view I associate with Rabbi Joseph Soloveitchik, a great Orthodox rabbi who wrote in the 1960s against engaging in theological dialogue with Christians. He described Judaism and Christianity as religiously antithetic. He felt that we could never come to understand the other religiously. But he favored dialogue on other issues of mutual interest, such as humanitarian social justice concerns, things that we share in common.

Anthony: I can see the Soloveitchik position making sense from the perspective of the 1960s about what dialogue is supposed to be. "Let's get together so we can get along, and in order to get along, we have to figure out what we have in common. The other stuff doesn't really matter." But I'm not there. I don't think that has worked. I think there are certain distinctions that need to be highlighted and respected. I think we should celebrate diversity and not pretend that we're all the same. I think there was an ideal, a hope, that these distinctions between religions, distinctions between cultures, would fall away, and we would transcend them as a culture. Not only does this dialogue not work, it's also a dialogue that is uninteresting to me. It seems like a very boring way to enter a conversation. Because I don't get to find out about the real you, and it seems somewhat patronizing. Are the only things that are important about me, the things that I have in common with you? That seems patronizing. That's my take on this. The idea is, there is a border, and it's not an obstacle. It doesn't necessarily get in the way.

Larry: I want to go back to the particular case of Jesus. I entered into dialogue after and during an extensive self-study of Christianity. Would you and I be sitting here if I hadn't done that? I don't think so.

Anthony: I don't agree with that.

Larry: Could it have happened in another way? Probably. But what made me an interesting dialogue partner to you? If I were expert in Isaiah, or Dead Sea Scrolls, that might have made me interesting to talk to. But once upon a time I said a few things interesting about Jesus, and that's why we're talking.

Anthony: I don't think so. I don't want to discount what you are saying.

Larry: Maybe I miscalculated back in the day, but years ago I'd thought that in order to be in dialogue with Christians, I had to be able to talk about this stuff.

Anthony: Your interest in Christianity led you to study Jesus, and my interest in Jesus led me to study Judaism. So that's an interesting symmetry. But I don't feel like you were an interesting dialogue partner because of anything you knew. I got into this because you were able to communicate your own experience in a certain way. I'm in it for your identity. I'm interested in talking with Larry, not to have abstract conversations about what Larry knows.

Larry: Oh yes. I did not mean to imply otherwise. But I could not communicate as I communicate now without having done that study.

Anthony: That's true. So we should be thanking Mel Gibson for this dialogue.

Larry: [*Laughs*] Absolutely. Part of this has to do with an asymmetry. Part of being Jewish is an ability to explain ourselves to outsiders. It's a survival skill; we've had to do this. We've lived primarily in a world of outsiders. But this doesn't work in reverse. I can't count on Christians being able to explain Christianity to me. You've pointed out that the average Christian has never met a Jew, so how would the Christian have developed the skill of communicating Christianity to Jews? So in order for me to be in dialogue and understand the Christianity of Christians, I needed to learn about Christianity first. And that takes us back to Jesus again, because I think Jesus is central to Christianity in the way that no single thing is central to Judaism.

Anthony: Well, your experience of Israel was somewhat transformative.

Larry: Oh, I agree. But if you don't get the centrality of Israel to the experience of many Jews, I'll say, "Fine. Toss that one out; I got nine more, and if you can relate to five of them, you'll understand a great deal of the Jewish experience."

Anthony: Whereas if you take Jesus out of the equation of being Christian . . .

Larry: I'm not getting anything that really matters.

Anthony: Interesting. Which is why you must have been so surprised earlier this year, when we had our e-mail discussion of Christianity, St. Francis, and nonviolence, and you heard my visceral reaction to our discussion of my pacifism.

Larry: Yes. In the past, we've talked about Jesus and pacifism, and you hadn't objected to my questioning Jesus' pacifism. You questioned it yourself. But when it came to St. Francis . . . I think I wrote to you something like, it was easy for St. Francis to be nonviolent, when his monasteries were effectively protected by violent, well-armed Christian knights. That wasn't a nice thing to say, nor was it accurate. I was completely ignorant of the lengths St. Francis had gone to put himself in harm's way in the name of peace. In any event, I said what I said to you in a private e-mail, and I feel somewhat free to say stupid things in private. Your normal reaction would have been to rebuke me, gently, with humor. You're not above sticking it to me every now and again. But instead, the reaction I provoked from you was more . . . visceral. It was clear I'd struck a nerve.

Anthony: I think I learned something about myself in that exchange. If someone had asked me, "What is more sacred to you, a nonviolent Christian way in the world, or the virgin birth?" I would have had to think about it. Why am I being forced to choose? But it's interesting to me, that I seem so much more invested in pacifism as sort of the central theme of Christian orthodoxy.

Larry: The interesting thing was the contrast. I remember having a conversation with you and your wife earlier that same year, and the topic of the virgin birth somehow came up, and I was trying to be sensitive about referring to Joseph as Jesus' father, or adoptive father, something like that. I was on my best behavior, because I wasn't sure if speaking about Joseph as Jesus' biological father might sound offensive to you, or to Sarah. I remember you laughing a bit at this, and saying, "Larry, you're among friends!"

Anthony: You *were* among friends!

Larry: I still am! I was "among friends" when I stepped on your toes about St. Francis. [*Laughs*] And the point of the matter is, we don't know. I think the best things to come out of dialogue are things like this, finding out what matters to us. Though I wouldn't want to be perceived as a guy always probing for soft points.

Anthony: Let me push back a little bit on this. Maybe this is a Jewish defense mechanism, but the way you spoke made me think, "There's no way Larry believes this; he's just saying this for my benefit."

Larry: Which part?

Anthony: Your feigned surprise that Joseph wasn't Jesus' biological father. I thought, "There's no way Larry believes this. Of course he doesn't believe in the virgin birth. This is something he's saying because he thinks he has to say it in polite company."

Larry: I tried to say it in a way that didn't indicate I believed it. I tried to talk about it in a way that allowed you to believe it.

Anthony: [*Laughs*] This is the problem. I would rather have the authentic Larry, and not the Larry projecting something he anticipates I would want him to project.

Larry: But the authentic Larry, and maybe this authentic Larry was Larry being authentically ignorant, said the things he said about St. Francis.

Anthony: So you're saying that being authentic Larry is risky no matter what.

Larry: I'm saying that being perfectly honest is not always a virtue.

Anthony: Not always, you're right, but we are risking something.

Larry: I think the point is: notwithstanding what a jerk I was, our conversation about St. Francis was terrific! But it would not have been great if that was our first encounter, because you have walked away thinking, "I don't want anything to do with that jerk."

Anthony: No, no.

Larry: And I would have thought, there's another Christian with a rod up his butt.

Anthony: [*Laughs*] The question is, which rod is it? It's not a question of whether there is one!

Larry: [*Laughs*] So they're interchangeable?

Anthony: Exactly. But, you're right. It's not a bad posture to have to suggest that being brutally honest 100 percent of the time is not good for dialogue. But, look, I'm reading this book of dialogue between Michael Lerner and Cornel West, and sparks are flying! The action is what brings us to places that are most edifying, I think. Maybe it's a personality thing.

Larry: I think it's more of a friendship thing. Remember that, historically, if a Jew is invited to dialogue by a Christian with the promise that "sparks will fly," the Jew will flee. We know that, historically, sparks are not a good thing. Historically, our first goal is to survive the dialogue encounter. At the end of the day, there's a lot that I hope for, but there's something like the physician's creed, a "do no harm" rule, at work here.

Anthony: Let's go back to *The Jew in the Lotus*, Rodger Kamenetz's book about a meeting between the Dalai Lama and representatives of Judaism. The Jews participating in this meeting represented a wide range of Jewish perspectives. The Dalai Lama wanted to ask these Jewish representatives: How do you maintain your religious identity in a diaspora, in exile?

Larry: I remember this now.

Anthony: Each Jewish representative had a different perspective on this. One perspective was that Jews built in ways to remember the loss of the Temple, the Shoah . . . Jews built in ways to remember these things in other rituals. So in a Jewish wedding, many Jews break a glass because it brings to mind the loss of the Temple. There is this wonderful moment, when the Dalai Lama says, "Now that you have returned to Israel, do these rituals still have meaning to you?" Because to say something like, "Next year in Jerusalem . . ."

Larry: Which we still say.

Anthony: Which you still say. It seems to have a different meaning than it did pre-1948.

Larry: Yes, absolutely, it does.

Anthony: So the rabbis responded, "No, we didn't take them out, we still say these things." Rodger Kamenetz wrote something like, this was the moment when he realized this wasn't a one-way conversation. This wasn't just Jews giving advice. This was reciprocal. For me, this brings up an interesting question. Even if Jews around the world can't claim to be in exile in the same way they might have claimed pre-1948, the remembrance of exile still serves an important function within Jewish life.

Larry: Yes it does, absolutely.

Anthony: There is something about Jewish identity that thrives within the identity of the exile.

Larry: I think that Jewish identity is impossible without a direct recollection of the feeling of exile, and it has to be something more than historic. There has to be something close to a personal sense of it.

Anthony: So it's something like the "Exile of History" and the "Diaspora of Faith"?[5]

Larry: I don't know how to break it down. I sometimes feel as a Jew that, for all of the horrible trials we have suffered, maybe the greatest threat to Jewish survival is success.

Anthony: Hmm.

Larry: I don't know if we can survive success. We don't seem to be . . . I don't know the right way to put this, particularly in a way that won't get someone really upset with me.

Anthony: Let's refer this to a different conversation. Cornel West was telling Michael Lerner, "Look, from our perspective, you guys have had enormous success in America." And Michael Lerner keeps on saying, "If that's who you think we are, you have misunderstood us. We are not that. Yes, we have had success, but that's not who we are." And Lerner keeps wanting to trump West with how much exile has been experienced by the Jewish people. It's almost as if to say, the success is superficial, and if you just measure us by this, you don't get what we are all about.

---

5. This was Anthony's attempt at nerd humor. He was playing with the well-worn distinction between the "Jesus of History" and the "Christ of Faith."

Larry: My reading of this conversation is a little different. I think what Lerner is concerned about is that Jews will be viewed through a particular lens, as the "successful immigrant group," the overachieving minority. Through this lens, we become part of that greater American story of how in a land of freedom and opportunity, our people were able to accomplish and contribute in ways that were impossible elsewhere. And within a particular American context, that *is* the Jewish story. If Lerner is saying that this is not how Jews see themselves in any way, shape, or form, well, his experience is different from mine. The point is that Jewish identity, at its heart, has to be the experience in Egypt, the experience in Sinai, that's the Bible through and through. This is the essential Jewish message of identity: Remember who you were, because that is who you are.

Anthony: Okay. Now we're getting somewhere. Then what's the trouble with Christians who identify with the passion experience? Christians who recreate the experience of alienation and suffering of Jesus on the cross? Let's be honest, we Christians are doing pretty well, but in order to tap into my identity as a Christian, I have to live into the passion narrative in a way. How is that different? How is it different than saying, "It was our generation who stood at the foot of Sinai"?

Larry: I have no trouble with Christians identifying with the passion, but this identification may not be the best way of communicating the essence of Christianity in dialogue. The Christian identification with this unfairly crucified, perfectly innocent man brings up the question of Jewish involvement and participation in the death of Jesus. How can I find commonality with you in the very historic experience that separates us and has created such animosity? I'd rather focus on the Sermon on the Mount, or some other Christian experience that's not so historically problematic.

Anthony: This goes back to a previous conversation we've had. I'm teaching a class called "New Testament and Suffering," and I've brought a lot of what we've talked about into the class. I invited Michael Cook—who is a rabbi, scholar, and expert in the New Testament—to lecture to my class. Cook teaches at Hebrew Union College, which is only about an hour away from where I teach. One important part of this class is to discuss the ways that the New Testament has been used by Christians to perpetrate violence. That's just one element, but it's one of the crucial elements of the class. Michael e-mailed me back to say that's not a Jewish thing.

Larry: What part is not Jewish?

Anthony: Suffering. He said, suffering is not a Jewish thing. He said, "That's a Christian thing." And he said, "I don't think I want to talk about it." I pushed back a little bit and said, "Certainly the Shoah is a really important identity marker." He replied, "That's not the Judaism we wish to discuss with Christians. We do not want to be perceived as victims. It doesn't help us to be seen as victims. What helps is for us to explain and critique how Christianity has been involved with this." I'm paraphrasing, of course.

Larry: Oh boy. Probably a year ago, I would have said, "Yeah, this is a quintessential Jewish-Christian difference: you guys think of pain as something like a positive religious experience, and we think of pain as something that should be avoided, not sought out."

Anthony: And this brings us back to your "Bordering Possibility" chapter about how you viewed the experience of suffering in a Christian worship setting.

Larry: It's one of the things about Jewish-Christian dialogue that I find transformative. I frequently discover aspects of Christianity and think, "Here is a stark Jewish-Christian difference. They do this and we do not." Then I later discover that you got it from us.

Anthony: Yeah, right.

Larry: For example, take original sin. I would say, "This is a stark Jewish-Christian difference, because Jews don't believe in original sin." Then I look at Jewish apocryphal literature and learn that this was a good Jewish belief in Jesus' time. Was this believed only by a handful of Jews during a particular period, or can we say that this was once a mainstream Jewish idea? In either event, it is clear that at some point, we turned away from that idea.

Anthony: Part of this relates to what you said about Jews not liking to define themselves in comparison to Christian belief. There are certain ideological elements Christians took on that became unattractive to Jews.

Larry: I don't think it's quite as simple as this. If you look at the literature of the first few centuries, it is remarkable how much the early Christians talked about Judaism, and how little the rabbis at that same time talked about Christianity.

Anthony: This is very telling to me. This relative silence is not speaking of a disinterest. It is a very loud silence.

Larry: We can't know this. What if it were the opposite, and these Jews talked about Christianity a lot? You would also conclude that this is evidence of an interest. What could we have done, then, to have proven disinterest to you?

Anthony: This may be an anachronism, but let me say this again. Jews live in a world of outsiders. If I went to twenty Jewish Sabbath services, how many times would I hear the name Jesus? Zero.

Larry: If I go to twenty Christian services, how many times would I hear a reference to Judaism, or Pharisees, or law, or Temple, or something that is core to Judaism?

Anthony: Fifteen times out of twenty.

Larry: In my experience, it's twenty out of twenty.

Anthony: I don't doubt it.

Larry: But I won't deny that Judaism is a syncretistic religion, meaning that we have adopted practices and beliefs from our neighbors. This can be conscious and unconscious. This goes as far back . . .

Anthony: . . . as Canaan.

Larry: Absolutely.

Anthony: Christians do the same thing.

Larry: Jews have been influenced by the larger, more powerful peoples that have surrounded us, and the influence works both ways. Sometimes we see this in evidence of things we do, and sometimes in things we don't do. Sometimes, our reaction was, "Christians are doing this, so we're not going to do this. Because there is a border, and we are distinct." Other times, we've done things because Christians were doing it. We don't always ask these questions out loud. Sometimes, we act under the influence without realizing it. I find it transformative to learn that many things I thought were exclusively Christian actually have Jewish roots, even if they are no longer a part of Judaism.

Anthony: This is the problem we are always going to run into when we try to talk about Jesus in Jewish-Christian dialogue. Jesus was Jewish, but he's now firmly placed on the Christian side of the Jewish-Christian border. For better or for worse, Jesus now belongs to the Christians. And if it's a Christian thing, Jews don't want anything to do with it.

Larry: It's an interesting thing, and I'm not sure exactly how to approach it. If not for Jesus, if not for Paul, certainly if not for Josephus and the apocryphal materials the church preserved, we would not know very much about the first-century Jewish experience.

Anthony: Yes. And for a long time, we Christians looked at first-century Judaism through the lens of the New Testament, because we didn't have a better lens.

Larry: From a Jewish scholarly perspective, we can use New Testament materials and come to a better understanding of this era. The first century is crucial to Jewish self-understanding, because this is the era when the Temple fell. This is not a random fifty to seventy years; this period is critical to a Jewish understanding of who we are and how we got here. Now, arguably, we can do this study without you. We can come back to that question. The next question is, can you really understand Jesus without our help?

Anthony: No, absolutely not.

Larry: Obviously, you're one of the very few Christians who would answer my question in this way. A few Christians would acknowledge that we might be of some assistance. I think most would respond, "What are you talking about? What I need to know is in the New Testament."

Anthony: I see the New Testament as consisting of Jewish documents, so I'm not going to be too sympathetic to those who say, "We don't need Jews because it's in the New Testament."

Larry: Here's an example of what I have in mind. I participated in a blog discussion recently where a good, sensitive Christian scholar had written about

Jesus healing in the synagogue on Shabbat. The discussion started badly, but ended quite well, I think. The blog post came out of Mark's Gospel, where Jesus heals on the Sabbath in opposition to the Pharisees. This blog author wrote that the Pharisees were hard-hearted, and that they had turned their practice into a wooden, automatic, legalistic sort of thing.

Anthony: They had forgotten what was important. This is a standard Christian way of thinking.

Larry: Right. I asked the question, "Didn't Jesus care about the fourth commandment, about remembering the Sabbath day and keeping it holy? Didn't Jesus think it was important not to work on the Sabbath?" The answer was, of course, that Jesus was a Ten Commandments guy: don't murder, don't covet neighbors' wives, all of that. So, we can easily imagine a Jesus who, like most Jews, took seriously the commandment not to work on the Sabbath. But that particular Sabbath, he simply couldn't bear the thought of praying all day next to a person who was suffering! Not working on Sabbath is important, but reacting to suffering is *really* important. Doesn't that give us a much richer portrait of who Jesus was? For me it does.

Anthony: It does. For me, it does too. My guess is that this author didn't mean to talk about Jesus or the Pharisees at all; that instead he wanted to make a point about people he views as present-day Christian legalists. He was using Jesus and the Pharisees both as tools to get to that rhetorical end. It's unfortunate.

Larry: Right. But whatever his purpose may have been, the message communicated about who Jesus really was . . .

Anthony: . . . was a cliché. I agree. Jesus becomes richer and more profound for Christian experience when we are in dialogue with Jews.

Larry: I acknowledge that there is a potential risk to all this. But we're talking about postures of friendship, hospitality, and reciprocity. I would like Christians to come out of Jewish-Christian dialogue, not with a feeling that they've gone to the dentist, that they've done something unpleasant they have to do every six months or so to fight spiritual decay . . .

Anthony: That's not a Christian posture.

Larry: I would like Christians to come out of dialogue thinking that it would be good for us spiritually if these Jewish people remained on the scene as good, sincere Jews, so we can continue this dialogue.

Part Three

Shoah

Things That Befell Us

Larry Behrendt

For my mother, a Jewish holiday like Hanukkah required a song from her childhood. Of course, I wanted to move from the ceremonial Hanukkah candlelighting straight to the Hanukkah gift receiving, but to please my mother, my sisters and I would sing a bit with her. So one of my earliest memories is my mother singing the following, in her thin, reedy voice:

Who can retell the things that befell us?
Who can count them?
In every age a hero or sage came to our aid.

We sang without thinking about what we were singing, just as we pledged allegiance to the American flag without knowing what "allegiance" meant. But as I grew older, I learned there were problems with the questions we sang on Hanukkah. I learned that the "things that befell us" included the systematic persecution and eventual mass murder of Jews in Europe by Nazi Germany, in an event known as the Holocaust, or the Shoah.[1] "Who can count them?" I learned that the "count" of Jews murdered in the Shoah

---

1. In this chapter, I will use the term "Shoah" in place of the term "Holocaust" to refer to the total of all anti-Jewish actions taken by Nazi Germany. "Shoah" is a Hebrew word meaning "destruction" or "catastrophe," and it has been the standard Hebrew term for this event since the 1940s. I prefer the term "Shoah," as the original meaning of "holocaust" includes a burnt sacrificial offering. See, for example, "The Holocaust," Yad Vashem, www.yadvashem.org/yv/en/holocaust/resource_center /the_holocaust.asp. I want to avoid any implication that European Jewry was "sacrificed" for any purpose, and I think that the more general term "Shoah" best avoids such an implication. In my experience, some English-speaking Jews speak of the "Shoah," while others use the term "Holocaust," and others use both terms interchangeably. I take no offense at use of the term "Holocaust," and I'm not aware of any Jew who insists that one of these terms be used exclusively.

reached six million, or two-thirds of the Jews living in Europe before World War II. I learned that, when it came to preventing this mass murder, no hero or sage had come to our aid.

There was also a problem with the song's reference to "retelling." We Jews are good at retelling, in this and every age. For example: my mother's side of the family came from Russia and immigrated to the United States around the turn of the twentieth century, and they talked a lot about pogroms, and Ellis Island, and struggling to succeed in the "Land of Opportunity." But on my father's side of the family, there was no retelling.

As a child, I knew this much: my father was born in Berlin in 1927. His mother died of cancer when he was little, shortly after Hitler came to power. He immigrated to the United States in 1936, along with his father, stepmother, sister, and step-siblings.[2]

I wanted to know more, but I didn't learn more until much later, well into my adulthood. This is my earliest memory of the Shoah: my mother told me not to ask my father anything about his boyhood in Nazi Germany. "He can't handle it," she told me.

It was the early 1960s, and I was around seven years old. To my seven-year-old self, my mother's request made no sense. My father seemed perfectly normal. He didn't talk as much as my mother, but when he did, the talk was about baseball, or his service in the military following World War II, or his achievements in the Boy Scouts. When I ask my boyhood friends about my father, they remember that he could play the piccolo and ukulele. "He threw the best curveball I ever saw."

How could it be that my father couldn't handle something? But I listened to my mother. Wouldn't she know? And over time, my view of my father changed. There were things about him that weren't "right." My mother told stories about "when I was your age." I knew the games she played as a child, and her favorite radio shows ("Who knows what evil lurks in the hearts of men? The Shadow knows"). She could describe her fear, listening to FDR's "Day of Infamy" speech and, later, learning that FDR had died. I heard little

---

2. After I wrote this chapter, I located ship passenger lists showing the immigration of the members of my father's family, and I discovered that my grandfather arrived in the United States on a ship that had departed from France in 1935. My father and the remainder of his family arrived in the United States on two separate ships departing from Germany at different times in 1936. My grandfather's 1935 departure from France tends to confirm a story I'd heard but never previously believed: that my grandfather escaped Germany in 1935 to avoid arrest by the Nazi special police, the SS.

comparable from my father. When he told his childhood stories, almost always they were later stories from his life in America. If I tried to imagine what he was like when he was my age, living in Germany, I drew a blank. There was a hole there.

A few years later, the hole was filled. One afternoon, my mother told me there was a show that evening on "educational TV." It was an adult show, but she thought I was old enough to handle it. Naturally, I was up for the challenge. Being "old enough" was usually a prelude to a good thing. Today, it's hard for me to believe that my mother gave me no more preparation than this. But how do you ready a ten-year-old to watch a documentary containing scenes from the Shoah?

At the appointed hour, my mother walked me into my parents' bedroom, turned on the TV, and shut the door behind her, leaving me alone. The door was closed so that my younger sisters would not wander in accidentally. They were not "old enough" to watch the show or be left alone, and my father wasn't home. All this added to the "adult" nature of whatever I was about to see.

What did I see? I only remember moments. I remember lines of naked Jewish bodies, their backs to the camera as they were shot, the momentum of the gunshots propelling the bodies into ditches the Jews had been forced to dig for their own burial, the lines being replaced by other lines of naked bodies to be shot and fall, while Nazi soldiers probed the ditch with bayonets to make sure all were dead. I remember the gas chambers of the death camps, disguised as showers, and the narrator intoning how the tiles near the doors of the chambers had to be periodically replaced because the Jews would frantically claw at them as they were being asphyxiated. I remember the ovens, and the remains of bodies in the ovens. I remember scenes of death camps as they were liberated, the survivors looking nothing like liberated human beings, the men indistinguishable from the women, all looking thinner than I'd imagine a person could look and still be alive. There was no joy at this liberation. The Jews looked into the cameras of their liberators as if to say, "Who are you? What are you going to do to us?"

I could not bear to watch, but I had to watch, because the documentary retold things that befell us. I could not bear to watch, but I had to watch, because millions of Jews had suffered and died, and all I was being asked to do was watch. I was afraid to watch, but more afraid of not watching. If I didn't watch, I would be no better than those millions of bystanders, in Germany and around the world, who turned away as my people were systematically butchered. I had to watch, because I had to do something, even if was something I desperately did not want to do.

As I watched, I thought of my father. *This is where he'd lived.* These were his home movies. Of course, my father had left Germany before these films were made. He'd never been in a concentration camp. He'd escaped the hell of Nazi Germany before it went into full operation. But he'd lived in hell while it was under construction.

My father could not handle talking about his boyhood in Germany? Of course he couldn't. Watching the documentary, I wondered how he could handle talking about anything at all. I was shaken to my core by a one-hour documentary, but he'd lived with the Nazis for more than three years. The hole in my understanding of my father's childhood filled with imagined stories, like a sand castle breached by high tide. Why had he never spoken like my mother of favorite childhood radio shows? Because his childhood radio was full of Hitler's screamed obscenities. I pictured his walk home from school, how he'd duck into doorways to avoid marauding Brownshirts in open trucks, only to be beaten with impunity by grinning schoolmates.[3] Most frightening was the thought that the Germans shown murdering Jews on TV were my father's neighbors. They drove the busses my father rode, delivered the mail to his apartment, even taught in the classrooms where my father sat. My father looked these people in the eye, day following day. How much rage, how much hatred, must my father have seen reflected there? How could anyone endure that kind of hatred?

I shut the TV off after the documentary ended. I'd had my fill of TV for that night. I left my parents' room to find my mother, to talk to her. But what could I have said to her? The right words must have failed me then, as they fail me now.

The documentary cemented the deal I'd made with my mother never to discuss Nazi Germany with my father. "He can't handle it." Of course he couldn't. Ask him the wrong question, even once, and he'd crumble to pieces.

---

3. The "Brownshirts," also known as the *Sturmabteilung* or stormtroopers, and more formally known as the SA, were a paramilitary group formed by the Nazi Party in 1920, many years before Hitler seized power in Germany. It was the job of the SA to use violent strong-arm tactics to intimidate the Nazi's political opponents. Much of the SA's activities were targeted against Jews. In the early days of Nazi Germany, the SA was used to enforce boycotts against Jewish businesses, physically attack Jewish lawyers and judges, and engage in other street violence against Jews and Nazi opponents.

※

Memory of the Shoah is an important component of modern Jewish identity, perhaps *the* most important. According to a recent Pew survey, when Jews in the United States are asked to name what is most essential to being Jewish, the number one answer is "remembering the Holocaust." Fully 73 percent of Jews surveyed named Shoah memory as "essential," a much higher number than those Jews who named "caring about Israel" (43 percent) or "observing Jewish law" (19 percent).[4]

If we want to understand present-day Jewish identity, then we must discuss Jewish Shoah memory. Lucky for me, my coauthor Anthony is both a terrific conversation partner and an expert on the subject of memory held by groups—what Anthony would call "social and collective memory." Strictly speaking, *all* memory is social: we share what we remember with others, and our memories of events are shaped by how others remember the same event. But when scholars like Anthony discuss "collective memory," they are referring to memories that members of a group share in common, memories that are used to help define a group and forge a sense of group identity.

As an example, consider how my mother made sure I watched that TV documentary about the Shoah. Evidently, my mother thought I needed to see this documentary to help me understand what it means to be Jewish. Doubtless there were hundreds of similar memories imparted to me during my childhood—memories of exodus from Egypt, prophets and kings, the destruction of two Temples, acts of oppression in the Diaspora, immigration to the United States, and formation of the modern State of Israel. Doubtless all parents pass similar memories on to their children, so that we understand what it means to belong to a certain religion, ethnic group, or nationality.

But there's something "off" in the story I've told above. How can social memory form if the thing remembered is not to be talked about? Social memory theorist Alan Kirk (relying on the foundational work of sociologist Maurice Halbwachs) describes patterns in the formation of social memory. Social memory begins with "face-to-face circulation of foundational memories" that are "biographically vested in those who experienced

---

4. "A Portrait of Jewish Americans," Pew Research Center, October 1, 2013, www.pewforum.org/2013/10/01/jewish-american-beliefs-attitudes-culture-survey/.

originating events."[5] This eyewitness-based memory is sometimes called "communicative memory," and obviously, communicative memory requires communication—the experience of the eyewitnesses must be communicated to the larger social group.[6]

Yet it was my experience that the Shoah was not talked about. I've long wondered if my experience was unique in my family. So I recently wrote my three siblings—two younger sisters and a much younger brother—to see what they remember learning about the Shoah from our parents. None of my siblings remember being told not to ask my father about the Shoah. But my sister Judy's response echoes the experience I remember:

> I don't remember Mom ever telling me not to ask Dad about his experiences growing up in Nazi Germany, but I did have the impression that it was not something Dad wanted to talk about. When I did ask him questions, he would say he didn't remember much. I always figured that a certain amount of dissociating was necessary for him to function effectively in society, let alone as the charming, fun-loving guy that Dad was for the most part.

I grew up thinking that the Shoah was something that should not be talked about, not with my father, and rarely with anyone else. What was there to say? Some of my friends had a parent or two who had escaped from Nazi Germany, and on occasion, we'd compare notes. "When did your father leave?" "When did yours?" It was not until high school that I met someone whose parent had escaped later than my father did—his father had immigrated illegally, on foot, across mountains.[7] We did not ask each other if our parents had been tormented, humiliated, beaten, or anything worse. The question was too personal, as inappropriate as asking a child abuse victim what the experience felt like. The pain of the Shoah was private back then. I remember visiting a tailor with my mother in New York City, and seeing the tattooed number on his forearm, then pretending I hadn't noticed as the tailor turned to hide the number. I remember leaving the tailor's shop, my mother's eyebrow cocked, gesturing back at the shop, as if to ask, "Did I see?" But it was not polite to notice.

---

5. Alan Kirk, "Social and Cultural Memory," in *Memory, Tradition, and Text: Uses of the Past in Early Christianity*, ed. Alan Kirk and Tom Thatcher, *Semeia Studies* 52 (Atlanta: Society of Biblical Literature, 2005), 5.

6. Kirk, *Memory, Tradition, and Text*, 3.

7. As I mentioned in a footnote above, it is possible that my grandfather also left Germany illegally, crossing the border into France to escape arrest.

I grew up thinking that my childhood experience of the Shoah was unique. But evidently, it wasn't. In her landmark book *Children of the Holocaust*, Helen Epstein wrote about her experience as the child of parents who survived the Nazi death camps, and she documented the memories of other such children. There is a common theme in nearly all of these memories: the Shoah was not discussed in the families of Shoah survivors. "We never addressed it by name."[8] Epstein reports that when she told others that her parents were concentration camp survivors, "the conversation usually died there. . . . *They were in concentration camp* was a warning. It meant don't step across this line I've drawn; watch the careless things you might otherwise say."[9]

Epstein's interviews with children of survivors reveal the same thing: the Shoah was not something to talk about. "I was never able to talk about it." "I couldn't talk about it." "He doesn't talk about it." "Terrible things had happened [to our parents], so terrible they didn't want us to know about them." "All I had to do was look at my mother's face and I know I'd better not ask questions." "It was my responsibility not to ask." "It was a strange feeling, not being able to ask questions where there were so many I wanted to ask." "I always wanted to talk about it with someone." "It never came up in school. It was taboo." "When people came over to our house and talked about the war, my parents always said '*Shah!* The children will hear us!'"[10]

Why was there so little discussion of the Shoah in survivor families? Epstein gives many reasons. The fact of the Shoah "was so obvious it did not require discussion." Discussion of the Shoah was painful, and survivor families were "quick to shield each other from pain." "Talk meant accepting that the war had happened and, more than anything else in the world, I wished it had not." . . . "The idea that my mother and my father had been forced out of their homes and made to live like animals—worse than animals—was too shameful to admit."[11]

Yet despite the silence, it is clear that the Shoah was the most significant event in the lives of these children of survivors. Their parents' experience of the Shoah dwarfed anything they themselves had experienced. Epstein describes one of her interviewees as emblematic of the rest:

---

8. Helen Epstein, *Children of the Holocaust: Conversations with Sons and Daughters of Survivors* (Lexington, MA: Kindle Edition, 2010), 15.

9. Epstein, *Children of the Holocaust*, 18.

10. Epstein, *Children of the Holocaust*, 18, 38, 198, 176, 37, 178, 192, 9, 28, 26, 243.

11. Epstein, *Children of the Holocaust*, 15, 21.

Like all the children of survivors I spoke with, he did not believe that any pain he had felt as a child could compare with what his parents lived through. His problems had been inconsequential compared to theirs; he did not wish people to think that he thought himself of the same stature as his parents. "I'm of no comparable stature," he repeated. "I didn't suffer."[12]

An odd parallel to Epstein's work is Katharina von Kellenbach's *The Mark of Cain: Guilt and Denial in the Post-War Lives of Nazi Perpetrators*.[13] Like Epstein, von Kellenbach is a member of the "second generation" following the Shoah, but her relationship to the Shoah is through German perpetrators, not Jewish victims. As a girl, von Kellenbach learned that her uncle was a Nazi SS officer in charge of the Jewish ghetto in Pinsk, Belarus, where he directed the execution of roughly thirty thousand Jews (mostly women and children). Von Kellenbach's uncle was not indicted for these crimes until the 1960s, and eventually he was declared incompetent to stand trial for medical reasons. While von Kellenbach "felt suspicious" of her uncle's acquittal, her inquiries to her family "resulted in angry harangues about the arrogance of the young, their lack of understanding and judgmental hypocrisy." As an adult, von Kellenbach studied the Nazi administration of Pinsk, hardly believing at first that such mass executions "could possibly have happened," before she learned to accept the truth about her uncle's role in the Shoah.

There is much in *The Mark of Cain* for Anthony and me to discuss—in particular, I am disturbed that the Lutheran and Roman Catholic Churches in post-war Germany argued for the unconditional forgiveness and reconciliation of many who were responsible for the mass murder of European Jewry. But here, I want to focus on what *The Mark of Cain* says about formation of social memory. While the Shoah victims described by Epstein were reluctant to discuss their experiences, the Shoah perpetrators in von Kellenbach's book would not do so *truthfully*. Von Kellenbach describes the perpetrators of the Shoah as "committed to forgetting, erasing, and burying the guilt of the past." On the whole, these perpetrators never acknowledged remorse or sought forgiveness. Like Epstein, von Kellenbach notes the impact of this suppression of memory on the children of those who experienced the Shoah firsthand. For von Kellenbach, the "German second generation"

---

12. Epstein, *Children of the Holocaust*, 177.

13. Katharina von Kellenbach, *The Mark of Cain: Guilt and Denial in the Post-War Lives of Nazi Perpetrators* (New York: Oxford University Press, 2013).

was "tainted" by the failure of Nazi perpetrators "to acknowledge culpable wrongdoing and moral corruption."[14]

All of this suppressed memory may sound surprising to people in Anthony's generation, people who grew up in the 1970s and later. In these years, the Shoah became the best documented and most widely remembered genocide in human history. But in the 1960s, the Shoah was not taught in school or synagogue. There were no Holocaust museums in the United States back then (and anecdotally, I understand that the American Jewish community initially opposed the construction of such museums, thinking that this was not how we wanted our neighbors to think about us). Elie Weisel's *Night* was published in English in 1960, but it sold only three thousand copies in the first three years after publication. Similarly, the work of Jewish philosopher and Shoah survivor Primo Levi was not yet widely known. Epstein recounts that when she conceived of the idea for her book, there was little initial enthusiasm. Her literary agent thought her topic was "depressing and unsalable." A friend of Epstein's, also a child of survivors, told her that she was "stirring up shit to no good purpose."[15]

It is perplexing how the Shoah could have been so keenly remembered in the 1960s of my childhood, and yet so infrequently talked about.

⌗

Over the years, I learned a few stories about my father's German experience—stories I assumed were edited to leave out the parts he couldn't handle. I continued to obey my mother's instructions, through childhood and into adulthood: I never asked my father about his experience in Nazi Germany.

I grew up and my parents grew older. I married and had a child of my own, and my small family lived an hour's drive from my parents' home in Los Angeles, close enough to visit one or two weekends a month. I remember one visit we made in the late 1990s, the four adults drinking wine in my parents' backyard while my daughter played. My mother was working on her crossword puzzle, and my wife and my father were deep into a conversation that would occasionally lapse into German, a language she can speak and I cannot. I wasn't paying close attention, so my wife's question to my father came seemingly out of nowhere.

14. Von Kellenbach, *The Mark of Cain*, 5, 6, 8, 30.
15. Epstein, *Children of the Holocaust*, 8, 20.

"Peter, what do you remember about your childhood in Germany?"

I sat up straight. Thoughts came to me in a jumble. "Don't ask your father about the Shoah. He can't handle it." I'd lived with this rule all my life, but I'd never spoken of it to my wife. It seemed so obvious to me, beyond need of mention. How could she have failed to realize that this was a question never to be asked? But of course she didn't realize. I had forgotten to tell her. It was my fault. And now it was too late. The question was out there. The damage was done.

I looked at my mother. Sorry, Mom, I wanted to say. But she did not look up from her crossword puzzle. I looked at my father. He had an odd expression on his face, odd for the fact that it was not far from his ordinary look. Did he seem upset? Surprised? It was as if he was thinking, "Funny. No one has asked me this before."

My father spoke as you might expect someone to speak when remembering ordinary childhood, from a perspective of distance and wistful bittersweetness, as if his childhood was spent someplace like an Iowa cornfield, and not in a chamber of horrors. He did not sound like a witness to the Shoah. In fact, he had few stories to tell. He was nine years old when he left Nazi Germany—if asked, how much can any of us recall from our first nine years of life? As I listened to his answer, I wondered if I might have misunderstood my mother some thirty years earlier, when she said my father could not handle discussing the Shoah.

My father remembered that he and Hitler shared the same birthday, and that he woke up one birthday to see Nazi flags flying everywhere outside his bedroom window, and that his mother told him the celebration was for him. My father remembered public school, how he began every school day with the "Heil Hitler" straight-armed salute to the Nazi flag. He also remembered how students sat in school in order of rank, the best performing students sitting in front, and how he was moved from the front of the class to somewhere in the middle. My father was competitive, proud of his class rank, but he knew that his teacher was trying to protect him, that it was no longer safe to have a Jew displayed with the classroom's best and brightest, and that his teacher was doing him a favor, allowing him to disappear into the undifferentiated middle of the room.

My wife asked the question I had answered for myself. Was my father physically persecuted in Nazi Germany? Did the other kids taunt him, threaten him, beat him? My father acknowledged that other Jewish kids were pushed around, hit, kicked, and abused. But it wasn't a question of systematic state-sponsored oppression. It was kids bullying other kids because they could get away with it. There were no adults involved, no Brownshirts. According to my father, the Jewish kids that got the worst treatment were the kids that were most "Jewish" in appearance: "bookish" kids with glasses. In contrast, my father had lighter hair, blue eyes, and was a good athlete. Then, as now, boys live in a playground culture where the strongest and fastest gain respect. When my father was targeted by older kids looking for Jews to beat up, his classmates stuck up for him. "Leave Peter alone," they'd say. "He's okay."

The way my father made it sound, his life in Germany was less "Diary of Anne Frank" and more "Lord of the Flies." His childhood was difficult, but not because of the Nazis. It was difficult because his father left home, and his mother died of cancer, after which he was awkwardly restored to his father's home, with a new mother and new step-siblings. Is this what my mother warned me not to ask my father? Not about Hitler, but about my grandfather?

What do I do with the memories I carried with me for so many years, about murderous stormtroopers and my father hiding in doorways? Those memories are not exactly false. My father was six years old in 1933, when Hitler took power. The Nazis built more than a hundred concentration camps in 1933, including the infamous camp at Dachau, though these camps were constructed initially to imprison political prisoners, not Jews. But the Nazis began to persecute Jews immediately upon taking power. In 1933, strict quotas were established for the number of Jews who could attend public school. The Brownshirts harassed Jews and those who shopped at Jewish stores. Julius Streicher's *Der Stürmer* newspaper was in wide circulation in 1933, publishing vile anti-Semitic propaganda with the enthusiastic approval of the Nazis. By the time my father left Germany in 1936, Jews had been stripped of German citizenship, banned from the civil service and other professions, and prohibited from marrying non-Jews.

So, the memory I'd held of my father's life in Germany was in a sense accurate. It was not far from the life he might have led. But it didn't match the memory my father reported to us some sixty years after the fact.

❊

We must discuss the Shoah in Jewish-Christian dialogue, as difficult as the discussion proves to be, if only because the Shoah is probably still the primary force that drives Jews and Christians together into discussion.

Regardless of whether we acknowledge it, and despite all previous conversation, the Shoah remains an unresolved item on the Christian-Jewish conversation agenda. We might say that Jews seek to distance themselves from the possibility that the Shoah might recur (many of us are familiar with the mantra "Never Again!"), while Christians seek to distance themselves from the anti-Jewish strain in Christianity that made the Shoah possible. In simplest terms, Jews look to Jewish-Christian dialogue for a sense of safety, and Christians look to this dialogue for a sense of absolution, but what Jews and Christians both seek from dialogue is a sense of distance. This makes the Shoah an unusual source of memory: we normally access memory to allow the past to inform the present, but in dialogue Jews and Christians recall the Shoah together primarily to ensure that nothing like it intrudes on our present.

The Shoah defies memory, because even with so much memory lost in the process of mass murder, we are overwhelmed by the quantity and intensity of the memory that has survived. We fall prey to the understandable desire to flee from such memory, and to the understandable desensitization that follows any sustained effort to examine this memory.

The Shoah defies memory, because it defies understanding. I tend to view the Shoah as one twelve-year-long event with a staggering body count. But as von Kellenbach points out, the Shoah is not "one singular event," but instead stands for six million individual murders, each "particular and committed by a specific person."[16]

Yet I fixate on a single Shoah location: the Nazi death camp at Auschwitz. In the roughly three years that the killing machine of Auschwitz was in operation, about 1.5 million people (mostly Jews) were murdered there. I try to see Auschwitz as von Kellenbach suggested—as 1.5 million separate acts of murder, only such understanding is impossible for me. I try to think of it by means of analogy: 1.5 million murders over three years comes out to 41,667 murders a month, or 1,370 murders a day, or fifty-seven murders an hour—roughly a murder a minute. This is roughly the present-day murder rate throughout the entire world[17]—slightly faster than the rate people died in armed conflict in the year 2000, slightly less than the worldwide rate of suicide. But I get no better sense of understanding by thinking in global terms.

---

16. Von Kellenbach, *The Mark of Cain*, 6.

17. Jaime Holguin, "A Murder A Minute," CBS News, October 2, 2002, www .cbsnews.com/news/a-murder-a-minute/.

I try an analogy to a single recent tragedy, one that triggered a personal sense of outrage: the December 2012 mass murder at Sandy Hook Elementary School. During the twenty minutes it took police to respond to the emergency calls from Sandy Hook, Adam Lanza killed twenty-six students and teachers. That's a rate of seventy-two murders an hour, again roughly one a minute. Was Auschwitz something like a Sandy Hook without end, continuous for three years, with no police response?

My question strikes me as obscene. Behind every murder at Auschwitz and Sandy Hook is an unquantifiable amount of grief and loss. Judaism teaches that taking a single person's life is like destroying the whole world, so the whole world was destroyed at both Auschwitz and Sandy Hook. It might matter to some how many times over this destruction took place, but not to any parent whose child died in either place.

Judaism also teaches that saving a single person's life is like saving the whole world.[18] I think of the teachers at Sandy Hook who risked their lives to save their students. I think of my father's teacher who kindly re-sat him in the middle of his class. This act was probably my father's primary childhood memory of Germany, so I owe it to my father to remember those acts of kindness performed by Germans on behalf of Jews. It is possible that this act saved my father—not his life, but whatever existed within him that allowed him to be the "charming, fun-loving guy" my family remembers.

I wish there were more such acts of German kindness to remember.

In my dialogue with Christians, I sometimes sense impatience when it comes to discussing the Shoah. *It's ancient history!* The Shoah belongs to an age before jet aircraft, commercial television, and the desegregation of U.S. public schools. Aren't we Jews *over it yet*? I hope this discussion helps explain why we Jews are not "over" the Shoah. Shoah memory was too difficult, too inexplicable, too painful to process immediately. It took over thirty years after the Shoah's end for Epstein's book to appear, nearly fifty years for Steven Spielberg to form the Shoah Foundation and begin taking testimony from Shoah survivors, and over fifty years before my father finally told us what his life was like in Nazi Germany. It took even longer before I began the process of making sense of my own childhood, fitting and fixing my memories within my father's retelling.

---

18. Babylonian Talmud Sanhedrin 37a. See, e.g., translation at http://www.on1foot.org/text/mishna-sanhedrin-45. While the text refers to those who destroy one "soul of Israel," my nonliteral and highly personal reading of the text is that it refers to any taking of life, whether Jew or Gentile.

It must be difficult for some to appreciate the perspective I'm describing. I don't always appreciate this perspective myself. When my father told my wife of his experiences in Nazi Germany, I wondered why I'd ever thought he was incapable of answering such questions. But I see now that with the passage of time, such questions became easier for us to ask, and for him to answer. In *The Generation of Postmemory*,[19] Marianne Hirsch describes family members who were reluctant to describe their experiences as Shoah survivors until they'd seen Claude Lanzmann's film *Shoah*. "*Shoah* authorized their acts of witness," writes Hirsch. "It made them feel that they had a story to tell and listeners who might be willing to acknowledge and receive it from them." I imagine that between my boyhood in the 1960s and my wife's conversation with my father in the 1990s, my father experienced similar events that "authorized" him to relate his memories to us.

And there was something else. By the time my wife asked my father about his boyhood in Nazi Germany, my father was nearly seventy years old. The generations that had lived through the Shoah were growing old, or had already passed from the scene. According to Alan Kirk, there is a "crisis" point in the formation of social memory that occurs roughly forty years after the remembered events in question, when it "becomes apparent that the cohort of living carriers of memory is disappearing," and when the community "must turn toward more enduring media capable of carrying memory in a vital manner across generations."[20] If Kirk is right, then sometime between 1973 and 1985 (forty years after the beginning and end of the Shoah), the Jewish community experienced a "crisis" where it felt a greater urgency to document the Shoah while there was still time to tap the memories of eyewitnesses. And arguably, much of the foundational documentation of the Shoah *was* produced in this period. Yeshiva University established the first academic chair for the history of the Holocaust in 1976.[21] The television series *Holocaust* was broadcast in 1978. Planning for the U.S. Holocaust Museum began in 1978. Epstein's *Children of the Holocaust* was first published in 1979. By this schedule, my wife's conversation with my father came late in the day!

---

19. Marianne Hirsch, *The Generation of Postmemory: Writing and Visual Culture after the Holocaust* (New York: Columbia University Press, 2012), 9.

20. Kirk, *Memory, Tradition, and Text*, 6.

21. William H. Honan, "First U.S. Doctoral Program on Holocaust Is Being Created," *New York Times*, October 12, 1997, www.nytimes.com/1997/10/12/us/fir st-us-doctoral-program-on-holocaust-is-being-created.html.

Theorists like Kirk provide an understanding of why it takes time for a community to incorporate an event, *any* event, into social memory. It makes sense that an even longer time will be required to process an event like the Shoah that is complex, traumatic, unimaginably destructive, and painful to consider. Of these factors, the complexity of the Shoah may be the least appreciated. Von Kellenbach's book cites historian Konrad Kweit's estimate that more than 500,000 Germans were "actively involved" in the various Nazi killing programs. Consider also that in 2013, scholars at the United States Holocaust Museum announced that they had cataloged some 42,500 Nazi ghettos and camps where the Shoah took place. These camps included not just "killing centers," but also 30,000 slave labor camps. The researchers themselves found this number to be "staggering" and "unbelievable." Just as staggering is the time it took the researchers to catalog these locations: *thirteen years*. And as of 2013, the work to catalog these sites was still ongoing.[22]

There are aspects of processing Shoah memory that we've barely begun to consider. For all of our pride in being "the people of the book," we Jews have always possessed a rich and significant oral culture. The Shoah murdered many Jewish teachers along with their students, interfering with the transmission of this culture. What was lost as a result? We don't know. I can think of this problem only in terms of how badly the Shoah disrupted Jewish life. Today, there are close to 14 million Jews worldwide, and over 80 percent of us live in Israel and the United States. But in 1933, something like 60 percent of world Jewry lived in Europe, mostly in Eastern Europe. In 1933, some 3.3 million Jews lived in Poland alone. Perhaps 12,000 Jews live in Poland today. In this dislocation, with this genocide, much must have been ripped from our collective memory.

This is one reason why I'm not comfortable with the Jewish rallying cry "Never Again!" When we say "Never Again," we mean to proclaim that never again will we Jews go "like sheep" to the slaughter of the death camps, at least not without putting up a fight. With this cry, we ignore (as Hannah Arendt pointed out so powerfully) that *no* group targeted for persecution or extermination by the Nazis put up more than token resistance.[23] But my

---

22. Eric Lichtblau, "The Holocaust Just Got More Shocking," *New York Times*, March 1, 2013, www.nytimes.com/2013/03/03/sunday-review/the-holocaust-just-got-more-shocking.html?pagewanted=all&_r=0.

23. Hannah Arendt, *Eichmann in Jerusalem: A Report on the Banality of Evil* (New York: Viking Press, 1963; repr., New York: Penguin Books, 2006). In the book's postscript, Arendt referred to the question of how Jewish victims of the Shoah "could or should have defended themselves," a question she regarded as "silly and cruel,"

problem with "Never Again!" goes beyond imagining that we Jews might have fought the Nazis more heroically. "Never Again!" makes me think that we will never again be who we were.

So no, we're not "over" the Shoah, not even as I write this, eighty years after Hitler came to power, not even with the passing of so many of the original generation who lived through the Shoah. But even if we're still processing Shoah remembrance, the growing distance between ourselves and the events of the Shoah is changing the nature of the memory process. The business of grappling with Shoah memory has fallen to a new(er) generation of authors and scholars who did not personally experience the Shoah but who (like Epstein and von Kellenbach) are children of Shoah victims, perpetrators, and bystanders.

This "second generation," sometimes called the "hinge generation" or the "generation after," is discussed by Marianne Hirsch (herself also a child of Shoah survivors) in *The Generation of Postmemory*.[24] According to Hirsch, the experience of the Shoah's second generation goes beyond a mere sense of connection to the prior generation of eyewitnesses who experienced the Shoah directly. Instead, Hirsch writes of the experience of the second generation in terms of what she calls "postmemory." Hirsch describes "postmemory" as follows:

> "Postmemory" describes the relationship that the "generation after" bears to the personal, collective, and cultural trauma of those who came before—to experiences they "remember" only by means of the stories, images, and behaviors among which they grew up. But these experiences were transmitted to them so deeply and affectively as to *seem* to constitute memories in their own right. Postmemory's connection to the past is thus actually mediated not by recall but by imaginative investment, projection, and creation. . . . [Growing up with postmemory] is to be shaped, however indirectly, by traumatic fragments of events that still defy narrative reconstruction and exceed comprehension. These events happened in the past, but their effects continue into the present. This is, I believe, the structure of postmemory and the process of its generation.[25]

I'm not sure what to make of "postmemory." I think Hirsch considers "postmemory" to have many of the qualities (and to carry much of the trauma) of the communicative memory possessed by Shoah eyewitnesses

---

since the failure of Jews to defend themselves "was not at all confined to the Jewish people and . . . therefore cannot be explained by specifically Jewish factors" (281).

24. Hirsch, *The Generation of Postmemory*, 1.

25. Hirsch, *The Generation of Postmemory*, 5.

(and, more controversially, by Shoah victims). I'd like to understand this better. But there's something in Hirsch's concept of postmemory that echoes my own relationship to my father's boyhood years in Nazi Germany. When Hirsch speaks of how postmemory is "mediated" by imaginative investment, I think of how I created a narrative for my father's Nazi experience that *felt* to me like memory even though (and even after learning that) the narrative did not match the one my father told near the end of his life.

⚜

I have taken time to describe the quality of my Shoah memory. All this is prelude to what I imagine will be my primary topic of conversation with Anthony: How do Jews and Christians remember the Shoah together? Anthony says that Jews and Christians have different memories of the Shoah. Should it then be our goal in dialogue to simply share these different memories, to make them understood, and leave it at that? Or are we after something more?

Before I consider these questions, I need to address another question that I think has dominated Jewish-Christian dialogue regarding the Shoah: namely, is Christianity responsible for the Shoah?

I cannot do justice to this question in this space. I cannot do much more than say that this question is controversial, even within the Jewish community. Perhaps the best-known Jewish statement on the question is contained in the 2002 document "Dabru Emet" (Hebrew for "Speak the Truth"), signed by over 220 Jewish rabbis and scholars. "Dabru Emet" addresses Jewish-Christian relations in general, but it also makes a specific statement about the Shoah, proclaiming that "Nazism was not a Christian phenomenon":

> Without the long history of Christian anti-Judaism and Christian violence against Jews, Nazi ideology could not have taken hold nor could it have been carried out. Too many Christians participated in, or were sympathetic to, Nazi atrocities against Jews. Other Christians did not protest sufficiently against these atrocities. But Nazism itself was not an inevitable outcome of Christianity. If the Nazi extermination of the Jews had been fully successful, it would have turned its murderous rage more directly to Christians. We recognize with gratitude those Christians who risked or sacrificed their lives to save Jews during the Nazi regime.[26]

---

26. "Dabru Emet," *Jewish-Christian Relations*, July 15, 2002, www.jcrelations.net/Dabru_Emet_-_A_Jewish_Statement_on_Christians_and_Christianity.2395.0.html.

Many Jews disagree with how Dabru Emet described the relationship between Christianity and the Shoah. Rabbi A. James Rudin called this description "inadequate and surprisingly diffident," and wondered why his Jewish colleagues did not address this question with the same "accuracy and power" as have some Christians. He pointed to this statement by the General Conference of the United Methodist Church:

> Especially critical for Christians . . . has been the struggle to recognize the horror of the Holocaust as the catastrophic culmination of a long history of anti-Jewish attitudes and actions in which Christians, and sometimes the Church itself, have been deeply implicated.[27]

If asked to summarize the history, my statement would go further. I would say that Christians participated in the Shoah in great numbers, and often with great enthusiasm. I would say that the main body of the German Lutheran Church supported Hitler, eager to prove that Christianity had much to offer to a Reich seeking to exterminate European Jewry. Even those Christians who opposed Hitler were often silent or quietly acquiescent when it came to persecution of Jews. There is simply no way that the vast machinery of the Shoah could have been manned by "willing executioners" if the church had not carefully taught its followers that the Jews are Christ-killers, a people cursed by G-d. Finally, even after the Shoah was over and the Nazis lost their power to silence and intimidate people of conscience, Christianity was slow to condemn the anti-Semitism and anti-Judaism that made the Shoah possible. As von Kellenbach points out in *The Mark of Cain*, it fell to the second generation of Germans and church leaders to begin to express remorse and seek forgiveness.

But I subscribe to Dabru Emet's description of the Christian relationship to the Shoah, for a reason that goes beyond how to best describe the history in a single paragraph. I see a determined attitude among my Christian dialogue partners that Christianity (at least as properly understood) is neither anti-Jewish nor anti-Semitic. Coupled with this attitude is the view that the Shoah and all it stood for was fundamentally anti-Christian—not merely in the sense that Hitler was an enemy of Christianity, but also that the goals and values of Nazism were diametrically opposed to those of Christianity. Yes, to be sure, this view paints a too-rosy historical picture of Christianity and

---

27. A. James Rudin, "'Dabru Emet': A Jewish Dissent," *Jewish-Christian Relations*, www.jcrelations.net/Dabru_Emet___A_Jewish_Dissent.2349.0.html?L=8&page=11.

its role in the Shoah, but it may best describe what Christianity is *today*. If today our Christian friends loathe Nazism, if they are sickened and appalled by the Shoah, if they wish to understand and define their Christianity in opposition to the forces and attitudes that made the Shoah possible, then this is a development to be welcomed and encouraged by all Jews.

It is for this reason that I'm not as interested as I might be in determining Christian responsibility for the Shoah. This being the case, it's fair to ask exactly what I hope to accomplish when we discuss the Shoah in Jewish-Christian dialogue. I hope for two outcomes. First, I'd like to see Christianity define itself as a pro-Jewish religion, so that anything found in Christianity that smacks of anti-Judaism or anti-Semitism is suspect and a candidate for reconsideration. This seems fair to me. If I'm willing to say that the Shoah was not a "Christian phenomenon," not an "inevitable outcome of Christianity," it's fair to ask my Christian friends to back me up and prove me right!

Second, I think that Jews and Christians together have to take a tougher stance against the kind of crime committed by the Nazis. I've already mentioned the Jewish rallying cry in response to the Shoah: "Never Again!" When I first heard this cry, it left me with mixed emotions. Never again? Of course not. But never what again, and to whom, and how to prevent it, and at what cost? The cry "Never Again!" rings hollow, now that the Shoah has been followed by genocide in Cambodia, Bosnia, Rwanda, and many other places. A determined and sustained effort to prevent further genocide must be part of any effort to remember the Shoah. Who can retell the things that befell us? We all can, and must, and to the purpose of affirming that saving a single person's life is like saving the whole world.

The Holocaust and Social Memory

Anthony Le Donne

For in the end, it is all about memory, its sources and its magnitude, and, of course, its consequences.

—Elie Wiesel, author of *Night*[1]

Remembering Together

We remember better together than we do as individuals. Remembering "better" can have the sense of remembering more accurately. But there is another important motive of memory. Remembering better can mean remembering successfully toward a purpose. Most often our purposes are mundane: I remember to set the alarm; I remember which route to take to work; I remember to pack a lunch. Other memories serve as identity markers: I remember my name; I remember my mother's kindness and discipline; I remember my children's birthdays. Some significant identity markers can be called "cultural memories." These are commemorative activities (memorial dates, annual celebrations, historic sites, meaningful stories, and so on) that are practiced collectively. Both as individuals and as groups, our memories define our identities.

Christian theologian Miroslav Volf writes, "Memory *defines the identities* of Jews and Christians. To be a Jew is to remember the Exodus. To be a Christian is to remember the death and resurrection of Christ."[2] Volf leans heavily on Jewish historian Yosef Hayim Yerushalmi. Yerushalmi explain that "memory draws from the past a series of situations into which one could be

---

1. Elie Wiesel, *Night*, trans. Stella Rodway (New York: Penguin Books, 1981), xv.
2. Miroslav Volf, *The End of Memory: Remembering Rightly in a Violent World* (Grand Rapids: Eerdmans, 2006), 97; emphasis original.

existentially drawn."[3] Both Volf and Yerushalmi devote a great deal of effort nuancing the importance and limits of memory. Volf grants that defining Jewishness and Christianity is much more complicated than remembering "the Exodus and the Passion," but "take away the memories of the Exodus and the Passion, and you have excised the pulsating heart that energizes and directs their action and forms their hopes."[4]

I was recently reminded of Volf's point as I again read Elie Wiesel's *Night*. This is a ruinous book. Every time. When we meet the boy who will witness the death of G-d at Auschwitz, he is a boy of profound belief. "During the day I studied the Talmud, and at night I ran to the synagogue to weep over the destruction of the Temple."[5] This is the first time Wiesel mentions "night," the key theme and title of his book. He hints of exile on page one and then more explicitly as night falls:

> The Week of Passover. The weather was wonderful. My mother bustled round her kitchen. There were no longer any synagogues open. We gathered in private houses: the Germans were not to be provoked.

> We drank, we ate we sang. The Bible bade us rejoice during the seven days of the feast, to be happy. But our hearts were not in it.

> On the seventh day of Passover the curtain rose. The Germans arrested the leaders of the Jewish community.

> From that moment, everything happened very quickly. The race toward death had begun.[6]

Wiesel's personal memory of being raced toward the death camps are framed in a cultural memory of the Exodus. On the seventh day of Passover, the day when the children of Israel commemorate the delivery from the Egyptian army, Wiesel's own exile begins. The failure of G-d to deliver the people enslaved at Auschwitz is set in stark contrast to the Jewish cultural memory of exodus. Whereas the cultural memory would suggest hope, Wiesel experiences only the opposite.

---

3. Yosef Hayim Yerushalmi, *Zakhor: Jewish History and Jewish Memory* (Seattle: University of Washington Press, 1982), 44.
4. Volf, *End of Memory*, 97.
5. Wiesel, *Night*, 13.
6. Wiesel, *Night*, 20–21.

Memory theorist Aleida Assmann would call this an intersection between cultural memory and communicative memory.[7] We measure our most significant personal memories against the great narratives and myths of our culture.

Christians do the same, but our memories are framed by our distinct identity "in Christ." (Here I borrow a key phrase from Paul the apostle.) We remember differently because we are different. Conversely, and cycling backward, we are different because we remember differently.

The Penguin edition of *Night* includes a foreword by Nobel laureate François Mauriac. Mauriac writes of his socially conditioned "memories of the Occupation." He explains: "It is not always the events we have been directly involved in that affect us the most . . . nothing I had seen during those somber years had left so deep a mark upon me as those trainloads of Jewish children standing at Austerlitz station. Yet I did not see them myself. My wife described them to me, her voice still filled with horror."[8]

Mauriac knows that these were not horrors that he witnessed personally, but his wife's memories became his own. This is a "communicative memory," clearly formed in social dialogue. Mauriac also frames the Holocaust in "cultural memory" (the type of memory passed down generationally). This is clearly seen as he relays a crucial passage from Wiesel's *Night*. Wiesel writes of the hanging of a child with "an angelic face," whose neck refused to snap, who swung suffocating on the gallows.

> For more than half an hour he stayed there, struggling between life and death, dying in slow agony under our eyes. And we had to look him full in the face. He was still alive when I passed in front of him. His tongue still red, his eyes were not yet glazed.
>
> Behind me I heard . . . "Where is G[-]d now?"
>
> And I heard a voice within me answer him:
>
> "Where is He? Here He is—He is hanging here on this gallows. . . ."
>
> That night the soup tasted of corpses.[9]

In his foreword, Mauriac reflects on Wiesel's story of literal and personal exile. Mauriac writes, "And I, who believe that G[-]d is love, what answer

---

7. Aleida Assmann, *Zeit und Tradition: Kulturelle Strategien der Dauer, Beiträge zur Geschichtskultur* 15 (Köln: Böhlau, 1999), 64.

8. François Mauriac, Foreword, in *Night*, trans. Stella Rodway (New York: Penguin Books, 1981), 7.

9. *Night*, 77.

could I give my young questioner, whose dark eyes still held the reflection of that angelic sadness which had appeared one day upon the face of the hanged child?" Mauriac, a Christian, continues, "What did I say to him? Did I speak of that other Israeli, his brother, who may have resembled him—the Crucified, whose Cross has conquered the world?"

Notice here that Mauriac must process the profundity and enormity of the story within his own cultural memory: that of Christ crucified but eventually victorious. Christians, as Volf tells us, tend to reinforce their identity in Christ by commemorating the passion.[10] I will return to Mauriac's distinctly Christian memory below, but more must be said about Jewish memory and identity first.

In his 2006 preface to *Night*, Wiesel writes:

> I do not know, or no longer know, what I wanted to achieve with my words. I only know that without this testimony, my life as a writer—or my life, period—would not have become what it is: that of a witness who believes he has a moral obligation to try to prevent the enemy from enjoying one last victory by allowing his crimes to be erased from human memory.[11]

For Wiesel, his memories of Auschwitz defined him. This much is clear. But notice also that the *process of writing* his account of Auschwitz also defined him. There is political and moral power in memorial practice. Wiesel's purpose in writing his story perhaps didn't become clear until years later. But his book was indeed an act of remembering that served a cultural purpose.

Memory also has the political and (a)moral power to define national identity. Wiesel concludes that Hitler and his political machine tried to define a new (Aryan) German identity. So part of Hitler's violence "was a war not only against Jewish, men, women, and children, but also against Jewish religion, Jewish culture, Jewish tradition, therefore Jewish memory."[12]

Hitler wanted to bury Jewish memory with counter-memories that would promote his vision for European culture. This is not uncommon among those who would be culture makers. Statues commemorating heroes

---

10. Consider also the words of Christian theologian Richard B. Hays, "The cross confounds all human religion and philosophy, all human wisdom. It is the strange instrument by which G[-]d has shattered the old world and brought a new one into being," *The New Interpreter's Bible: Second Corinthians–Philemon*, vol. 11 (Nashville: Abingdon Press, 2000), 316.

11. Wiesel, *Night*, viii.

12. Wiesel, *Night*, viii.

galvanize civic identity. The same statues are torn down during times of revolution. City names change from Saint Petersburg to Leningrad and then back again. On this topic, Martin Luther's ultimate advice concerning the Jews is revealing. Luther instructed the German government in 1543 "to set fire to their synagogues or schools and to bury and cover with dirt whatever will not burn, so that no man will ever again see a stone or cinder of them."[13] Erasing culture and identity requires the erasure of memory and tradition. This tells us quite forcefully that memory creates identity.

Consider the findings of the 2013 survey by the Pew Research Center:

> A key aim of the Pew Research Center survey is to explore Jewish identity: What does being Jewish mean in America today? Large majorities of U.S. Jews say that remembering the Holocaust (73 percent) and leading an ethical life (69 percent) are essential to their sense of Jewishness.[14]

Other major factors contributing to Jewish self-identification included "working for justice and equality," "caring about Israel," and "a good sense of humor." For American Jews, remembering the Holocaust (73 percent) is significantly more important than "observing Jewish law" (19 percent). I would argue that memory is essential in each of these factors, but the first and most prominent among these identity markers appeals to "remembering" explicitly.

I would push the significance of this data a bit further. I would suggest that it is impossible to be an adult, educated person who identities as Jewish without being connected in some way to Shoah memory. For Jews, remembering the Shoah is a central and essential identity marker. I would also suggest that most Christians do not know this. We Christians, by and large, know very little about the Holocaust and know even less how important remembering it is to our Jewish neighbors. The implication here should be clear: *We don't know the first thing about Jews.*

Let's return to Mauriac's Christian reading of *Night*. As I've said, we measure our most significant experiences against our most meaningful cultural memories. Mauriac, to use Yerushalmi's phrase, was "existentially drawn" into Wiesel's story. In this process, the saving act of Jesus on the cross became the dominant symbol in Mauriac's interpretation. Mauriac writes that Christ's connection to human suffering is "the key to that impenetrable

---

13. I will address Luther's anti-Semitic advice more fully below.

14. "A Portrait of Jewish Americans," Pew Research Center, October 1, 2013, www.pewforum.org/2013/10/01/jewish-american-beliefs-attitudes-culture-survey/.

mystery." In context: "Did I affirm that the stumbling block to his faith was the cornerstone of mine, and that the conformity between the Cross and the suffering of men was in my eyes the key to that impenetrable mystery whereon the faith of his childhood had perished?"[15]

Is this an appropriate way to remember the Holocaust? I tend to think not. As I first read Mauriac's particularly Christian move from crucifixion to resurrection in a single breath, I confess that I recoiled. Why must Christians project Christ and triumph onto this catastrophe? But I read on.

> Zion, however, has risen up again from the crematories and the charnel houses. The Jewish nation has been resurrected from among its thousands of dead. It is through them that it lives again. We do not know the worth of one single drop of blood, one single tear. All is grace. If the Eternal is the Eternal, the last word for each one of us belongs to Him. This is what I should have told this Jewish child. But I could only embrace him weeping.[16]

The Christian story (borrowing from Jewish literature) is that of resurrection.[17] How can I blame Mauriac for creating a meaningful memory from within this commemorative narrative? It is not just how our memories work; it is who we are.

In Wiesel's original draft of *Night* (now quoted in his 2006 foreword) he wrote, "And now, scarcely ten years after Buchenwald, I realize that the world forgets quickly."[18] The world has forgotten quickly and far too many Christians reflect this cultural amnesia. We have forgotten our role in the Holocaust. And for lack of a better memory, we have returned to a projection of triumph—of Christ crucified and risen. If we Christians are left to our own devices, we will misremember stories like the one told by Elie Wiesel. But when we—as Jews and Christians—have the opportunity to remember together, we remember better.

---

15. Mauriac, Foreword, in *Night*, 10.

16. Mauriac, Foreword, in *Night*, 11. I would also add that in Wiesel's account of this exchange, Mauriac was not shy about his Christology during this meeting. Indeed, according to Wiesel, Mauriac referred to Christ repeatedly. "Every reference led back to him." (See Mary Boys, "When Elie Wiesel Met François Mauriac," *America: The National Catholic Review*, July 2016, http://www.americamagazine. org/content/all-things/when-elie-wiesel-met-francois-mauriac.)

17. On this point, see Jon D. Levenson, *The Death and Resurrection of the Beloved Son: The Transformation of Child Sacrifice in Judaism and Christianity* (New Haven: Yale University Press, 1993).

18. Wiesel, *Night*, vii.

Two Thin Books That I Cannot Unread

The following is a cut-and-paste job that sets passages from (1) a little book by Martin Luther against passages from (2) the little book by Elie Wiesel mentioned above. The former represents Luther's advice to German government officials in 1543. The latter represents Wiesel's memories and reflections of his time in Germany from 1941 to 1945.

Some will read what follows and see that I am being unjust to Luther's legacy.[19] Martin Luther was a complicated person and personality; the act of cutting and pasting rarely does justice to a great thinker's life or work.[20] Others will read what follows and recognize that I am truncating Wiesel's great work of literature—reducing it to sound bites. Moreover, there is no way to cut and paste from Wiesel's account of the Holocaust and do justice to its darkness. So what follows is probably unjust on a number of levels.

I set these quotations together only to show how my own memory is arranged. I cannot remember Luther and not think of Wiesel. I cannot remember Wiesel and not think of Luther.

Luther: In brief, dear princes and lords, those of you who have Jews under your rule—if my counsel does not please you, find better advice, so that you and we all can be rid of the unbearable, devilish burden of the Jews. . . . First, to set fire to their synagogues or schools and to bury and cover with dirt

---

19. Some would argue this point forcefully. See Uwe Siemon-Netto, *The Fabricated Luther: Refuting Nazi Connections and Modern Myths*, 2nd ed. (St. Louis: Concordia, 2007).

20. David Nirenberg writes: "Luther launched an armada of arguments whose force led to the acceptance of his way of reading [Scripture] by many and its violent rejection by many more. It was the active prosecution of this conflict of ideas that reshaped the ways in which European Christians experienced their world, and heightened the dangerous significance of Jews and Judaism in that world." *Anti-Judaism: The Western Tradition* (New York: W. W. Norton & Company), 256. Also: "Luther's reconceptualization of the ways in which language mediates between G[-]d and creation was achieved by thinking with, about, and against Jews and Judaism. Insofar as these reconfigurations diminished the utility and heightened the dangers Jews posed to the Christian world, they had the potential to transform figures of Judaism and their fates. How powerful this potential might be, and what work it might perform in the future, were not Luther's to control" (267). Nirenberg rightly draws a connection between Luther's (hermeneutic toward the) reading of Scripture and the foil he creates in Judaism. To his credit Nirenberg also avoids a simplistic distinction between the "early Luther" and the "later Luther." Helpfully, he begins by examining Luther's anti-Jewish work on the Psalms, a work representing the "early Luther."

whatever will not burn, so that no man will ever again see a stone or cinder of them. This is to be done in honor of our L[-]rd and of Christendom. . . . Second, I advise that their houses also be razed and destroyed. . . . This will bring home to them that they are not masters in our country, as they boast, but that they are living in exile and in captivity, as they incessantly wail and lament about us before G[-]d.[21]

> **Wiesel:** The commandant announced that we had already covered forty-two miles since we left. . . . We sank down as one man in the snow. My father shook me. "Not here. . . . Get up. . . . A little farther on. There's a shed over there . . . come on." I had neither the will nor the strength to get up. Nevertheless I obeyed. It was not a shed, but a brick factory with a caved-in roof, broken windows, walls filthy with soot. It was not easy to get in. Hundreds of prisoners were crowding at the door.[22]

Luther: Third, I advise that all their prayer books and Talmudic writings, in which such idolatry, lies, cursing and blasphemy are taught, be taken from them.[23]

> **Wiesel:** It is obvious that the war which Hitler and his accomplices waged was a war not only against Jewish, men, women, and children, but also against Jewish religion, Jewish culture, Jewish tradition, therefore Jewish memory.[24]

Luther: Fourth, I advise that their rabbis be forbidden to teach henceforth on pain of loss of life and limb.[25]

> **Wiesel:** On the seventh day of Passover the curtain rose. The Germans arrested the leaders of the Jewish community.[26]

Luther: Fifth, I advise that safe-conduct on the highways be abolished completely for the Jews.[27]

---

21. Martin Luther, *On the Jews and Their Lies* (1543; repr., East Sussex: Historical Review Press, 2011), 111.

22. Wiesel, *Night*, 99–100.

23. Luther, *On the Jews and Their Lies*, 111.

24. Wiesel, *Night*, viii.

25. Luther, *On the Jews and Their Lies*, 111.

26. Wiesel, *Night*, 21.

27. Luther, *On the Jews and Their Lies*, 111.

Wiesel: There are anti-Semitic incidents every day, in the streets, in the trains. . . . The situation is getting very serious.[28]

Our terror was about to burst the sides of the train. Our nerves were at breaking point. Our flesh was creeping. . . . The heat, the thirst, the pestilential stench, the suffocating lack of air. . . . But we had reached a station. Those who were next to the windows told us its name: "Auschwitz."[29]

Luther: Sixth, I advise that usury be prohibited to them, and that all cash and treasure of silver and gold be taken from them and put aside for safekeeping.[30]

Wiesel: That same day the Hungarian police burst into all the Jewish houses in the street. A Jew no longer had the right to keep in his house gold, jewels, or any objects of value. Everything had to be handed over to the authorities—on pain of death. My father went down into the cellar and buried our savings.[31]

"Look, take this knife," he said to me. "I don't need it any longer. It might be useful to you. And take this spoon as well. Don't sell them. Quickly! Go on take what I'm giving you!" The inheritance. "Don't talk like that, father." (I felt that I would break into sobs.) "I don't want to hear you say that. Keep the spoon and the knife. You need them as much as I do. . . ." He looked at me with eyes that veiled despair.[32]

Luther: Seventh, I commend putting a flail, an axe, a hoe, a spade, a distaff, or a spindle into the hands of young, strong Jews and Jewesses and letting them earn their bread in the sweat of their brow, as was imposed on the children of Adam.[33]

Wiesel: "Remember this," he went on. "Remember it forever. Engrave it into your minds. You are at Auschwitz. And Auschwitz is not a convalescent home. It's a concentration camp. Here, you have got to work. If

---

28. Wiesel, *Night*, 19.

29. Wiesel, *Night*, 36–37.

30. Luther, *On the Jews and Their Lies*, 112.

31. Wiesel, *Night*, 21.

32. Wiesel, *Night*, 86.

33. Luther, *On the Jews and Their Lies*, 114.

not, you will go straight to the furnace. To the crematory. Work or the crematory—the choice is in your hands."[34]

All the skilled workers had already been sent to other camps. There were only about a hundred of us ordinary labourers left. . . . We were surrounded by about ten SS. On the door the plaque: "*Work is liberty.*" We were counted.[35]

Luther: I wish and I ask that our rulers who have Jewish subjects exercise a sharp mercy toward these wretched people, as suggested above, to see whether this might not help (though it is doubtful). They must act like a good physician who, when gangrene has set in, proceeds without mercy to cut, saw, and burn flesh, veins, bone, and marrow. Such a procedure must also be followed in this instance. Burn down their synagogues, forbid all that I enumerated earlier, force them to work, and deal harshly with them, as Moses did in the wilderness, slaying three thousand lest the whole people perish.[36]

David Nirenberg explains that even before Luther published *On the Jews and Their Lies*, he "directly provoked the expulsion of the Jews from the electoral of Saxony in 1537 and from the towns of Thuringia in 1540, and sparked riots against the Jews in Brunswick in 1543."[37] Luther might not have drawn the "blueprint" for the violence and arrests that launched the Holocaust, but he certainly contributed to the climate wherein the Holocaust was made conceivable (even desirable) among German Christians.[38] In many cases, Luther's advice was appealed to explicitly by Christians in Nazi Germany to justify the "dejudaization" of Germany and the Church.[39] Theology professor Martin Redeker voiced an all too common notion among Nazi Christians: "The contemporary fulfillment of German politics and political leadership that we are enabled to experience in National Socialist Germany

---

34. Wiesel, *Night*, 50.

35. Wiesel, *Night*, 57.

36. Luther, *On the Jews and Their Lies*, 131.

37. Nirenberg, *Anti-Judaism*, 262.

38. See Diarmaid MacCulloch, *Reformation: Europe's House Divided, 1490–1700* (New York: Penguin Books, 2004), 666–67.

39. See discussion in Susannah Heschel, *The Aryan Jesus* (Princeton: Princeton University Press, 2008), 76–77, 140.

is the fulfillment of [proto-]German themes that broke forth with Luther and through Luther experienced religious and moral substantiation."[40]

A more thorough discussion might devote as much time to the theological influence of Marcion or draw parallels between *Night* and the words of Christian patriarch, John of Chrysostom. I focus on Luther's rhetoric (and selectively so) because his is the voice that haunts me when I remember the Holocaust.

A Singular Catastrophe

I have argued that memory shapes identity. Some might state this more boldly; some might say that *memory is identity*. For now, I will adopt softer language: *memory shapes identity*. I've also suggested a circular relationship: *identity shapes memory*.

I am also convinced that the *ways* we remember are just as identity-forming (and informed by identity) as the content of our memories. I think that the ways that Christians and Jews remember the Holocaust differently is very telling. Folks who use the term "Shoah" tend to remember it differently, with a different purpose, and reinforced with different social frameworks.

Before detailing a few of these differences, allow me to state clearly: I believe that there is significant overlap between the words *Shoah* and *Holocaust*. Shoah is a Hebrew word that can be translated as "catastrophe" or "destruction." But as the term "Shoah" has made its way into English vocabulary, it has become a synonym for the Holocaust. I believe that there is some nuance required. The concept of Shoah, in my view, reveals a particularly Jewish way of remembering that exists within the larger cultural memory of the Holocaust in secular history. So we could say that Shoah memory is a subset of Holocaust memory.

For many Jews, the Shoah is a singular event that caps centuries of persecution, murderous violence, and attempted genocide. Christians find it difficult to identify with the cultural memory in the same way. For most Christians, it is not family history. This much is expected. But I will push a bit further. If (1) memory shapes identity and (2) our memories differ, then our very identities (who we are and who we will be) have become increasingly divergent. This brings me to my point: *Jews and Christians have remembered our common history divergently and have become alienated from each other in this process.*

---

40. Quoted from Heschel, *The Aryan Jesus*, 173–74.

In the summer of 2005, I was invited to speak to a group of well-educated and intellectually eager Presbyterians in Santa Rosa, California. The organizers let me choose my own topic. The lecture I ended up giving was titled "New Testament Judaism: Atoning for 400 Years of Anti-Semitism in Biblical Studies." I explored the ways that anti-Judaism and anti-Semitism have biased New Testament scholars.

Trying to provide a bit of perspective on traditionally Christian ways of reading the Bible, I wrote of our collective failures. I wrote of the impact that our ways of reading the New Testament have had on a "long and dark history of religious misgivings and polemics punctuated by violence, forced displacement, pogroms, and holocausts."

Notice here that I used "holocausts" in the plural.

My research for this lecture set me on a path toward two essays that I completed in 2011. A friend, a Jewish professor of New Testament, was kind enough to send me feedback before these essays were published. And so it happened that I first learned of my misstep. My friend gently corrected me:

> Jews believe that "Holocaust" must always be capitalized and always be singular and NEVER be used to refer to anything but the Nazi regime—in other words, there was but one Holocaust, and the word is cheapened if applied differently— one of the reasons Shoah came into usage.

In trying to convey the longer history of persecution, I used "holocausts" in the plural. After all—I thought—highlighting only the catastrophic genocide in World War II Europe neglects the many other mass killings of Jews in Christian history. Count Emicho's slogan for the German Crusade of 1096 gnawed at me: "Why fight Christ's enemies abroad when they are living among us?" Over five thousand Jews were killed in this episode alone.

In my study, I came to the conclusion that Christian-perpetrated mass murder is too easily forgotten by Christians. If we remember them at all, we tend to do so in ways that absolve ourselves from any complicity. Such historical amnesia/delusion allows us to make the same mistakes we have always made when we read our sacred texts. It seemed to me then—as I carefully chose the plural form "holocausts"—that I was helping in some small way to correct an ongoing Christian oversight. From my posture of righteous indignation (no doubt, I aggrandized myself in the process), it was clear that "holocausts" was the correct term.

What I thought of as a corrective was corrected from a Jewish perspective. For many Jews, it is the singularity of the Holocaust that punctuates its significance and promotes a right remembering of a long history of anti-Semitism. Indeed, as my friend explained to me, many Jews now use the word *Shoah* rather than Holocaust to further promote a sense of singularity. Larry has also suggested to me that part of the appeal of "Shoah" is that it doesn't get appropriated so often in a way that cheapens the use of the word.

We must keep in mind that not all Jews use this term. Nor do all who use the term "Shoah" do so to convey a sense of singularity. But the fact that there was a recognized need among many Jews to retitle this historical event indicates something important about how it is remembered among Jews.

Consider the definitions below. I've offered two different definitions of "Shoah" from online resources. I've also included Merriam-Webster's online definition of "holocaust":

Shoah: The Hebrew word meaning "catastrophe," denoting the catastrophic destruction of European Jewry during World War II. The term is used in Israel, and the Knesset (the Israeli Parliament) has designated an official day, called Yom ha-Shoah, as a day of commemorating the Shoah or Holocaust.[41]

Shoah: Shoah is the standard Hebrew term used to refer to the murder of European Jews by the Nazis—the event commonly referred to as "the Holocaust" in English. Some people object to use of the term "Holocaust," as one of the primary meanings of the word "holocaust" is a sacrifice consumed by fire. The idea that millions of people died as a sacrifice to G-d is too horrible for me to contemplate. I think it is better to refer to this catastrophe in a way that does not suggest whether or how the catastrophe fit into a divine plan. However, I fully understand that people use the term "the Holocaust" with the greatest respect for the Jewish people (and for humankind), and without intending to make a theological statement, and I am in no way offended by others' use of this term.[42]

holocaust: The killing of millions of Jews and other people by the Nazis during World War II

: an event or situation in which many people are killed and many things are destroyed especially by fire

1 : a sacrifice consumed by fire

2 : a thorough destruction involving extensive loss of life especially through fire <a nuclear *holocaust*>

---

41. A *Teacher's Guide to the Holocaust;* http://fcit.usf.edu/holocaust/DEFN/shoah.htm; Shoah is often translated as "destruction"; see, e.g., "The Holocaust," Yad Vashem, www.yadvashem.org/yv/en/holocaust/resource_center/the_holocaust.asp.
42. Larry Behrendt, "Never Forget," *Jewish-Christian Intersections*, December 8, 2013, http://jewishchristianintersections.com/?p=394.

3 **a** *often capitalized* : the mass slaughter of European civilians and especially Jews by the Nazis during World War II—usually used with *the*

b : a mass slaughter of people; *especially* : genocide[43]

By the two "Shoah" definitions, we would be reminded that six million Jews were murdered. Contrast this definition with the definition of "holocaust."

As used when it is capitalized, the Holocaust is widely understood as the mass murder of civilians (especially Jews) in European (especially German) death camps. "Holocaust" does indeed call to mind a primarily Jewish catastrophe. But it also includes non-Jewish victims as well. The phrase "Jews and other people" is significant.[44] Using this definition, we are reminded that eleven million civilians were murdered, including Jews, Roma, communists, gays, Roman Catholics, Greek Orthodox, Jehovah's Witnesses, and other people deemed ideologically dangerous to the "common good." The mentally ill and the disabled were also selected for extermination.

So if you simply want a numerical difference between *Holocaust* and *Shoah*, it could be counted in the millions.

But there is another important difference to be drawn here. Your average Christian—lamentably!—tends to think of the Holocaust as a politically motivated war crime. Here I use the phrase "politically motivated" to indicate that most Christians see the Holocaust as an entirely secular tragedy. Most Christians (if they've thought about it at all) believe that it was not committed by Christians at all, but by an archetypal enemy: the Nazis. They believe that the Nazis might have used religion as political leverage, but they were not themselves Christians. This point is crucial and worth explaining. Most Christians see the Nazis as enemies of Christianity.[45] Your average Christian

---

43. Merriam-Webster's online dictionary, http://www.merriam-webster.com/dictionary/holocaust.

44. The Yad Vashem website refers to "non-Jewish victims of persecution in Germany" instead of non-Jewish victims of the Holocaust: "Non-Jewish Victims of Persecution in Germany," www.yadvashem.org/holocaust/about/nazi-germany-1933-39/non-jewish-victims. Does this move to use the language of victimization suggest an exclusion of non-Jews from the defined parameters of Shoah? By contrast, notice the inclusion of non-Jews within this definition: Terese Pencak Schwartz, "The Holocaust: Non-Jewish Victims," www.jewishvirtuallibrary.org/non-jewish-victims-of-the-holocaust.

45. World War II historian Martin Gilbert self-identifies as Jewish. Many Christians I've met echo him on this point: "Although the Jew was Nazism's particular

refuses to believe—even among those Nazis who claimed allegiance to
Christ—that true Christians would commit mass murder. In my experience,
this is the Christian narrative.

Indeed, I have heard often from my fellow worshipers that the "true
Christians" were heroic during this period. Let that notion settle in for a
moment: *Christians tend to remember Christian heroism when we think of
the Holocaust!* I would guess that those who use the term "Shoah" do not
remember it in this way.

Two observations are warranted. The first is that most Christians are
woefully uneducated when it comes to the Holocaust. The second is a bit
more complicated: within this general lack of data, the little that we do know
about the Holocaust focuses on Oscar Schindler and Dietrich Bonhoeffer
types. The narrative created within this "Christian" way of remembering the
Holocaust is incorrect and irresponsible.

Sometimes facts lie. It is a fact that Irena Sendler, a Roman Catholic nurse
and social worker, saved close to 2,500 Jewish children from the death camps.
It is a fact that Christian theologian Dietrich Bonhoeffer was murdered by
Nazis for his resistance. But facts like this can create a fiction. They are facts
that perpetuate the Christian tendency to remember the Holocaust in heroic
terms. These true stories cannot possibly give us a realistic picture of how
Christianity relates to the Holocaust.

In large part, Christians remain unaware of the theological currents
that made the Holocaust possible. Perhaps it is impossible for Christians to
identify with the Holocaust to the extent that Jews do, but we would do well
to bring a *Shoah* definition corrective to our narratives.

As those who use the term "Shoah" will remind us, the Holocaust is a
catastrophic climax in a long trajectory of anti-Semitism. What has been lost
in Christian memory is the fact that a great deal of this anti-Semitic history
is Christian history. However painful it might be to admit it, the Holocaust
betrays the fingerprints of Christianity. Indeed European Christians and
clergy were actively involved in the erasure of Jewish culture long before
World War II began.

I don't doubt that most Christians are simply unaware of their own
history and thus unaware of the great parade of Christian failures leading

---

enemy, Nazism was also the enemy of not only Jews and Judaism, but of true Christianity, and of all liberal, ethical and moral values, totally opposed in everything it did
to the Judaeo-Christian ethic." See Martin Gilbert, "Christians and the Holocaust,"
Jewish-Christian Relations, www.jcrelations.net/"?id=2249."

to the Holocaust. But it would be incorrect to speak only of our sins of omission. In many ways, our misinformation is a result of political spin and active suppression. Many SS officers and soldiers were not Christians, but far too many were.

Hans Frank, governor-general of Poland, was convicted of war crimes at Nuremberg. Frank came to the conclusion that he, alongside those left behind by Hitler, was the real victim. Frank likened Germany to Christ. He wrote that Germany "is now experiencing the most grueling passion. It is scorned, flogged, and nailed to the cross."[46] I can hardly think of a more repugnant way to remember the ruin left by Christian-sponsored Nazism. Even so, we see again the Christian tendency to remember in a way that reinforces our identity "in Christ."

Adding to the problem of Christian amnesia is the untold thousands of Christians who covered up their war crimes. Both Protestant and Catholic clergy were anxious to forgive and forget. Matthias Defregger (1915–1995) was the Roman Catholic auxiliary bishop of Bavaria. Defregger "retreated into apologetic assertions that Christian forgiveness of sins should 'cover up' the memory of the offense."[47] In this case, we see that not only was the Holocaust theologically motivated, post-Holocaust amnesia was also theologically motivated.

For Christians, remembering better must involve an account of the vast majority of Christians in that time and place who were complicit or guilty of genocide. Unless properly told within the larger narrative, our fond memories of Sendler and Bonhoeffer betray them and what they stood for. Moreover, however we tell their stories, the larger narrative must end in catastrophe. There might have been a few heroes along the way, but the purpose of the story should not be to venerate heroes. Christians will continue to be ill-equipped to dialogue with Jews until this point is understood.

Those who use the term "Shoah" do not remember for the sake of Christians. All the same, we Christians need help remembering. I would suggest that remembering better means remembering together.

---

46. Hans Frank, *Im Angesicht des Galgens* (Munich: Beck Verlag, 1954), 431. Cf. K. von Kellenbach, *The Mark of Cain: Guilt and Denial in the Post-War Lives of Nazi Perpetrators* (New York: Oxford University Press, 2013), 113–14.

47. Von Kellenbach, *The Mark of Cain*, 190.

Shoah

Dialogue

Larry: Let's start with something that our two chapters share in common. You want us to remember the Shoah together. So do I.

Anthony: For Christians, our failure to remember the Holocaust together with Jews comes perilously close to a kind of forgetting. I'm not sure that Jews need Christian help in remembering the Shoah, but when it comes to Christian memory, there's so much we don't know. We tend to fill in the gaps to reinforce our positive self-image.

Larry: I have to say, this gets into what was a difficult and challenging part of your chapter for me. You've said to me before that Jews and Christians have different memories of the Shoah, and I'd always reacted, "Of course." How could it be otherwise? But in your chapter, you quoted Miroslav Volf to say that Jews remember through the lens of the Exodus, and Christians through the lens of Jesus' crucifixion and resurrection. It's jarring for me to consider the Shoah through this Christian lens.

Anthony: To tell the truth, I felt some reluctance bringing this up. It doesn't feel right to me, to compare the Holocaust to the crucifixion. Comparing one death, no matter how significant, to the death of six million . . . really, there is no comparison.

Larry: I'm not talking about the numbers, or at least, I'm not just talking about the numbers. You titled the first section in your chapter "Remembering Together," and there's a part of me that says, "Fine." But to remember together, we first have to learn how we've remembered separately. If you want to learn something of how Jews remember the Shoah, you can go to just about any Holocaust museum, or read Wiesel or any other number of

Jewish writers, or go online to Spielberg's Shoah Foundation and listen to witness testimony.

Anthony: That's no substitute for Jews talking to Christians, face to face—answering our questions and telling us how you really feel about Christian fault and Christian guilt.

Larry: No, it's not a substitute. But my point is, there's not nearly as much out there about what Christians are thinking. To have the dialogue you seek, first, Jews need to understand something of the Christian memory of the Shoah. We can't go to a Holocaust museum to learn this; you need to tell us. So, I'll start with what I think is a simple question: Using whatever definition of memory you like, what is your memory of the Holocaust?

Anthony: In order for me to use the word *memory*, it has to be in the broadest possible way. I'm thirty-eight years old. I've never met a Holocaust survivor. In order to use "memory" at all, we're talking about collective memory: how my culture has chosen to remember and commemorate the Holocaust. I can draw from several places, like when my sisters got to stay up past nine o'clock to watch a made-for-TV movie about Anne Frank. My sisters were six and four years older than me, and I remember my parents arguing about whether the topic was too adult for my older sisters. But for me, there was no question: I was too young; I had to go to bed. Of course, as soon as I heard that there was something adult that my sisters got to watch, I wanted to watch it. My room was upstairs, and I used to sneak out and sit on the top step and look through one of the grates of the railing. They couldn't see me, but I could hear what was on television, and if I wanted I could peek over and see what was happening. And there was nothing scandalous at all! Because it was all over my head.

Larry: How old do you think you were?

Anthony: I was around eight years old. So, even before I knew what the word *Holocaust* meant, my first exposure to the narrative was the name Anne Frank. And knowing that it was really a very adult story.

Larry: Which made it interesting.

Anthony: Which made it fascinating. So, whatever I gathered as a child about what happened in National Socialism from 1933 to 1945, whatever I knew about that time in Europe, was shaped by that initial framework of the all-too-adult story of Anne Frank, the child.

Larry: Were you aware as an eight-year-old that Anne Frank was a child?

Anthony: Yes, because I remember thinking, what's so adult about this? What are they saying, like a curse word or something? So I asked, what's it about? And then, the most unhelpful answer ever given by a parent, my Mom told me, "It's a story about a little girl and her diary." And that sounded like the greatest injustice in the world, because what could be more appropriate for an eight-year-old to watch, something as benign as a young girl and her diary? So, I didn't get it. I totally didn't get why it was not for children's consumption. I don't remember much more about that experience. I guess that the next stage would have been in junior high, hearing other people talk about a documentary they had seen, and hearing them talk on the playground about the horror of all the naked bodies being piled up. It was something I hadn't seen, but I responded through their emotional responses. *It was serious, it was horrific, it was disgusting.* So that became a cultural filter. The same goes for how I framed the Nazis: they are so archetypically evil that the iconic *Star Wars* trilogy models their bad guys after the Nazis.

Larry: This is before you knew what happened.

Anthony: This is before I knew what happened. This is before I had any content, before I heard the number "six million."

Larry: This is before you knew it had anything to do with Jews?

Anthony: This is before I had any idea it had anything to do with Jews.

Larry: But you have a filter in place by which you are inclined to view Jews sympathetically, before you know where to apply the filter.

Anthony: I think this is what happens for most cultural memory. For instance, before Christians are able to read the Bible, they know it is something sacred. You're already positioned with a particular posture; you are set on a particular path by which you will read the Bible in reverence. In a similar way, I knew what I was going to think about Martin Luther King long before I had heard anything about Martin Luther King. These categories were already framed before I had any specific data.

Larry: Martin Luther King is a really good example. Martin Luther King's "I Have a Dream" speech was my eighth birthday. I remember hearing that Martin Luther King was a troublemaker, that change would come but that he was making things more difficult. But remember, Martin Luther King was assassinated when I was thirteen years old, so it is relatively easy for me to revise that narrative.

Anthony: Let me make sure we are both on the same page: the revision of the narrative is not necessarily a bad thing.

Larry: No, it is a good thing. After 1968, you couldn't apply the old racism to Martin Luther King, because the filter has already been applied.

Anthony: The filter has already been applied, right. I will say this: I was a party to a certain kind of anti-Judaism at church at times. I did not connect this with the Holocaust. This was not a connection I would have been able to make, but in learning about Jesus and the Pharisees at a very early age, the image was that the Pharisees were killjoys, they wanted to stop people from having fun and being healed. They wanted to follow the letter of the law. What kid wants more laws in their life?

Larry: So the Pharisees are the vice principals of the New Testament?

Anthony: Exactly. [*Laughing*]. And Jesus is Martin Luther King! He is setting up against the establishment, saying that their rules and laws are unjust.

Larry: But at that moment in your life, you have had no experience of American Judaism.

Anthony: Never met a Jew. The first thing I was taught about Jews is that they didn't believe Jesus was the Messiah, and that they are still waiting for the Messiah. Which sounded silly. It was something that was so ingrained in us at such an early age: it was so clear, so obvious that Jesus was the Messiah. He fulfilled all the ancient prophecies, my goodness, he was resurrected on the third day, what better proof do you need? You have to be hardheaded, hardhearted . . .

Larry: Stiff-necked?

Anthony: Stiff-necked, not to believe that Jesus was the Messiah. So the first time I learned that there was a modern people who identified as Jews, it was in this negative connotation. Even though the Shoah paradigm was in place, which would initially cause me to feel sympathy for the Jewish people, I did have another paradigm that was particularly anti-Jewish. I would not say anti-Semitic.

Larry: At what point are you making the connection between the people you felt sympathy for, because they were victims of the Holocaust, and the people who have this silly belief about the Messiah?

Anthony: There was a point in which it didn't really matter to me what the Jews believed; it was just a tragedy that the Holocaust had happened. Nothing like this should happen to anyone, no matter what they believe. These things start to converge, to the point where it was very clear to me, starting around my high school years, that saying anything anti-Jewish was not okay. Because, who are the archetypal villains in my world? The people who wear white hoods like the Ku Klux Klan, the Nazis, the stormtroopers. These archetypal bad guys are the guys against the Jews.

Larry: I wonder what the dividing line is between your generation and earlier generations that seemingly were willing to continue in their anti-Judaism even after learning about the events of the Shoah. What if you'd learned about Anne Frank ten years later than you did, or twenty years later, or thirty?

Anthony: I think that the discovery of the Holocaust created a certain sympathy for modern Jews that crossed all generational lines. I don't know if this "sympathy" is particularly Christian . . .

Larry: . . . but there is a difference between your attitude toward Judaism and that of earlier generations of Christians.

Anthony: Every new generation is going to have to process the Holocaust in its own way. It could be that the way the first generation processes these events is always going to be inadequate. For example, think about the Rwandan genocide. Before the movie came out, *Hotel Rwanda*, how often it was in the news? Do you remember?

Larry: Not very much.

Anthony: This was before the Internet really took off; we did not have a twenty-four-hour news cycle or, at least if we did, I wasn't aware of it. We cared about Rwanda once every couple of weeks, maybe for a three-month period. But I don't remember thinking, "This is one of the worst things I've ever heard in my life."

Larry: It was not, "How can we be revisiting this again?"

Anthony: Yes, exactly. Here's how I think of it. I have memory patterns that help me survive during the day. I can remember where I put my car keys, I remember how to get to the office, I remember where to find the food in the refrigerator. I remember my life in terms of patterns. The mental space I have for tragedy exists between seven and eight o'clock for the evening news period of my life. So it's very hard to mobilize a people who think in patterns that are so mundane. But for Jews with family memories of the Shoah, you didn't have the luxury of not having it dramatically change the way you saw the world. It was the unthinkable.

Larry: The odd thing about something being unthinkable is, if you don't think about it, it's about the same thing as ignoring it.

Anthony: Right, if you don't how to process the information . . .

Larry: . . . and one of the things that you've said to me in conversation is that Jews and Christians can't forget the Holocaust in the same way. Are we at a point where we should think about forgetting the Holocaust in *any* way?

Anthony: Let me ask you this question. Are you familiar with Martin Luther's little book *On the Jews and Their Lies*?

Larry: That's one of his later books, the one that recommends burning down synagogues and that sort of thing?

Anthony: *On the Jews and Their Lies* was very late in Luther's career. The book commands "don't suffer them usury," which is another way of saying Jews shouldn't hold currency. "They should not be able to have free passage on the highways"; that's another way of saying, "We don't care if Jews live or die." We know who is on the highways: bandits and murderers. And the Jews don't deserve protection. "Permit not a rabbi to teach on pain of life and limb." *If a rabbi teaches, he should be dismembered or killed?* "Their holy books should be burnt and buried and their synagogues should be torn down." So when did that idea, that Luther was anti-Semitic, first enter your personal knowledge?

Larry: My first encounter with Christian thinkers was in my study of political theory in college. In a political theory class, Luther's anti-Semitism doesn't come up. I enjoyed reading Luther in college. I mean, Luther is a good read.

Anthony: If he lived today, he would be a good blogger.

Larry: Exactly. So I did not learn about Luther's anti-Semitism until I studied him in a religious context.

Anthony: Let me tell you how I learned about Luther's anti-Semitism. As a kid growing up, my church was very anti-creed. We didn't recite a statement of belief every Sunday like other churches did. We believed that the things you need to know to be a Christian should be simple enough for a ten-year-old to understand to be baptized. The one thing we knew, the one thing on the back of our church bulletin every week, was a two-line statement that explained our beliefs: In the 1500s, Martin Luther and other Christians decided to return to the practices of New Testament Christianity, and we believe in the Bible. Basically, that was our creed, although we wouldn't have called it a creed. So I never had an image of Martin Luther that was anything other than positive. But for me, Luther comes up when I'm in college, and I'm reading Jewish websites.

Larry: Why are you reading Jewish websites?

Anthony: Why not?

Larry: Well, *why?* Why not read a good Agatha Christie mystery? There are a lot of things you can read.

Anthony: Well, this is probably a different conversation, but the nutshell version is that I'm fascinated by Jesus, and the people who are writing the things that make the most sense about Jesus are the people who are describing him in a first-century Jewish context. The thing that is most fascinating to me about Jesus is his Judaism, so it becomes very clear to me that I need to learn a lot more about Judaism.

Larry: And the Jewish websites are detailing Martin Luther's anti-Semitism?

Anthony: They're detailing Christian anti-Semitism throughout the ages. It just so happened that there was an online version of *On the Jews and Their*

Lies. It's not very long. You can read the whole tract in about an hour if you want. If you're feeling particularly anti-Semitic someday, you could do that.

Larry: If you're feeling anti-Semitic, it probably only takes forty-five minutes.

Anthony: So that was a transformational experience for me, to learn that the person I've always associated as the father of the movement by which I've encountered G-d for my whole life is a hate-monger, in the most repugnant way. You might as well just be Hitler. This is my initial reaction, thinking that here's this guy recommending the killing of rabbis and the burning of synagogues, and this is exactly what the Nazis did. Oh, the other thing that Luther said was to round up the Jews and put spades in their hands and make them work by the sweat of their brow. That sounded like the concentration camps. So how can I not connect Luther to Lutheran Germany in the 1930s? Christian memory had all but forgotten Luther's anti-Semitism.

Larry: But how could it have?

Anthony: Let me put it this way. I probably met ten thousand Christians in my life. And I had debated about Luther a lot. We were talking about Luther versus Calvin, we were talking about the funny things Luther said, how he loved to talk about farting, how he died while sitting on the toilet. He's just a really fascinating character. So it's not like we knew nothing! But none of the ten thousand Christians I had encountered in my lifetime conveyed to me the memory of his anti-Semitism. My guess is that 99 percent of those people had no idea. However, and this is my point, this is a long, convoluted answer to your question . . .

Larry: I don't remember my question.

Anthony: Your question was, why does it matter if Christians and Jews forget the Shoah differently? It was Jewish memory of Luther that created a transformational experience for me. If there was no Jewish memory, there would be no reason for anyone but Luther scholars in the ivory tower to have any knowledge of Luther's anti-Semitism. So the vast majority of Christians are completely unaware of that aspect of Luther. It makes it possible for Christians to say things that are insensitive, and to continue to venerate Luther in a way that is inappropriate. Christians' forgetfulness of the Shoah is problematic for the same reason that forgetfulness of the things that Luther said is problematic. This forgetfulness contributed in large part to the world that was created whereby the Jews could be exterminated.

Larry: This gets back to where we started, about remembering together as Jews and Christians.

Anthony: Because forgetting something like Luther's anti-Semitism can have catastrophic consequences.

Larry: I would put it simply: We have a unique ability to help each other remember. We each possess counter-memories that are potentially important to the other. But it's a separate question how to best provide this help. There's a part of me that says that the content of Christianity should be determined by Christians, and if you need our help, ask for it. There's another part of me that says that Christianity is way too important to be determined solely by Christians.

Anthony: I've said this too: We Christians can't be trusted with the New Testament.

Larry: I vacillate on this point, in part because I don't want to give Christians a symmetrical right to tell us how to be Jews.

Anthony: I'm okay with the idea of a corrective to Christianity. The comparison I'm drawing to Luther is, what if the Lutheran Church in Germany in 1920 had come out with an official statement that condemned *On the Jews and Their Lies*? Lutheran churches have done this in recent years. If this had happened in 1920s Germany, I don't know how much good it would have done, but it would have been an important effort against the Christians who attempted to "dejudaize" Christianity during this period.

Larry: I don't know what effect it would have had, but it would have had some positive effect. There might have been a half-dozen more righteous Gentiles who would have offered to hide Jews in their basements. One life saved is saving the whole world, so a few more righteous Gentiles would have had enormous consequences. I don't know if this would have prevented the Shoah from happening—that is a little hard for me to believe.

Anthony: Who knows what would have happened? But if four hundred years from now, Christianity has no clue that there was a theological impetus behind the Holocaust . . . gosh, Christianity *right now*—in large part—does not believe that there was a theological undergirding to Nazi ideology. Too many Christians today think that the "true Christians" were against the Nazis. If it's that way now, that sets us on a horrible trajectory.

Larry: I have had dialogue with Christians like the one I'm about to describe. A hypothetical Christian might say that there weren't Christians who were involved in the Holocaust, because anybody who was ostensibly Christian and participated in the Holocaust wasn't Christian. No Christian *could do that*. This hypothetical Christian tells me: We Christians are friends of the Jews, have always been friends to the Jews, and always will be friends to the Jews, and what the Nazis did was the most anti-Christian act conceivable or possible. My hypothetical Christian says: Everything that Christianity stands for is opposite to everything the Nazis stood for. There's a part of me that reacts: Great! I want Christians to be anti-Nazi. Why would I want to talk this hypothetical Christian out of this belief?

Anthony: Because you could easily correct the narrative in a way that doesn't ruin the outcome.

Larry: Could I?

Anthony: You think if you take this one toothpick out of the formation, the whole thing is going to crumble?

Larry: It could. I mean, it's not that easy to acknowledge guilt, to say that the generation of my parents or my grandparents did horrible, unspeakable things in the name of Christianity, and I repudiate that Christianity. At some point, guilt defines you, you go from having *done* bad to *being* bad, and the identification with being bad becomes who you are.

Anthony: I guess I'm just saying that I feel like we're at a certain moment where the climate is right for ideological shifts, and it seems that for whatever reason there are more Jews and Christians willing to have conversations. I don't know if there are more than in any time in history, but it seems like there's a lot more than there were in many other times in history.

Larry: This is the best time in history for me to write my blog. If I tried to write this blog in the thirteenth century, it never would've gotten off the ground.

Anthony: So for me, it's crucial that we take the opportunity to compare narratives. And I think, at least from the Christian side, I've found that Christians are actually quite appalled at the amount of damage that Christianity has done. They know very vaguely about the Crusades . . .

Larry: . . . and you believe that the Crusades are now viewed in Christianity as a negative thing.

Anthony: [*Laughing*] Oh, absolutely.

Larry: It was not a heroic effort to wrestle the Holy Land from the infidel?

Anthony: No, no.[1]

Larry: Okay. What if I were to say that Christianity was solely responsible for the Shoah? I don't believe that today, but there was probably a time in my life when I did believe it.

Anthony: Now we're getting somewhere. I'm assuming that there are other Jews in the world who might say that very thing.

Larry: Some, I would guess. I'm not sure how many.

Anthony: If there are Jews who would say, "Christianity is solely responsible for the Shoah," and most Christians think that Christianity was in *no way* responsible for the Shoah, then this is an enormous obstacle for Jewish-Christian dialogue . . .

Larry: That's why this subject has to be on the table . . .

Anthony: . . . that will only be solved if we talk about it together.

Larry: Before we get to that position . . .

Anthony: I'm already there. But go ahead anyway.

Larry: Is the statement "I consider Christianity to be responsible for the Shoah" offensive to you?

---

1. Shortly after this dialogue, Anthony encountered (with dismay) an interview with a Christian historian who attempted to place a positive spin on the Crusades. This just supports further the general rule that one cannot speak for any religion as a whole.

Anthony: [*Sighs*] It's not offensive to me. I don't think it tells the whole story, but I understand why someone might say that. In fact, I've gone so far as to say, "Luther is just as responsible as Hitler." I've said that in the past. And I've been shouted down by Christians for offering that narrative.

Larry: I think this is a question of the narrative that best explains events for us. For a moment, let's consider the Jewish narrative. I just visited Yad Vashem, the Shoah memorial museum in Jerusalem. We got there when it opened, and we stayed there until it closed. We were there the day of the week they were open the latest. And as it was, we had to race through 1942 through 1944, because there just wasn't time. And we saw only the main exhibit. My guess is that this is a particularly Jewish tourist's visit. But I'm sensitive to the need to remember the Shoah with an appropriate narrative. Because it's too big.

Anthony: Right.

Larry: You can't simply absorb fact after fact and be a mere repository of all that has been documented. The only way to process all this is in the form of a narrative.

Anthony: I agree, and I would also suggest that whatever narrative we construct, it has to be one that ends with catastrophe. The story of the Shoah has to be catastrophic. There can't be a happy ending.

Larry: You're probably right, but the consequences of the catastrophic ending are different for Christians than they are for Jews. Jews have lived with a number of dominant narratives that we have been playing "revisionist history" with from their inception. One such narrative is "the sheep that went to the slaughter." That we did not resist the Nazi effort to exterminate us.

Anthony: This is not true?

Larry: It's a question of how you frame the narrative. There is truth to the narrative of "sheep to the slaughter." But there is also truth to the narrative that there was Jewish resistance in terms of armed struggle and sabotage, and there was also resistance in a hundred thousand little ways: people keeping the commandments, producing art in the camps . . . this is a much better narrative to have as a legacy, in my opinion. Yad Vashem also presents as a narrative that the only logical response to the Shoah was the formation of the State of Israel, that you move from Auschwitz to Israel's 1948 War of Independence seamlessly and without alternative. This obviously serves a purpose for Jews and for Israel. As problematic as the formation of the State of Israel has proven to be, as intractable as the peace process has proven to be, there wasn't any other way to respond to the Shoah. That's a kind of narrative.

Anthony: How does the Jewish narrative of the Holocaust include the five million people non-Jewish victims who were murdered by the Nazis alongside the Jews?

Larry: We have this problem: on a certain level, Jews want to "own" the Holocaust. If you read the material at Yad Vashem or on the website for the U.S. Holocaust Memorial Museum, and the nuance here is important: some of this material talks about the Jews who died in the Holocaust and the non-Jews who died in the *violence that accompanied the Holocaust.* Here is where I struggle to find the right language. Were we disproportionately victims of a "crime against humanity," or are we talking about a crime primarily aimed against Jews and Judaism, with five million ancillary victims? How do we express this?

Anthony: Why can't both be true simultaneously? It seems like that's where you would like to go: you would like to say that proper remembrance of the Shoah leads to a stance against genocide everywhere.

Larry: For me, that has to be part of the commemoration, or I distrust the commemoration. But I can come to that conclusion even if there wasn't a single non-Jew killed in the Holocaust.

Anthony: That's right.

Larry: My wife Stephanie spent a great deal of time in East Germany before the wall fell. East Germany offered stipends and opportunities for total language immersion to German teachers, and Stephanie participated in these programs when most of the other participants were Poles and others from behind the Iron Curtain. So, she knows the East German experience reasonably well, and she describes the East German narrative as: Jews were not targeted in the Holocaust; the Holocaust was aimed at Communists and other political dissidents, and of course there were Jews who fell into these categories; but the Holocaust was aimed at Hitler's political enemies. We are very much afraid of this, that if we frame the Shoah narrative in terms of a crime against humanity, or a crime resulting from totalitarian rule, then the Jews who died will lose what little identity they still have.

Anthony: Let me ask you this: I've heard you use the word *we* or *us* several times. This is an interesting difference between Christians and Jews, and the Shoah is an interesting litmus test for this. There's a sense even among third-generation Jews, but especially among second-generation Jews, that this is something that happened to *us*. In fact, the title of your chapter is "Things That Befell Us."

Larry: That's the title of a song.

Anthony: Yes, right. There's a sense in which you are using this as a double entendre, right?

Larry: Yes.

Anthony: So, it would not be controversial to say that most second-generation Jews would refer to the Shoah or Holocaust as something that happened to "us."

Larry: How many generations has it been since the Exodus?

Anthony: Right, this is something that happened to "us."

Larry: We're *commanded*. During the Passover Seder, we tell the story of the four sons: a wise son, a wicked son, a simple son, and a son who does not know how to ask. Each son is taught the Passover story in a way appropriate for him. But the wicked son displays wickedness by asking about the Passover Seder, "Why are *you* doing these things?" To *you*, and not to *him*. You betray your wickedness by thinking of the Jewish people as "you." And this is a big deal: the wicked son is cutting himself off from the Jewish people! So in my writing, there are times I have to refer to the Jewish people as "we," and other times when I think, "Who am I talking about?" In 586 BCE, the first Temple was destroyed and the Jews were exiled to Babylon, but can I say that "we" were exiled to Babylon? It feels weird to say that. That's 2,600 years ago. Yet it is a question in my mind: Were those Jews "them" or "us"?

Anthony: But that is an interesting memory thing, because the Exodus from Egypt is still something that befell "us."

Larry: Yes. And the "us" thing is stronger with the Shoah, because my father was born in Berlin, so I had a living connection. I have to be careful here, because there is a difference between my story, as the son of a Shoah escapee, somebody who experienced the Shoah but only the first few years of it . . .

Anthony: . . . and to be clear, your father would not be considered a survivor, because he was never in a camp.

Larry: That's correct. But technically speaking, my father and grandfather experienced the Shoah, because the Shoah is dated to 1933, and they were both still in Germany at the time. There were no death camps in 1933. But the Nazis burned books in 1933, they built concentration camps, the Brownshirts were in operation, there were organized boycotts of Jewish businesses . . .

Anthony: What do you mean by "Brownshirts"?

Larry: The Brownshirts were the SA; they were Nazi thugs. My father later told some of his childhood stories, how he began every school day with the straight-armed salute to the Nazi flag, shouting "Heil Hitler!" My grandfather escaped arrest by the Gestapo in 1935, bringing his family to New York in stages over the next year. The immediate family escaped, but I know of many relatives who died in the camps. As I describe in my chapter, I carry my father's Shoah memories around with me, even if I made some of them up because he didn't talk about them until I was an adult.

Anthony: For lack of a full story, you filled in gaps. I mean, it's the way memory always functions. You were trying to draw a connection with your father's experience, in a sympathetic way.

Larry: Yes. And that sympathy means that the Shoah most certainly happened to "us," in a way that even the Exodus didn't happen to "us." Though, of course, I cannot compare my experience to anyone in the camps.

Anthony: I don't know that Christians have something similar to this. There's nothing that occupies our commemoration that happened to "us." We believe that Christ died for us, that G-d did things for us, but I can't think of something that was done to "us" that we commemorate. It was done to "them," like a long time ago people threw Christians to the lions, and you can question the historicity of that if you want to. But it's not like I would say, "They threw *us* to the lions," and have that have any reasonable meaning in the Christian narrative.

Larry: Would you feel comfortable saying, "They threw *them* to the lions"?

Anthony: Sure! I mean, that's really what happened. [*Laughs*] This is interesting, because what I'm finding is that Christians seem to perpetuate this triumphant narrative, where we come out as heroic, we're on the winning side at the end. When I see a Christian post something on Facebook that relates to the Holocaust, inevitably it's about some kindhearted nun or Christian social worker who acted heroically during National Socialism. There's nothing about what Christians remember that doesn't make us look good in the end. Because in our memory, the Nazis are not Christian, the Nazis are the archetypal bad guy. You see what I'm saying?

Larry: It's so complicated what you're saying. Here's my outsider perspective: I want to understand the question of Christian complicity in the Shoah. But I have to say as the Jewish conversation partner here, if I had been given the opportunity to be a "righteous Gentile" during the Shoah, I don't know that I would have taken the opportunity.

Anthony: You don't know?

Larry: I do not know that I would have been brave enough to do what Wallenberg did, or what Schindler did. I know that's what I would have been supposed to do. I know what it is that I wish I would have done. But not having been in that circumstance, I cannot say that I would have been a righteous Gentile. I hope to G-d that I would not have been a war criminal.

Anthony: No, no, it's one of those things that you don't know. When you are living through the end of the world, there's no guidebook to tell you how you might act.

Larry: If you've been consigned to hell, the chances are that you're going to act pretty much like the average person consigned to hell. The chances that I would be the kind of resident of hell that heaven could be proud of . . . I don't know.

Anthony: My guess is, you want to figure out some way to get out of hell. To do whatever you can to get you and the people you love out.

Larry: And I don't know at what point I would say that I would rather have the machine crush me than to continue to participate in the machine. I just can't say, sitting here, that my intrinsic goodness and wonderfulness would have guaranteed my having been a righteous Gentile. I hope that's what I would have been, but that's the most I can say. That does not, of course, create any moral equivalence between perpetrator and victim. It's simply a matter of understanding the difference between the two.

Anthony: Let me try to answer your question about Christian complicity. It has to be a really complicated answer. It depends on when you want to begin the discussion. I have no problem with saying that the New Testament itself has been used as a bludgeon in very real ways to do violence to the Jewish people. I am absolutely certain that this is not what Jesus had in mind, or what Paul had in mind, but it is the way their words have been coopted. The world that Christianity created in Europe was hostile to Jews, often producing violence against Jews in an attempt to convert or kill. The extent to which Christianity is responsible for the Holocaust is unbelievable. I don't think Hitler was a Christian, but I think that Christianity alongside ten other factors combined to produce the Shoah, like race theory and Nietzschian master-slave morality.

Larry: I want to throw two pieces of nuance onto your answer: one that exacerbates Christian responsibility, and one that alleviates it to some extent. The exacerbation factor is, I don't think there needs to be a single Christian in Europe for Christianity to have a substantial responsibility for the Shoah. It is simply a cultural legacy.

Anthony: I would agree with that. Even if we were to say that every Nazi gave up their Christianity . . .

Larry: . . . and renounced it. . . .

Anthony: . . . Christianity would still be in large part responsible for the Shoah. I would agree with that.

Larry: It's one of the reasons why I want to move away from the question of the responsibility of Christians for the Shoah, and toward the question of the responsibility of Christianity. But there's a second factor here that I think we have to recognize: if we are looking at where we stand today, if we're looking at the recent thirty to fifty years of Jewish-Christian relations, at the academic push to understand the Jewish Jesus, then I have to believe that the primary impetus for this golden age of Jewish-Christian relations is the Shoah. I am trying to figure out why.

Anthony: Yeah.

Larry: And what you said about Christians in your generation receiving a "Shoah filter" before they received any Shoah information . . .

Anthony: I was talking autobiographically, but I would guess that I'm not the only one who had that experience.

Larry: Right. That's part of my explanation, that the Shoah is the first overtly anti-Jewish, anti-Semitic act that Christianity, or modern Christianity, can look upon from a perspective. *Is that what anti-Judaism, anti-Semitism looks like when someone else does it?* The perspective is possible because on some level, the Shoah is not something that Christianity did. So Christians can say, "If that's what this looks like, we want no part of it."

Anthony: If you're saying this is the first time in history that this is the case, that's a pretty big statement. But you might be able to say that, because of media culture, Christians could experience the Holocaust in 1945 in a way that made them not only sympathetic but empathetic to Jews in 1938, or 1943 . . .

Larry: Let me put it in a different way. The filter you talked about, the early "what is this" information you received about the Shoah, was that (1) this was horrible, and (2) the people who perpetrated this were the worst people on earth?

Anthony: Yeah.

Larry: They are the moral equivalent of the stormtroopers from *Star Wars*— whatever the movie is, they are the ultimate villain of the movie. If you had learned instead the Shoah was something that Christians did, you were not going to process the event in the same way.

Anthony: There would have been a tremendous element of guilt.

Larry: But if you had learned that this was something that Christians did, you might easily have processed it the way Christians had traditionally processed prior disasters that happened to the Jews: "This is terrible, but this is the fate of the Jews."

Anthony: That's impossible.

Larry: Is it possible for you to imagine it?

Anthony: No, no. Let me just tell you that for my generation, it's impossible.[2] I can give you a few examples, off the top of my head, where a similar thing happened, and it didn't result in that. As a second grader, I was told about the Pilgrims and the first Thanksgiving. But for my generation, in the California public school system, we immediately learned about the plight of the Native Americans. So from that early age, as a second grader, I knew that there was a counter-narrative that had to correct the dominant narrative, and that I was the villain in that counter-narrative. I even remember my second-grade teachers debating this. They wondered how much of the counter-narrative they ought to introduce. I heard the same counter-narrative when we learned about women's suffrage. I'm white, I'm male, I feel guilt. I remember talking to my mom one day, we were in the kitchen, sitting at the table, I don't know how old I am, it must've been around fourth or fifth grade, and I remember saying something like, "Mom, I'm just tired of being the bad guy." She said, "What are you talking about?" I said, "Well, I'm American, I'm white, I'm male . . ."

Larry: When you first learned about the Shoah, did you feel guilty?

Anthony: Absolutely not.

Larry: Because you thought, *Americans didn't do this.*

Anthony: Right. No, bad guys did it.

---

2. In retrospect, Anthony confesses, "I'm a bit ashamed that I doubled down on this point. The word *impossible* is much too strong. During and after the 2016 presidential election, I've observed an uptick in anti-Semitic public displays: spray-painted swastikas, political references to 'global elites' and 'America First,' organized marches, etc. It is clear to me now that 'my generation' is no less immune to anti-Semitism than any other. This does not erase the improvements in Jewish-Christian relations over the last few decades. It should, however, remind us that good feelings between Jews and Christians in America carry no guarantee of durability or longevity."

Larry: So the Shoah is a different event for you, in terms of your guilt complex, than Pilgrims coming to America?

Anthony: If the first two things I knew about the Shoah were that it was a terrible thing and it was perpetrated by Christians, I know I would have felt guilt, because I had these other examples. But I didn't think it was perpetrated by Christians. I always thought that those people who've villainized Christianity misunderstood Christianity, though there were probably a few bad Christians throughout history. But I thought, don't confuse those bad guys with who we really are. That was the idea. But the Martin Luther revelation was quite jarring to me, because he's the guy! He's the guy who founded the movement I was a part of.

Larry: When you learned this, did you feel the same sense of guilt you felt when you learned about the Pilgrims?

Anthony: No. I remember feeling angry that I had never been taught this. How could I never have been taught this about Martin Luther? Surely, someone else knew about this in my church.

Larry: I'm sure they did.

Anthony: Well . . . I don't know that that's true; it could be that no one knew this information.

Larry: How could anyone have gone to seminary and studied Martin Luther and not known this?

Anthony: Luther's anti-Semitism was not part of my seminary education. And I've taught seminarians who don't know this. I'm their first exposure. I taught this to a group of Presbyterians, most with graduate educations. Presbyterians in general are white-collar, educated people, and this was something I taught to a room of seventy retired Presbyterians, and jaws dropped! And stomachs were upset. Unless you do a thesis in Reformation Christianity, you might never be exposed to this aspect of Martin Luther.

Larry: How can that be? I took a Teaching Company class on Martin Luther, and there was an entire lecture devoted to his anti-Semitism.

Anthony: You didn't take it in a church or a seminary. Now, if you study Martin Luther specifically, you might learn this stuff. But a seminarian can go all the way through seminary and never take a class specifically on Martin Luther.

Larry: Even a Presbyterian?

Anthony: Absolutely. It would be more likely that we would take a class on Calvin.

Larry: Ha! Live and learn. So, the identity formation I'm asking you to represent resists the idea that there's any connection between the Holocaust and Christianity. It took a shocking revelation to drive the point home, one that left you feeling you'd been deceived.

Anthony: Yeah. I felt anger because *how could I have never been taught this?*

Larry: What is it that you would like Christians to understand, in terms of Holocaust memory?

Anthony: That their narrative is woefully incomplete and ultimately misleading.

Larry: Is there anything you would like to tell Jews about Shoah memory?

Anthony: You think I could have something corrective to say about Jewish Shoah memory?

Larry: When I listen to your narrative, it's mostly about what you wish your fellow Christians understood.

Anthony: That's right. However, I think that one of the key points in my chapter, at least what I try to convey, is that one good purpose of Jewish memory of the Shoah is to correct Christian memory, and we are at a moment in history when our ears are open and Christians are teachable. A lot of us aren't, but some of us are. So I try to suggest that it is lamentable that some Jewish educators think "Jews just know, so we don't have to talk about it anymore." It's particularly lamentable from a Christian point of view, when it's absolutely crucial that we are in dialogue together.

Larry: Then what is it that you want to hear from me? Your answer could be, "I don't have a clue until we talk." But I suspect that isn't your answer.

Anthony: I think it would be an effective rhetorical move if you were to say, "I think most Jews blame Christians for the Holocaust."

Larry: Yeah, I know, but I'm not going to say that. It's interesting, because when I asked you what is it that we can do to improve Christian memory, you asked me to make a statement about what Jews think. I think I can return the favor. Understanding that no religion should be judged on the worst behavior of its followers, and acknowledging that the Holocaust was produced by many complex factors, should the memory that Jews have of Christianity be of an anti-Jewish religion?

Anthony: [*Sighs*] Christian anti-Judaism is an element, a very prominent thread that runs through Christianity that needs to be understood, but to simply equate Christianity with anti-Semitism or anti-Judaism is not helpful. I would say that Christianity has included anti-Judaism and anti-Semitism.

Larry: Okay. What do we do with that?

Anthony: We try to create a better world together.

Larry: Do I help create that better world by emphasizing the anti-Jewish component that is in Christianity so that Christians can see it better? Or do I do the opposite, and try to stress that my vision of Christianity is not as an anti-Jewish religion?

Anthony: I think it depends on who your dialogue partner is; I think it depends on what point you're trying to make; I think that both of those things definitely can be true, depending on the context in which they are said. You don't want to become a one-note singer. It's a complicated issue; it deserves a complicated conversation.

Larry: If you don't want me to play the one note of Christian anti-Judaism, then why do you want me to say that most Jews blame Christianity for the Holocaust?

Anthony: Because that is the note we haven't heard yet. Because of this, we simply don't understand you. One of the reasons we don't understand you is that in large part, and maybe for good reason, Judaism has retreated from Christian interaction. So we have no idea—most of us—that you even associate Christianity with the Holocaust. And from a Christian perspective, it can seem hypersensitive. But if we knew why, it would make more sense to us. In my experience, the ignorance of Christians on the topic of Christian complicity is massive, and so I guess what I'm asking is simply to talk.[3] It almost doesn't matter as much what is said, so long as the lines of communication are open. It would be a revelation to most Christians to know that there is still a certain amount of blame being assigned to Christianity.

Larry: This hasn't come up in dialogue? From your experience in Jewish-Christian dialogue, I'm the first person to have ever said this?

Anthony: In my experience of dialogue, Shoah/Holocaust has not come up. We mostly talk about "Old Testament" texts, because it's something we share in common. Often, the goal is a Kumbaya sort of thing, and I don't know that people benefit from that as much as sitting in a room where people can be honest about what the real issue is. It seems like, in large part, the real issue is the Shoah. And Christians think it's about Jesus. We think, that's the one thing that divides Jews and Christians: it's all about Jesus. And that may be a big issue.

Larry: It is a big issue.

Anthony: It is a big issue, and that's the one Christians know about. And maybe we should discuss that one too, I don't know. All I know is the one that I haven't heard discussed is the Holocaust. And that might be the biggest obstacle to dialogue.

Larry: Isn't there a danger that—what was it that you said to your mom?

Anthony: "I'm tired of being the bad guy." I mean, the alternative to that story is, I never learn about the plight of the American Indian, I never learn about women's suffrage, I never learn about the war in Vietnam. Yeah, there's going to be some Christian guilt.

Larry: And a Christian backlash?[4]

---

3. This comment is meant to reflect Anthony's experience of regular Christian folk. He is aware that some Christians are very well-studied on the Holocaust and aware of Christian complicity.

4. In our dialogue, we did not explore what we meant by "backlash." Our concern is that certain historical narratives can be so uncomfortable (or embarrassing,

Anthony: And there may be that. But it's better than what we have right now, because Christians are blissfully ignorant, and Jews are withdrawn in many cases.

Larry: What I hear you saying when you ask us to share Shoah memories, we have to be honest with you.

Anthony: We have to start talking, and you have to be honest with us.

Larry: When we talk about the Shoah, are we holding back? I'll have to think about that one. But you have to remember: we have a bad history when we have been honest with you.

Anthony: I know. We are both risking something in the conversation, and it may be that you are risking a lot more. But I think you are risking a great deal more by not having the conversation.

---

or guilt-ridden) that they become difficult or impossible to be remembered as such. Instead, the narratives are reconceived so that they can be retold more comfortably. We can most easily recognize this reframing when it is at its most extreme: for example, when a white supremacist describes the slavery of African-Americans as the "feeding and housing" of slaves. See Jake Miller, "Suggestion to segregate black Republicans draws controversy," CBS News, March 16, 2013, http://www.cbsnews.com/news/suggestion-to-segregate-black-republicans-draws-controversy. We've also seen this phenomenon recently, when French presidential candidate Marine Le Pen suggested that France was not responsible for the wartime round-up of French Jews sent by French police to Nazi death camps, because these police were Nazi collaborators and thus "not France." James Masters and Margaux Deygas, "Marine Le Pen sparks outrage over Holocaust comments," CNN, April 10, 2017, http://www.cnn.com/2017/04/10/europe/france-marine-le-pen-holocaust/index.html. Both of these are examples of dishonesty, if not out-and-out lying. But we're not always conscious of how we reframe or reshape our narratives. For example, Anthony refers in his chapter to Christians who understand the Holocaust as being an evil perpetrated by non-Christians, because in the Christian imagination, Christians could not have been Nazis. It's not likely that Christians who so understand the Holocaust are engaging in intentional dishonesty; it's more likely that Christians have emphasized the role of Christian Holocaust "good guys" to the relative exclusion of the rest of the story. Then again, the selective Christian memory of the Holocaust described in Anthony's chapter may itself be a "backlash" against the conscious or subliminal Christian memory of the role played by real-life Christians in Nazi genocide. Thus Anthony's desire to correct Christian memory of the Holocaust may run up against Larry's expressed fear that there may be limits to our ability to think the worst of ourselves.

Part Four

Posture

Take a Stand, Have a Seat:
Questions of Posture

Anthony Le Donne

"I do not know what a Jew is. I know only human beings."

—André Trocmé

In this chapter, I will offer a few possibilities for how Jews and Christians might stand together. Included here are two prominent examples of activism from a distinctly Christian perspective. I will discuss Korean *han* theology and an episode of Christian pacifism at Le Chambon, France.[1] These are, in my view, examples of Christian virtue extending from rhythms and inclinations of an authentic Christian life. Moreover, not only are these examples of Christian virtue, I believe that they give hope for the possibility of mutual benefit in our joined stance for righteousness and against injustice. I will then suggest that standing up for a cause—even if virtuous, righteous, and often necessary—is not the ideal posture for interreligious dialogue. While dialogue can happen from the posture of advocacy, it opens more possible

---

1. The quotation by André Trocmé that leads off this chapter is in reference to the value of human life when dealing in life-or-death circumstances. It is borne out of Trocmé's experience of saving Jewish lives in France during WWII. I should acknowledge at the start that this quotation smacks of "color blindness" (wherein the unique problems of American blackness are overlooked). While Trocmé certainly did not have American race relations in mind when he spoke these words, I would like to point out that this quotation may well be offensive to some of my readers and for good reason. Larry and I discuss this briefly in our scripted dialogue about "posture." I would also point out that Trocmé, while noble and courageous in many ways, was far from perfect. "Under the Wings of the Church: Protestant Pastor Andre Trocme," Yad Vashem: http://www.yadvashem.org/yv/en/exhibitions/righteous/trocme.asp.

outcomes in the sitting position. While there are certain things that can be accomplished only from the standing position, there are others that are best accomplished from the sitting position.

Exterior and Interior Postures

I have heard it said that nonverbal cues reveal thoughts and feelings. I don't know how much these cues reveal or in what ways. Surely a psycho-physiologist, a behavioral investigator, or a body language trainer (these are real jobs) would be able to explain posture better than a biblical scholar. Here is what I can tell you with certainty: I learn more about you when we are face to face. I learn much less when we encounter each other via phone call. And I learn much, much less when I encounter you as a social media persona.

Conversely, I imagine that I reveal much more of myself in person. Where do my eyes go when you're talking? How am I sitting in my chair? Are my arms folded? Have I furrowed my brows or narrowed my eyes? Does my posture convey strength, or nervousness, or skepticism? Have I adopted a posture to mask or defend something else about me? While I am no expert, I know enough to know that my posture expresses information about me without me knowing it. My posture can also affect the moods of those around me without them knowing it. To my mind, these are examples of exterior postures; these are expressions of otherwise invisible inclinations of the mind. Importantly, these exterior postures often express how your interior life is oriented.

The idea of "interior posture" might seem strange. Perhaps "inclina-tion" or "attitude" or "habitual thought pattern" or "constant feeling" better conveys what I mean by interior posture. To illustrate interior posture, let's imagine that we are on a first date. Let's imagine further that I strike you as particularly unattractive and boorish. These feelings or convictions you have about me exist within your interior. These may or may not manifest as external expressions. Your exterior posture can express these interior parts of you by pulling your hand away when I touch it or leaning away from me at the theater. In this case, the exterior posture is the physical recoil, while the interior posture is the sense of recoil.

Some interior postures are developed by repeating a thought or feeling over the course of a lifetime. Let's imagine that you have an accent from West Texas. Let's imagine further that I've met a few West Texans in my life and that they were racists. Perhaps my association with the accent has been reinforced by a myriad of television, film, and fictitious portraits of racist Southerners. Might I be inclined to think that you, with your West Texas accent, are a racist? In this case, it could be that my interior posture is oriented by an assumption. Might our external expressions be affected by these interior dynamics?

Or let's say that you are one of my Californian friends. What if you use the phrase "a whole nother thing" as if "nother" is a real word? Do I feel bad about myself for correcting your grammar in my nonverbal, internal dialogue? *What kind of arrogant tool cares that "nother" isn't a real word? How much of our conversation have I missed while concluding that I am an arrogant tool?* When I'm slumped in my chair, biting my bottom lip, and grimacing while despairing my toolishness (also not a real word), do you think I'm upset with you? Perhaps you have misunderstood my exterior postures; perhaps they do not express my interior postures precisely enough. In this case, I am more upset with myself but you read my posture as if I am upset with you.

So much of our physiological cues and verbal expressions are beyond our conscious control. I consider all of these examples of exterior posture. By expanding posture to something that happens on the interior, I am thinking of posture in the broadest possible terms. By interior posture, I mean *one's conscious intentions and unconscious inclinations toward the perceived other.*

I believe this topic is of crucial importance because so much of the conversation is determined by the posture we have adopted before we enter the room.

My Sentinel Mind

There is a half-truth popularized by the modern, scientific spirit that observers can be and ought to be objective. This is the interior posture of attempted detachment and neutrality. From this view, emotional or existential investment in a subject taints one's output. In short, a trustworthy observer is one who is free from bias. As I have indicated, this is partially true. There are times when bias becomes prejudice, when presuppositions become predetermined conclusions. There are times when we must aim to be as objective as possible. In this way, Jon Levenson is correct that objectivity is "a necessary ideal," even if it cannot be achieved absolutely. Levenson argues that there is an important distinction between saying "We all have biases" and saying "All we have is biases." Of course, "The first is true; the second is false."[2] So, *yes*, we all have biases and should attempt to locate them, name them, and (at times) attempt to bracket them. And, *no*, we cannot achieve objectivity in the way that many Enlightenment thinkers thought we might.

When it comes to the topic of Jewish-Christian dialogue, not only is the posture of objectivity untenable, it is not even ideal. My investment in the education and spiritual development of Christians is part of the reason why the conversation is worthwhile. My investment in the longevity and well-being of Jews and Judaism is part of what makes the conversation human and humane. These are examples of necessary and virtuous biases. Empathy for and with the perceived other is the better ideal when engaging in interreligious dialogue.

Ethicist and historian Philip Hallie wrote of his own struggle with posture as he researched the Holocaust. His research, at least initially, focused on the forms and functions of human cruelty. Before he stumbled upon the exceptional good done in the village of Le Chambon during WWII, Hallie's research was focused on "the torture experiments the Nazis conducted upon the bodies of small children in those death camps." He confesses:

> Across these studies, the pattern of the strong crushing the weak kept repeating itself and repeating itself, so that when I was not bitterly angry, I was bored of the repetition of the patterns of persecution. When I was not desiring to be cruel with the cruel, I was a monster—like, perhaps, many others around me—who could look upon torture and death without a shudder, and who looked upon life without a belief in its perniciousness. My study of evil incarnate had become a prison whose bars were my bitterness toward the violent, and whose walls were my horrified indifference to slow murder. Between the bars and the walls I revolved like a madman. Reading about the damned I was damned myself, as damned as the murderers, and as damned as their victims.[3]

Hallie's defensive posture against his study was anything but neutral. Even his indifference was a "horrified indifference." When he retreated from bitterness and anger, he became something like a monster, detached from the humanity of his subject. Hallie attempted to insulate himself from a subjective posture and found himself emotionally contorted.

2. Jon D. Levenson, "The Perils of Engaged Scholarship: A Rejoinder to Jorge Pixley," in *Jews, Christians, and the Theology of the Hebrew Scriptures*, ed. A. Ogden Bellis and J. S. Kaminsky (Atlanta: Society of Biblical Literature, 2000), 241.

3. Philip P. Hallie, *Lest Innocent Blood Be Shed: The Story of the Village of Le Chambon and How Goodness Happened There* (New York: Harper & Row, 1979), 2.

His ideal of objectivity becomes even clearer when confronted with a story of ethical virtue. When he discovered the goodness done at the French town of Le Chambon, he again tried to adopt an internal posture of dispassion. So not only did he attempt to retreat from bitterness and anger, he also attempted to bracket his feelings of "painful joy." Hallie, in the midst of a research project on human cruelty, discovered the story of a French village that "provided refuge for an estimated 5,000 people. This number included an estimated 3,000–3,500 Jews who were fleeing from the Vichy authorities and the Germans."[4] In Hallie's words:

> As usual, I was reading the pages with an effort at objectivity. . . . About halfway down the third page of the account of this village, I was annoyed by a strange sensation on my cheeks. The story was so simple and so factual that I had found it easy to concentrate upon *it*, not upon my own feelings. And so, still following the story, and thinking about how neatly some of it fit into the old patterns of persecution, I reached up to my cheek to wipe away a bit of dust, and I felt tears upon my fingertips. Not one or two drops; my whole cheek was wet.
>
> "Oh," my sentinel mind told me, "you are losing your grasp on things again. Instead of learning about cruelty, you are becoming one more of its victims. You are doing it again." I was disgusted with myself for daring to intrude.[5]

What Hallie calls his "sentinel mind"—the part of him that chided him for emotional investment—illustrates the ideal of objectivity. What Hallie discovered by breaking his ideal of objectivity was a new posture. Indeed, I believe that he adopted the only posture that would allow him to discover the humanity in another: he was finally willing to embrace his own humanity. "Those involuntary tears had been an expression of moral praise, praise pressed out of my whole personality like the juice of a grape."[6]

What I hope is clear by now is that our postures can be overlooked—perhaps they are usually unknown to us, but no person is without them. In times of intense emotional investment, adopting an authentically humane posture is almost required. Perhaps it takes an unexpected expression of pain or painful joy to lay our unseen inclinations bare. But whether we recognize our postures or not, we always extend ourselves into the world in particular ways, and this makes absolute objectivity impossible. One's own social placement and embodiment affects perspective.

---

4. "Le Chambon-Sur-Lignon," *Holocaust Encyclopedia*, https://www.ushmm.org/wlc/en/article.php?ModuleId=10007518.

5. Hallie, *Lest Innocent Blood Be Shed*, 2–3.

6. Hallie, *Lest Innocent Blood Be Shed*, 4.

It is sometimes important to try to be "more objective" rather than less. I would argue that it is more important to be honest. The honesty I envision is twofold: (1) We ought to deal honestly with whatever discussion or study is before us; and (2) we ought to be honest about our own investments and biases. In other words, we must be just as interested in self-discovery as we are about the discovery of the world around us. I believe that this twofold commitment to honesty is crucial for Jewish-Christian dialogue.

Han

In my chapter on borders in this book, I claimed (historically speaking) that Christians tend to trespass carelessly and without much thought for indigenous landscapes, natives, or neighbors. But—also acknowledged within these pages—Christians are quite diverse, and we should not mistake European or North American Christians with Christians as a whole. Christians are not always the colonists, oppressors, or ignorant travelers with more power than is healthy. In fact, it would be a mistake to apply my commentary on Christians and border-crossings to struggling Christians in the majority world.[7] This is an important point to make in Jewish-Christian dialogue, because approximately 80 percent of all Jews worldwide live in America and Israel. This means that the contemporary Jewish experience of Christian neighbors tends to be more impacted by affluent, privileged, and comfortable Christians. Put another way, how would this dialogue be different if the three-hundred-plus-million Christians of South America were represented?

One of the many ways I am privileged is that I share a hallway with one of the most influential thinkers in liberation theology: Andrew Park. Much of Dr. Park's early career was devoted to bringing a South Korean voice into conversation with Gustavo Gutiérrez (Peruvian theologian) and James Hal Cone (African-American theologian). Gutiérrez, Cone, Park, and others challenged theologians to think about Christianity from the perspective of the oppressed. Liberation theologians are not immune to mistakes, but their challenge has been a necessary corrective. Park writes, "As the United States

---

7. By "majority world" I mean the developing nations of Africa, Asia, and Latin America. I prefer this terminology (while not perfect) over the outmoded label "Third World."

and the West control biblical scholarship and theology, their interpretation and theology can easily be that of conquerors."[8]

As a New Testament scholar, I value these theologians because the earliest Christian writings emerged from a group of people who lacked social privilege, political influence, military strength, and so on. Christianity emerged from a culture that was significantly dissimilar to the modern West. So I have much to learn about these texts from the voices of others. And in the process of self-discovery, I find myself bringing something unexpected (for me at least) to Jewish-Christian dialogue: by "standing up" for the majority world (and the many Christians represented within it), I find myself standing alongside Jewish friends who are also committed to social justice and humanitarian efforts. In short, I have learned that the Jewish-Christian encounter can look like Jews and Christians *sitting* on opposite sides of the table; it can also look like Jews and Christians *standing* on the same side of a cause.

Andrew Park's family, along with a few others, escaped a concentration camp that bordered North and South Korea. His older brother (now a Baptist minister in Texas) was an infant when his parents snuck away in a boat. The refugees there were so afraid of being caught and murdered by North Korean soldiers that some of their fellow escapees demanded that Andrew's brother be drowned. If the baby was drowned, he would not cry out. Mrs. Park refused. To their good fortune, the baby didn't cry. The Parks were able to boat down the river and into political exile. Andrew Park was born in South Korea shortly after this escape. The Park family immigrated to the United States in 1973.

Dr. Park tells me, "In its 5000+ year history, Korea has been invaded over 930 times. In all of this time, Korea has never invaded another country." This legacy of oppression has created an inclination of lament in South Korean culture (an example of interior posture). While difficult to translate into English, Dr. Park refers to this interior posture as *han*.

---

8. Andrew Sung Park, "The Bible and Han," in *The Other Side of Sin: Woundedness from the Perspective of the Sinned-Against*, ed. A. S. Park and S. L. Nelson (Albany: State University of New York Press, 2001), 46. To place this quotation in context, Park explains, "We are living in a world of enormous division between rich and poor countries. The United States is the most powerful nation on earth. Its wealth and military strength surpasses that of all mighty nations in history. When these wealthy and well-to-do people interpret the Bible, they tend to comprehend it from their experience."

The experience of the powerless, the marginalized, and the voiceless in the world can be summed up as han. Since women have experienced the long suffering of dehumanization, their han is deeper than men's. In Korea, hundreds of years of Confucian oppression have created the sociobiography of woman's han. Han is the suffering of the innocent who are caught in the wicked situation of helplessness. It is the void of the soul that cannot be filled with any superficial patch. This void is the abysmal darkness of wounded human beings. In other words, han is a physical, mental, and spiritual repercussion to a terrible injustice done to a person, eliciting a deep ache, a wrenching of all the organs, and intense internalized or externalized rage, a vengeful obsession, and the sense of helplessness and hopelessness.[9]

As Dr. Park describes it to me, he balls his hand into a fist, holding it against his chest. *Han* has the power to determine one's experience of the other; it can predetermine perceptions, responses, actions, and inactions. *Han* can influence cultural expressions and collective identities. It is an interior posture that builds toward exterior expressions like in language and art.

For example, "Arirang" is a folksong composed to commemorate a hill where, during the Li dynasty, tens of thousands of Koreans were executed over the course of hundreds of years.[10] "Arirang" is so popular among South Koreans, it is often called the "unofficial national anthem." Dr. Park considers the popularity of this song to be an exterior expression of *han*. *Han* can also influence language. Dr. Park tells me that clouds do not rain in Korea, they weep. Birds do not sing or tweet in Korea, they cry. Han is not just the experience of long and intense suffering; it is the interior posture created by such suffering that orients a person or a culture to the world.

Such interior postures can be bottled up for centuries. But *han* eventually demands external expressions or resolutions. C. S. Song writes, "*Han* is the rhythm of passion welling out of restless souls in the world of dead, the wrongs done to them unrequited."[11]

---

9. Park, "The Bible and Han," 47–48. Related to Park's reference to the *han* of women, C. S. Song clarifies, "In the traditional Chinese family system, the culture of suffering concentrates on the daughter-in-law. It is she who absorbs centuries of deep bitterness in her bones, muscles, and heart. The story of her suffering, living under the same roof as her parents-in-law, her husband's brothers and sisters, is endless." *Theology from the Womb of Asia* (Eugene: Wipf & Stock, 2005), 71. Speaking for myself, I do not know enough about the Korean-Chinese encounter to know the nuance and/or variation of this practice.

10. Song, *Theology from the Womb of Asia*, 95–98.

11. Song, *Theology from the Womb of Asia*, 70.

If neither interior posture nor inclination communicates my focus in this chapter, perhaps "rhythm" is better. Life rhythms incline us to particular patterns of thought and courses of action. In this case, the rhythm in question creates the possibility of revolution.

> The *han* accumulated for five thousand years must be a powerful *han*. It has been accumulating from one generation to the next. It has been accumulating in Korean stomachs, lungs, livers, and hearts. It has been filling the entire being of the Korean people. . . . And the time comes when human bodies cannot contain it any longer, when the fabric of society can no longer stand it, when the texture of the nation cannot endure it. That is the time when *han*, brewing in the soul of the people and seething in the abyss of the nation, breaks out into revolt and revolution.[12]

Here we see an example of an interior posture (or rhythm) that extends into an exterior posture (or expression).

Among South Korean Christian theologians, *han* has become an important topic as it connects the Korean culture to the topics of suffering, persecution, and subversion of hierarchies found in the New Testament. *Han* theology is related to the experiences and perspectives of the common folk, or what is called *Minjung*. *Minjung* theology, then, is the theology of the common folk who are excluded from elite social status.[13] Park reminds me that when *han* breaks out into revolution, common folk can find themselves with ruling status (seemingly) overnight. Those who were once considered *minjung* now possess a new and dangerous political power. People of *han* can and sometimes do become oppressors. The postures that incline us toward violent revolution can be difficult to unlearn once *minjung* status is overcome.

But lest we think that *han* is absolutely determinative or necessarily leads to violence, Park writes:

---

12. Song, *Theology from the Womb of Asia*, 71.

13. Tong H. Moon offers a fuller definition: "The term [*Minjung*] came to be used first during the Yi dynasty (1392–1910) when the common people were oppressed by [the] *Yangban* class, the ruling class of the time. . . . At that time anyone who was excluded from the *Yangban* class was a *Minjung*. During the Japanese occupation (1910–1945), most Koreans were reduced to *Minjung* status except for a small group who collaborated with the Japanese imperialists. Today the term *Minjung* may be used for all those who are excluded from the elite system." As quoted from A. Sung Park, "Minjung Theology: A Korean Contextual Theology," *The Indian Journal of Theology* 33 (1984): 1–11, citing 2. See also, Kim Yong Bock, *Minjung Theology People as the Subjects of History* (Singapore: Christian Conference of Asia, 1981).

Han can be resolved destructively or constructively. In its destructive resolution, a person of han seeks to avenge one's enemy. In its constructive resolution, the person of han can use it as the source of transforming the root causes of han.[14]

He explained further in our personal conversation that *han* "can explode negatively by destroying and taking revenge or be used as the energy to heal others (2 Cor. 1:4) and to build up G[-]d's community, but G[-]d can ultimately heal or dissolve it by G[-]d's Presence. For me, that is the reason Jesus became incarnate and was crucified."

When Park talks about constructive *han*, I am reminded of one of the first things that Larry told me about Holocaust memory. Larry told me that "Never Forget" is an oft-repeated reference to the Shoah. But Larry worries that "Never Forget" is not specific enough. In other words—if I may paraphrase—*what is the point of remembering the Shoah if the memory isn't constructive?* In his view, whatever "Never Forget" means, it ought to motivate us not to allow genocide of any kind ever again. I also wonder whether *han* theology is comparable to Holocaust theology in other ways.

For the purpose of this chapter, however, I am more interested in how our postures can mirror, counterbalance, or correct each other. I occupy a place of privilege as an American Christian, a male, as a person with excellent educational opportunities, and so on. As such, I will never experience *han* in any of the ways described above. Yet studying *han* theology reveals something about my own social placement and brings a new level of complexity to my identity as a Christian. By observing the posture(s) of South Korean Christianity, I am given an opportunity to reflect on my own. Perhaps more importantly, I believe I have a greater capacity for compassion with having been stretched by *han* theology. When I experience fear, anger, melancholy, pessimism, retreat, or defensiveness in others, *han* theology challenges me to see beyond external expressions.

One more point is apropos. Larry and I have often noted that Jewish-Christian dialogue tends to fall into the awkward postures of historic perpetrator versus historic victim. Neither of us are comfortable with these default positions. Even so, it is necessary to be honest about the histories of our peoples. In my investment in the well-being of Jews and Judaism, it has been necessary for me to learn to see the Jewish people as something other than victimized. I have also (at times) reminded Larry that I do not and cannot represent global Christianity. But the more I become invested in the well-

---

14. Park, "The Bible and Han," 48.

being of my siblings in Asia, Africa, and South America, the less inclined I am to affirm the classic default positions between Jews and Christians. This is a simple recognition that the world is much more complex than the default positions of perpetrator versus victim. In this recognition, I feel that I move beyond stereotypes and toward a better view of our common humanity.

A Conviction Deeper than Words

For better or worse, Christians are largely defined by belief. For as long as Christianity has existed, many of these convictions were borrowed from or set in contrast to those of Judaism (or a caricature of Judaism). Most of our beliefs about Jews and Judaism have been either too negative or too idealistic to reflect the truth. Richard Rubenstein touches on an important point: "It has been said that English literature has portrayed the Jew as the best of saints and the worst of sinners but never as the simple human being. This characterizes more than English literature; it characterizes the Christian view of Israel."[15] Even if this is an overstatement, Rubenstein's concern is justified. Gary Porton suggests that if Rubenstein is correct, then "Christianity cannot imagine the Jew as a normal human being."[16] This all-too-Christian inclination is tragic because both views—either idealized or demonized—have had the effect of dehumanization.

None of my Christian friends are overtly anti-Semitic. But it is quite common for Christian convictions to have unforeseen consequences. And I see these convictions (interior postures) manifest at times in external expressions. Below is a short list of Christian beliefs about Jews and Judaism. I have selected them arbitrarily, in no particular order, and based on my idiosyncratic experience and study of Christianity.

- Israel will play a key role in the soon-coming end of days.

- Jews are just like Christians, lacking only the belief that Jesus is L-rd.

- Jews have an inordinate amount of influence over the media.

- Judaism is a religion of trying to earn one's way into heaven.

- The Jews are to blame for the death of Christ.

---

15. Richard L. Rubenstein, *After Auschwitz: Radical Theology and Contemporary Judaism* (Indianapolis: Bobbs-Merrill, 1966), 68.

16. Gary Porton, "Judaism and Christianity: After the Holocaust," http://www.myjewishlearning.com/article/judaism-and-christianity-after-the-holocaust/.

Some of these beliefs lead to ideological stances. History tells us that the last belief listed created a hardened and often aggressive stance against Jews. Repeated over and over again for centuries, the conviction that Jews carry blame for the death of Christ has perpetrated incalculable harm.[17] Thus the interior posture against Jews leads to the exterior expression of violence. It is probably no coincidence that this belief has become less important for Christians at a time when Jewish-Christian friendship is experiencing a renaissance.

So sometimes beliefs lead to interior and exterior postures. To complete the cycle, some postures lead to beliefs. For example, the postures of myopia and self-centeredness contribute to the false belief that Jews are just like Christians, lacking only the belief that Jesus is L-rd. Again, not every Christian is inclined toward myopia and self-centeredness. Sometimes the internal and external patterns of Christian living have resulted in remarkable acts of empathy and courage.

With the hope that I can point my fellow Christians in the right direction, I will use a positive example of Christian posture. Sometimes reminding a people of a past goodness can encourage a similar posture in the future.

In his research on the nonviolent resistance of Nazism at Le Chambon, Hallie found that the people of that village experienced no great ethical crisis. They did not need to weigh the costs and benefits of hiding refugees. They hid people who would otherwise be murdered not because it was *the right thing to do*, but because it seemed to be *the only thing to do*. So steeped was their investment in the value of human life that they had already inclined themselves toward goodness long before any particular decision was required.

The villagers, alongside the leadership of André and Magda Trocmé, were inclined to believe that all human life is precious.[18] This fit hand-in-glove with André Trocmé's public expression of passivism. "The Chambonnais showed their allegiance to this presumption by disturbing the center of their domestic lives and endangering their own existence to protect the lives of human beings, and in the process they never sought to do grievous harm to anyone."[19] But whatever disturbance the Trocmés might have felt, it was not enough to belabor the decision. In order to understand the ethics

---

17. The Catholic Church publically renounced this belief in Vatican II.

18. Charles Guillon seems to have created space for such a life ethic before the arrival of the Trocmés. Roger Darcissac and Reverend Edouard Theis also guided the effort to host and hide refugees.

19. Hallie, *Lest Innocent Blood Be Shed*, 273.

of Le Chambon, one must imagine Magda Trocmé "rushing in her frenetic way from the kitchen to the presbytery door, turning the doorknob, and opening the door for a refugee with 'Naturally, come in, and come in.' "[20] The word *naturally* is important here. Inviting in a refugee wasn't the *right* thing to do as much as it was the *natural* thing to do. An ethic of reverence for human life created a regular interior posture and an exterior (albeit mundane) life rhythm.

> To her dying day Mrs. Trocmé could not comprehend a world that regarded it as in any way remarkable that she, her husband, and thousands of other residents of the village of Le Chambon-sur-Lignon in the plateau region of southern France had risked their lives to feed, clothe, hide and protect those who would have died without their help. . . . To her mind, at least, she had done nothing more than provide the obvious help to those in obvious need. She no more understood the fuss over her efforts to rescue Jews than the consterna- tion she caused her neighbors when policemen came to arrest her husband (he was later released) and she served them dinner. "I don't understand," she said. "It was dinner time."[21]

This interior posture toward human life and to the regular, exterior rhythms of life extended also to the Nazis and the Vichy regime. The Trocmés and many other villagers of Le Chambon believed that murder was evil. By deceiving the police, the villagers were helping their enemies by preventing them from committing murder.[22]

---

20. Hallie, *Lest Innocent Blood Be Shed*, 284.

21. Robert McG. Thomas Jr., "Magda Trocmé, 94, Is Dead; Sheltered Victims of Nazis," *The New York Times*, http://www.nytimes.com/1996/10/19/world/magda-trocme-94-is-dead-sheltered-victims-of-nazis.html; accessed: March 11, 2016.

22. It must be said that Christianity and pacifism were uneasy bedfellows in 1930s Europe. It may well be true that the Trocmés were acting out a conviction that was a natural extension of their lives as Christian pacifists. It is also true that their inclinations toward pacifism made them exceptional among European Protestants. In fact, preachers within the Reformed Church of France were prohibited from preaching nonviolence from the pulpit. Shortly after André Trocmé was ordained, the national synod passed a provision disallowing the ordination of declared paci- fists. Trocmé was feeling increased pressure not to discuss his pacifism openly. This was part of the reason Trocmé relocated to the remote village of Le Chambon. He was hoping to "find a little parish where such preaching would not be so plainly visible to the national synod" and so relocated from Sin-le-Noble to Le Chambon in 1934 (Hallie, *Lest Innocent Blood Be Shed*, 71). André Trocmé was not only inclined toward the preciousness of human life, but he had also developed a morality that

Hallie writes that this deep conviction of the preciousness of human life was an extension of the more common belief that a child's life is priceless. Not priceless in a way that it can be sold at great expense. A child's life is priceless in the sense that its very existence defies monetary value. To most parents, such a conviction seems only natural. This posture toward human life can be extended, but it needs to be fleshed out.

> How much money would we take in ordinary times in exchange for giving up the breathing, the eating, the drinking we usually hardly notice? Without noticing it, our bodies and our minds are usually celebrating a conviction deeper than words can express, a conviction that life is incomparably more valuable to us than death. When we are awake and when we are asleep, the heart in each of us pushes to beat, the lungs push to be filled.[23]

Hallie continues, "The moral leadership of André Trocmé consisted in keeping this perception green in his own life and in the lives of the other Chambonnais." In welcoming people in peril, the Trocmés were "celebrating a conviction deeper than words can express."[24] This deep reverence for human life is, I think, an example of interior posture.

We now have the context to understand André Trocmé's most famous quotation: "I do not know what a Jew is. I know only human beings." This statement, I think, reveals the Trocmés reverence for all human life. André and Magda did not host and help refugees simply because they were "the people of the Bible"; their view of Jewish life fit hand-in-glove with their view of all human life.[25] Here we witness, I would argue, a correction to a common Christian posture toward Jews and Judaism: neither idealized nor demonized; imbued with value simply because of our common humanity.

Activism and Dialogue

In this chapter, I have put forth two kinds of interior posture. First, *han* draws from the wells of Korean experience with the hope to create a dialogue posture of constructive compassion. Second, the conviction that

---

ran contrary to the establishment. Could this have contributed also to his stance against the Vichy regime and Nazism in France?

23. Hallie, *Lest Innocent Blood Be Shed*, 275–76.

24. Hallie, *Lest Innocent Blood Be Shed*, 277.

25. "André and Magda Trocmé, Daniel Trocmé," Yad Vashem; www.yadvashem.org/righteous/stories/trocme.

all human life is precious inclined the Trocmés to act on behalf of refugees in grave peril. Both in my view are positive examples of interior postures resulting in activism. More importantly for my interests, I am interested in the interior postures (e.g., *han* and valuing human life) that point people in such directions.

Here I must make a distinction between *activism* and *dialogue*. I would consider *han*-inspired revolution and quiet subversion of Nazi policy to be forms of activism. I try my best to support activism that enhances the well-being of oppressed people and the preservation of human life. Neither, it must be said, are ideal expressions of dialogue. Activism exerts pressure. It pushes for a cause, often defiantly and relentlessly. It wins arguments and acts subversively. Activism can take the shape of civil disobedience, media manipulation, or uprising. These exterior postures, while necessary and righteous at times, are not ideal for dialogue in the long term. The Jewish-Christian encounter can benefit greatly from joint activism. But periodically we will need to sit down together for the sake of learning about and from each other. And in sitting down together we open the possibility of learning more about ourselves. When I sit down with Larry, I don't want to exert pressure, push defiantly and relentlessly, win arguments, and act subversively.

Consider this anecdote from the life of André Trocmé, whom Hallie describes as "a man of enlivening and sometimes terrifying passion."

> Long after the war, he was giving one of his many lectures on nonviolence outside of Le Chambon when a certain member of the audience began to turn to his neighbor and whisper audibly whenever Trocmé made an interesting point. It turned out later that he admired what Trocmé was saying. After a few such whispers, Trocmé stopped his lecture suddenly, walked up to the vivacious whisperer, fixed his blue eyes down upon his upturned, stupefied face, and shouted, his fair, baby-soft face flushed with rage, "Out of the room! Get out of the room!" And with a massive arm he pointed the way to the door while calling over his shoulder for an usher to conduct the miscreant out. The lecture had been about nonviolence.[26]

This is an unfortunate example of exterior posture. In this setting, Trocmé was *taking a stand*. One might say that Trocmé's nonviolence, his traumatic experience of war, his reading of the Sermon on the Mount, and so on were put to best use when he was taking a stand. Thank G-d he was the sort of man who took a stand! I wish more Christians did during these

---

26. Hallie, *Lest Innocent Blood Be Shed*, 46–47.

years. Standing up against an oppressor is at time necessary and righteous. But *standing up against* is not an ideal posture for dialogue.

Dr. Park explains that a people of *han* can express their interior posture by "standing up or standing under." By "standing under" he means that *han* can motivate one's desire to "understand" the other. When looked on in this way, the interior posture of *standing* can create the possibility of under*standing*. Dr. Park believes that understanding can sometimes lead to healing. And here Dr. Park and Larry may have something in common. Larry has suggested in our personal correspondence that "activism and dialogue are not mutually exclusive. . . . Dialogue can be a part of a person's activism—a pacifist might engage in dialogue to reduce tension between warring groups."

I now must acknowledge a problem with my idealized call to dialogue from the sitting position. Given my place of privilege, my distinction between dialogue and advocacy might betray a power asymmetry. We people of privilege might be more comfortable in dialogue if the other person isn't standing at the table, pushing an agenda, or using ALL CAPS. But, as Dr. Park tells me, "forced sitting" is detrimental on any number of levels. Dr. Park echoes Qohelet and The Byrds, "There is a time for standing and a time for sitting."

I do not mean to suggest that Jews and Christians should refrain from advocacy. Indeed, in this chapter I have argued forcefully for two examples of "standing up." I believe that there is virtue and necessity in advocacy. I do believe, however, that we need episodes of dialogue for the sake of dialogue. This is perhaps the best way I can describe dialogue from the sitting position: it is dialogue for the sake of dialogue. Of course, this does not mean dispassion, neutrality, or objectivity. It simply means being open to where the conversation leads, rather than setting a goal beforehand and pushing the conversation in that direction.

Have a Seat

I will conclude with a story about my friend named John Castelein. John is a Chicago-educated theologian. He was raised in Belgium and converted to Christianity as a teen. Sharpness of mind often presents the opportunity for an insufferable ego, but not in John's case. I have met few people more sincere, humble, and willing to follow their research honestly. John has become a hero of mine, as he has to many of his students over a forty-year career as a seminary professor. In a private conversation, John told me the following story. I will summarize it here from memory, which is far from perfect. This is, at least, what I took from the conversation.

> When first became a Christian, I was a young man. My ministers and teachers encouraged me to stand up for Jesus. When I went to Christian college, I was told to stand up for the Gospel. When I went to Christian Seminary, I was taught how to stand behind a pulpit. Then I went to the University of Chicago and met Martin Marty. Professor Marty invited me to have a seat.

John told me this story to illustrate the necessary posture of honest research. At the risk of simplifying John's story, I will suggest that it is more difficult to learn and listen from the standing posture. Being willing to stand up for something of value speaks positively of one's character; it can even be courageous in the right context. There are times and places that require people of roused conscience to stand up. There are also times for taking a seat. The sitting posture, in my view, is more conversational, less urgent, less determined to be right. The sitting posture suggests an exchange of ideas rather than a unidirectional conveyance of truth. Sermons are delivered in the standing posture. Research takes place in the sitting posture. John, in sharing his story with me, affirmed that my research has value even when it does not result in a sermon or produce a confession of faith. I believe that the best dialogues are most often in the *have-a-seat* posture.

Since my conversation with John, I've given a great deal of thought to questions of posture. When should I stand or sit when I lecture in the classroom? What does my body language say about my hospitality? Why am I inclined toward certain kinds of research? What tone of voice should I adopt if I want to invite a two-way conversation? Do I expect to need to defend myself or my faith? Do I expect to learn something new about my neighbor and myself? To my mind, these are all questions of posture. Posture can tell us a great deal about how a person relates to their environment and their counterparts. It can also predetermine how a conversation unfolds. If I present an idea from a posture of deference and curiosity, I am likely to receive a different sort of reply than if I speak with utter conviction. Becoming conscious of my posture in a conversation has proven invaluable for me in interreligious dialogue. What is more, I've found that a happy byproduct to a seated posture in dialogue is that my theology takes on a more dynamic character.

In a seated posture, there is always more to learn, more to hear, more to be said. When seated, I am perhaps in less control of the theological discourse. But—sometimes—having less control produces more interesting results.

Shadow Posture

Larry Behrendt

Some years ago, I offered a course on the history of Judaism at a Protestant seminary in the midwestern United States. . . . I found it gratifying that my course fulfilled a distribution requirement in church history at the seminary; the genuine interest of Christian divinity students in my Judaic subject encouraged me no less. Surprisingly, however, my interaction with the president, the dean and some faculty colleagues at the school proved less gratifying. . . . [T]hey habitually focused on the satisfaction they derived from my presence at their seminary, from having, as they put it, "a Jew in our midst." . . . For these colleagues, who welcomed me onto their campus with genuine memorable warmth, I functioned less as the historian I construed myself to be and more as a player on a theological stage set long before my arrival.

—Jeremy Cohen[1]

I have a new friend, Rabbi Sarah Bassin. I'm about thirty years older than Sarah, but she is already a veteran of interfaith dialogue. Sarah focuses on discussion between Jews and Muslims,[2] and sometimes we get together to compare notes. One thing Sarah likes about Jewish-Muslim dialogue is its reciprocity: "When Jews say 'we are victims,' and Muslims reply with 'we are victims too,' it's a new paradigm for us as Jews," Sarah told me. "Ultimately, we can emerge from this shared experience with mutual empathy and understanding."

---

1. Jeremy Cohen, *Living Letters of the Law: Ideas of the Jew in Medieval Christianity* (Berkeley: University of California Press, 1999), 1.

2. Rabbi Bassin is the former executive director of NewGround, a Muslim-Jewish Partnership for Change, where she still serves on the Board of Directors. You can read about this terrific organization at http://mjnewground.org/.

Sarah and I sadly acknowledge that the old paradigm set by Jewish-Christian dialogue does not establish a similar reciprocity. Sarah's experience may not be the same as mine. But in my experience, when Jews say to Christians, "We are victims," we're not expecting to hear parallel stories of Christians being victimized. Instead, we expect the conversation to focus on the history of Christian anti-Semitism and anti-Judaism. Our Jewish stories function as a kind of accusation against our Christian dialogue partners, and not surprisingly, good dialogue rarely begins with an accusation. Even if Christians offer up an apology, it does not satisfy. Indeed, how could it satisfy? There can be only a handful of Jews and Christians present at any instance of dialogue. The missing include Christians who don't think they owe an apology to anyone, and Christians who understand original sin to require everyone to apologize to everyone else. The missing include Jews who don't believe in interfaith dialogue . . . and of course, Jews who perished in anti-Jewish persecution without receiving an apology of any kind.

Humans have conventions in place, allowing one person to apologize to another. But we haven't nailed this process down when the victims and perpetrators number in the millions, and consist of the living and the dead. Without such a process in place, Jewish-Christian dialogue can't get past those first few items on the agenda, the quest for meaningful apology, forgiveness, and reconciliation. The dialogue proceeds on nevertheless, but the residue of recrimination and regret lingers, like smoke in a windowless room.

A while back, Anthony asked me to write a chapter about "posture" in dialogue. I resisted. For a person of my generation, "posture" evokes the image of a seven-year-old boy stuffed into a button-down shirt and clip-on tie, being told "Stand up straight" and "Take your hands out of your pockets." I'm sure Anthony had something else in mind when he made this request, something more like a "posture" of welcome and hospitality. But when Anthony recently repeated this request, I thought of my conversation with Rabbi Bassin, and about the paradigm of persecutors and victims.

And I thought to myself, "I'm sick of this paradigm. Isn't there any way out of this?"

❄

Why am I sick of the posture of victim? Well, for one thing, it makes for dull dialogue. I'm not making light of the history of Jewish suffering, but I doubt my Christian dialogue partners can help me understand this history better than I already do. If Christians need to better understand this history, then they can ask me about it. I don't need to wave this history in their faces.

Moreover, I'm not being completely true to my history when I assume the posture of victim. The preeminent twentieth-century historian of Judaism, Salo Baron, famously criticized the "lachrymose theory" that Jewish history is a thousands-year-old string of unbroken suffering.[3] While Jewish life under Islamic and Christian rule was certainly no picnic, we *did* manage to emerge into present time with *two* Talmuds, a collection of Midrash, a library of scriptural commentary, more than 20 percent of the Nobel Prizes,[4] Sigmund Freud, Albert Einstein, and Barry Manilow. Evidently, I can choose to stand in dialogue for something other than persecution.

Another problem is that no one wants to be persecutor or victim forever. The only purpose I can see in perpetrator-victim dialogue is to get to where the air is cleared, all residual persecution is eliminated, and the forgiveness agenda I referred to above is figured out. But what if we actually managed to do this? What if the elusive apology was issued and accepted, and all remaining anti-Semitism had been eliminated? What would we do next? Join hands, sing "Reach Out of the Darkness,"[5] and go home? Well . . . I don't engage in dialogue with the goal of putting it to an end. I *like* talking to Christians. Since I enjoy the talking and listening, and given that this apology business is proving difficult, why not jump the gun, drop the victim posture, and start the kind of conversation we want to have post-reconciliation?

I might feel a need to take a victim's posture, out of respect for those Jews of blessed memory who suffered under historic Christian anti-Judaism. But it doesn't make sense to commemorate the persecuted by pointing a finger at the children of their persecutors. If given the chance, those persecuted Jews would have welcomed the opportunity to live with their then-contemporary

---

3. Salo Wittmayer Baron, "Ghetto and Emancipation: Shall We Revise the Traditional View?" *Menorah Journal* 14 (1928): 515–26. It is available online at https://jewsandjudaism.files.wordpress.com/2012/07/baronghettoandemancipation.pdf.

4. "Jewish Biographies: Nobel Prize Laureates," Jewish Virtual Library, www.jewishvirtuallibrary.org/jewish-nobel-prize-laureates.

5. "Reach Out of the Darkness," Jim Post, Copyright Sony/ATV Songs LLC. This song was recorded by the folk duo Friend and Lover in 1968, and reached #10 on the Billboard charts. The lyrics include, "I knew a man that I did not care for,/ And then one day this man gave me a call,/ We sat and talked about things on our mind,/ And now this man he is a friend of mine./ Reach out in the darkness . . . and you may find a friend." If you're not familiar with this song, you might substitute "Kumbaya" in its place, with similar effect.

Christian neighbors as something other than victims. Who would want to protract a posture of suffering and persecution, except maybe the persecutors, whose wishes should be the *last* thing we should seek to honor.

There's one other small matter to mention. [Pause, while I embarrassedly shuffle my feet.] Thing is . . . I've never personally been persecuted. Quite the contrary. My sixty-odd years on Planet Earth have been remarkably blessed, and among my blessings are this: I can't identify a single incident when I was the victim of anti-Semitism. I don't know if I am blind to such things or if my experience is typical, but what I feel is what I feel. The Christians I know have been remarkably nice to me. *Exactly what is it that I have to complain about?*

So why would I assume a victim's posture? The answer has to do with Jewish history. When Jews approach Christians in dialogue, we do so conscious of the history of those who came to dialogue before us. By and large, *that* history *is* lachrymose.

※

I do not know any well-accepted work on the history of Jewish-Christian dialogue, but much has been written about Jewish-Christian *disputation*. The three best known of these disputations are named by the cities where they took place: Paris (1240), Barcelona (1263), and Tortosa (1413–14). The best work I know on these disputes is Hyam Maccoby's *Judaism on Trial*,[6] and indeed, Maccoby's title is a good summary of what occurred on these three occasions. In Paris, the disputation-trial took place before Christian judges and with a Christian prosecutor (who, like the prosecutors in Barcelona and Tortosa, was a Jew who had converted to Christianity); the Jewish disputants-defendants were held in prison during the dispute, interrogated separately in the manner of the Inquisition, and forced to defend a series of charges made against the Talmud, which was found guilty and burned by the cartload.[7] The Tortosa Disputation was worse: it was a drawn-out twenty-one-month-long

---

6. Hyam Maccoby, *Judaism on Trial: Jewish-Christian Disputations in the Middle Ages* (London: The Littman Library of Jewish Civilization, 1993). My discussion here of Jewish-Christian disputations is based largely on Maccoby's work.

7. Maccoby, *Judaism on Trial*, 19–38; see also Judah M. Rosenthal, "The Talmud on Trial: The Disputation at Paris in the Year 1240," *The Jewish Quarterly Review* 47.1 (1956): 58–76.

exercise in terror, where the rabbis summoned to this proceeding feared for their lives and the lives of their families, while church officials bullied into conversion large portions of the Jewish communities these rabbis were forced to leave behind.[8] The Barcelona Disputation was the only one of the three where Jews experienced anything like freedom of speech, but even this disputation concluded with exile of the Jewish disputant (the famous Rabbi Moses ben Nachman[9]) and the burning of his account of the dispute.[10]

Perhaps it is the bitter memory of these disputations that has led many scholars to date the beginning of Jewish-Christian dialogue to the twentieth century.[11] Some sources admit to "burgeoning" forms of Jewish-Christian dialogue extending back into the nineteenth century,[12] while others imply that this dialogue did not take hold in a significant way until the mid-twentieth century, after the Shoah.[13] The assumption that Jewish-Christian dialogue is a relatively recent phenomenon might make sense if we think of "dialogue" as something polite or constructive. Thus Catherine Cornille writes that "the common denominator" in all forms of interreligious dialogue "is mutual respect and openness to the possibility of learning from the other."[14]

Cornille may have "written the book" on interreligious dialogue (or at least, she edited it!), but I don't agree that dialogue is dialogue only if it is positive and uplifting. Instead, I'll go with a definition of "dialogue" as any

---

8. Maccoby, *Judaism on Trial*, 82–84.

9. Rabbi ben Nachman was also known by his Greek name Nahmanides and the Hebrew acronym Ramban.

10. Maccoby, *Judaism on Trial*, 39–75.

11. Thus Yaakov Ariel wrote that attempts at Jewish-Christian dialogue "began at the turn of the twentieth century." "Jewish-Christian Dialogue," in *The Wiley-Blackwell Companion to Inter-Religious Dialogue*, ed. Catherine Cornille (London: Blackwell, 2013), 208.

12. See, for example, Yehudah Mirsky, "Jewish-Christian Dialogue Today," *Jewish Ideas Daily*, February 21, 2011, www.jewishideasdaily.com/826/features /jewish-christian-dialogue-today/.

13. The terrific Jewish-Christian Relations webpage for Scarboro Missions contains biographies for fifteen "Dialogue Pioneers," all of whom are twentieth-century figures, and most of whom were principally active in dialogue after World War II. Scarboro Missions, "Pioneers of Dialogue in the Modern Jewish-Christian Relationship," https://www.scarboromissions.ca/interfaith-dialogue/jewish-christian-relations/pioneers-of-dialogue-in-the-modern-jewish-christian-relationship. Spring Hill College's online Theology Library for Jewish-Christian Dialogue does not list a document written prior to 1941. "Theology Library at Spring Hill College, Jewish-Christian Dialogue," http://theolibrary.shc.edu/jewish.htm.

14. Cornille, *The Wiley-Blackwell Companion to Inter-Religious Dialogue*, xii.

conversation between two or more people,[15] and insist that even the medieval disputations outlined above were forms of dialogue. Indeed, I don't think it's possible to understand the Jewish attitude toward Jewish-Christian dialogue without keeping in mind the awful precedent set in Paris, Tortosa, and Barcelona.

From my definition, we should date the beginning of Jewish-Christian dialogue well before the twentieth century, and even well before the medieval disputations. I think it obvious that Jews and Christians must have been in some form of conversation, civil or not, going back to the first-century beginnings of Christianity as a late Second Temple Jewish sect. Recent scholarship indicates that the "parting of the ways" between Judaism and Christianity took some time—perhaps a few hundred years, perhaps longer—before Judaism and Christianity emerged as clearly separate religions.[16] Certainly there must have been discussion between these more-or-less differentiated Jews-Christians as the "ways parted," and even for some time after that. But what was said during these conversations? For the most part, we don't know.

The church has handed down a number of Jewish-Christian "dialogues," all penned by Christian authors during the second through sixth centuries. The most famous of these is Justin Martyr's *Dialogue with Trypho the Jew*;[17] lesser known works include the dialogue of *Athanasius and Zacchaeus*, the dialogue of *Simon and Theophilus*, and the dialogue of *Timothy and Aquila*.[18] At times, the discussion in these dialogues seems quite friendly! At other times, harsh accusation flies freely. For example, Trypho accuses Justin of

---

15. The online Merriam-Webster dictionary defines "dialogue" as (a) the things that are said by the characters in a story, movie, play, etc., (b) a discussion or series of discussions that two groups or countries have in order to end a disagreement, and (c) a conversation between two or more people. "Dialogue," Merriam-Webster, https://www.merriam-webster.com/dictionary/dialogue. Only the second of these definitions points to a form of dialogue that ideally should be civil.

16. See generally, Adam H. Becker and Annette Yoshiko Reed, eds., *The Ways That Never Parted: Jews and Christians in Late Antiquity and the Early Middle Ages* (Minneapolis: Fortress Press, 2007). Reed and Becker's introduction to this book is a particularly good summary of this scholarship.

17. A translation of this dialogue is available at "Justin Martyr: Dialogue with Trypho," *Early Christian Writings*, www.earlychristianwritings.com/text/justinmartyr-dialoguetrypho.html.

18. These works are described in William Varner, "In the wake of Trypho: Jewish-Christian dialogues in the third to the sixth centuries," *Evangelical Quarterly* 80.3 (2008): 219–36.

having been "deceived by false words" and having "forsaken G[-]d."[19] In turn, Justin tells Trypho that Jews were circumcised "as a sign," to mark them for persecution: "that you may be separated from other nations, and from us; and that you alone may suffer that which you now justly suffer."[20] Despite these harsh words, Trypho and Justin amicably part company after their dialogue, with Trypho proclaiming that he was "particularly pleased" with the discussion, and with both sides expressing the wish that the conversation might continue.[21] (Evidently, the ancients had more tolerance for polemic than we do today!) Trypho remains committed to Judaism throughout Justin's dialogue; in contrast, the Jews Zacchaeus, Simon, and Aquila all convert to Christianity at the conclusion of their respective dialogues.

What should we make of these dialogues? Scholars debate whether any of these dialogues report actual discussions between Christians and Jews. Most scholars have concluded that the lesser-known dialogues were fabricated by their Christian authors for the purpose of presenting a positive picture of Christianity to unbelievers, or as instructional texts for Christians new to the faith.[22] Perhaps a more important question is whether these dialogues present a realistic picture of what a Jewish-Christian conversation might have sounded like in the early centuries of Christianity. Here, count me among the skeptics. Scholars place these dialogues within a broad category of so-called *contra Iudaeos* ("against Judaism") writing, described by my dialogue partner Anthony as "idealized portraits of Christian apologists deconstructing Jewish straw men" and ending with "accounts of defeated Jews submitting to baptism."[23] Even those scholars who see these dialogues as based on real-life conversations readily admit that the authors often crafted Jewish arguments to "allow the spokesman for Christianity an easy victory."[24]

To me, the more interesting question is why these dialogues were penned in the first place. We might think that the early Jewish-Christian encounter

---

19. *Dialogue* VIII.

20. *Dialogue* XVI.

21. *Dialogue* CXLII.

22. Varner, 223n19.

23. Anthony Le Donne, "Remapping Schweitzer's Quest," in Bruce Chilton, Anthony Le Donne and Jacob Neusner, eds., *Soundings in the Religion of Jesus: Perspectives and Methods in Jewish and Christian Scholarship* (Minneapolis: Fortress Press, 2012), 116–17.

24. Varner, "In the wake," 222. The quote is from Marcel Simon, *Verus Israel*, trans. H. McKeating (Oxford: Oxford University Press, 1986), 140.

would have been inherently interesting to all concerned, but it doesn't seem to have held particular interest to the *Jews* in these encounters,[25] as we don't have any Jewish-Christian dialogues from this period that were written by Jewish authors.[26] In fact, the rich Jewish library of the first centuries CE contain little discussion of Jesus or Christianity.[27] Why, then, do the Christians of this period talk so frequently about Jews and Judaism? One answer, suggested by Paula Fredriksen, is that Christians were not interested in Jews and Judaism per se. Instead, the *contra Iudaeos* literature reflects debates *between Christians* on matters of emerging Christian doctrine, where the Christian author discredited the position of his Christian nemesis by describing it as *Jewish*. Fredriksen describes this phenomenon as "intra-Christian exchanges of anti-Jewish insults," and refers to the Jews in this literature as "rhetorical Jews"—they are not intended to represent a realistic portrait of Jews and Judaism, but instead to show the extent of the heresy of the author's Christian opponents.[28]

Fredriksen's point here is taken up in a big way by David Nirenberg in his *Anti-Judaism—The Western Tradition*.[29] Nirenberg reads Justin's dialogue not as an argument against Jews and Judaism, but as an attack against Justin's Christian contemporary, the arch-heretic Marcion. A brief discussion of Marcion is in order here, in part because his version of Christianity was *itself* deeply rooted in anti-Judaism. Marcion read the Old Testament literally and asked, how could an omnipotent G-d have to call out to Adam in Genesis, asking where he was?[30] Or, how could a supremely good G-d admit in Isaiah

---

25. Thus Stephen Wilson writes that "initially Christians were much more interested in Judaism than Jews were in Christianity." Stephen G. Wilson, *Related Strangers: Jews and Christians 70–170 C.E.* (Minneapolis: Fortress Press, 1995), 170.

26. Stephen Wilson mentions that scholars know of early dialogues between Jews and Christians that were written by Jewish authors, but these dialogues no longer exist (*Related Strangers*, ch. 6).

27. *Related Strangers*, 170–71; see also Peter Schäfer, *Jesus in the Talmud* (Princeton: Princeton University Press, 2007), 2. (Mentions of Jesus in early Jewish literature are so sparing, they can be compared to the proverbial drop in the ocean.)

28. Paula Fredriksen, "Jewish Romans, Christian Romans, and the Post-Roman West: The Social Correlates of the *contra Iudaeos* Tradition," in Israel Jacob Yuval and Ram Ben-Shalom, eds., *Conflict and Religious Conversation in Latin Christendom: Studies in Honour of Ora Limor* (Turnhout: Brepols Publishers, 2014), 29, available at http://www.bu.edu/religion/files/2010/03/Jewish-Romans-PF-6-14.pdf.

29. David Nirenberg, *Anti-Judaism: The Western Tradition* (New York: W. W. Norton & Company, 2013), 92.

30. Genesis 3:9.

that he created evil?[31] Marcion concluded that the Jewish G-d could not be
the same G-d represented by Jesus in the New Testament. Likewise, Marcion
concluded that the Old Testament (full of judgment, punishment, and death)
was inferior to the New Testament gospel (full of love and mercy). From
this, Marcion concluded that Christianity should be purged of everything
Jewish, including the Old Testament and its G-d.[32] Justin and other orthodox
church fathers responded to Marcion's anti-Judaism with anti-Judaism of
their own. Per Justin, the correct way to understand the Old Testament is
spiritually and allegorically, and not literally like Marcion had done. But who
did Justin use to represent Marcion's literalism in dialogue? Not Marcion
himself! Instead, it is Justin's "rhetorical Jew" Trypho[33] who insisted that
Justin could not obtain mercy from G-d unless he obeyed "all things which
have been written in the law."[34]

Nirenberg's book cites an impressive, if depressingly long, list of other
rhetorical Jews used throughout Christian history to score Christian points.
As one example, the theological battle between Catholics and Protestants
featured use of rhetorical Jews by both sides. Martin Luther attacked the
church's "legalistic understanding" of Scripture, complaining that it forced
the obedient Catholic to "almost have to become a Jew."[35] The Roman Church,
wrote Luther, was "the Devil's Synagogue."[36] Luther's Catholic opponents
responded by claiming that Protestants learned their doctrines from the Jews
and that the Jews encouraged Luther to rebel against the papacy. Indeed,
a Jewish contemporary of Luther wrote that Luther's plunge into virulent

---

31. Isaiah 45:7, according to the King James Version, the JPS Tanakh, and
other translations. Not every Bible translation reads Isaiah 45:7 in this way. For
example, the New Revised Standard Version of the Bible translates 45:7 as G-d
creating "woe," and the New International Version of the Bible translates 45:7 as
G-d creating "disaster." The Hebrew word being translated here is רע, pronounced
"ra," which is defined in the Kohlenberger/Mounce Concise Hebrew-Aramaic
Dictionary of the Old Testament as "bad, disagreeable, inferior in quality; by
extension: evil, wicked in ethical quality." It is reasonable to read Isaiah 45:7 as
stating that G-d created evil.

32. Bart D. Ehrman, *Lost Christianities: The Battles for Scripture and the Faiths
We Never Knew* (Oxford: Oxford University Press, 2003), 104–6.

33. Nirenberg, *Anti-Judaism*, 99–100.

34. *Dialogue* VIII.

35. Nirenberg, *Anti-Judaism*, 251. Here, Nirenberg is quoting Luther's *That Jesus
Christ was Born a Jew*.

36. Nirenberg, *Anti-Judaism*, 260. Here, Nirenberg is quoting Luther's *On the
Jews and their Lies*.

anti-Judaism was a reaction to his opponents "defaming him and saying that his mind inclines to the faith of the Israelites."[37]

If I were to write a longer history of Jewish-Christian dialogue, I'd focus at least *some* attention on *positive* premodern encounters between Jews and Christians. For example, we know of cooperative efforts between Jewish and Christian scholars, going back at least as far as the fourth century, when Saint Jerome used the assistance of rabbis to help prepare the Vulgate, the church's definitive Latin translation of the Bible. We might search for early examples of Jewish-Christian friendship, like that between the eighteenth century Jewish philosopher Moses Mendelssohn and the Christian playwright Gotthold Lessing. But at least from my present-day perspective, the negatives I've described overwhelm the positives. Many Jews (myself included) see the specter of disputation, persecution, and forced conversion continuing into the present day in the mission of some Christians to convert Jews to Christianity. But worse in my view is the persistence of the Christian idea of the "rhetorical Jew," and this persistence is worth more discussion here.

※

In our dialogue, Anthony and I have noted a marked asymmetry when it comes to the attention our religions pay to each other in our worship services. You might attend regular Jewish worship services for ten years, or twenty, without hearing Jesus or the New Testament invoked in a rabbi's sermon. Amy-Jill Levine jokes that she's heard Reform and Conservative rabbis cite Homer ("both the Greek poet and Bart's father"), Plato, the Buddha, Muhammad, Gandhi, Martin Luther King Jr., the Dalai Lama, and even Madonna ("the Kabbalah-besotted singer, not the mother of Jesus") from the Bimah[38] . . . so why not Jesus?[39] But Jesus is rarely mentioned in synagogue, except perhaps in adult education about world religions, or when Mel Gibson makes a Jesus movie. In contrast, I don't think I've ever attended a church service without hearing Judaism referred to in one way or another. In my experience, present-day Christians most frequently invoke Judaism by reference to the Pharisees.

---

37. Nirenberg, *Anti-Judaism*, 261.

38. Hebrew for "pulpit."

39. Amy-Jill Levine, *The Misunderstood Jew: The Church and the Scandal of the Jewish Jesus* (New York: HarperCollins, 2006), 8.

Who were the Pharisees? We probably know less about the Pharisees than we think we know.[40] We can safely say that the Pharisees were a group of Jews in ancient Israel during the latter portion of the Second Temple era. But the Pharisees are described differently in different places: sometimes as a political party, sometimes as a school of thought, and sometimes as a social movement.[41] I'll rely here on a description of the Pharisees provided by Scot McKnight: the Pharisees were (1) devoted to Torah, (2) known as the most accurate (and also the most liberal) interpreters of Jewish law, and (3) devoted to living life as closely as possible according to Jewish law.[42] Some believe that the Pharisees were relatively popular among the Jewish people. One source calls the Pharisees "blue-collar Jews,"[43] which might be accurate (if anachronistic!). Rabbinic Judaism, the Judaism that emerged after the fall of the Second Temple and the exile of Jews from Israel under Roman rule, is assumed by many to rely on the teachings and traditions of the Pharisees, though rabbinic literature never so claims.[44] Perhaps without good cause, I am one of many Jews who considers the Pharisees to be my spiritual ancestors.

But for many Christians, "Pharisee" has a different meaning. In the New Testament, some of Jesus' opponents are Pharisees, and Jesus' criticism of these Pharisees is withering:

> "But woe to you, scribes and Pharisees, hypocrites! For you lock people out of the kingdom of heaven. For you do not go in yourselves, and when others are going in, you stop them. Woe to you, scribes and Pharisees, hypocrites! For you cross sea and land to make a single convert, and you make the new convert twice as much a child of hell as yourselves." (Matt. 23:13–15)

Still, even if we were to limit our view of the Pharisees to what we find in the New Testament, we'd conclude that the evidence there is mixed. The named Pharisees in the New Testament—Nicodemus (John 3:1–21; 7:50–51; 19:39–42), Gamaliel (Acts 5:34–39), and the apostle Paul (Phil 3:5; Acts

---

40. See, for example, William Scott Green's essay "What Do We Really Know about the Pharisees, and How Do We Know It?" in Jacob Neusner and Bruce D. Chilton, eds., *In Quest of the Historical Pharisees* (Waco: Baylor University Press, 2007), 409–24.

41. Neusner and Chilton, Preface, *In Quest of the Historical Pharisees*, vii.

42. Scot McKnight, "Pharisees: Revisiting an Old Problem," *Jesus Creed*, February 4, 2013, www.patheos.com/blogs/jesuscreed/2013/02/04/pharisees/.

43. "Ancient Jewish History: Pharisees, Sadducees & Essenes," Jewish Virtual Library, http://www.jewishvirtuallibrary.org/jsource/History/sadducees_pharisees_essenes.html.

44. Green, "What Do We Really Know," 418–19.

23:6)—all come across as reasonably good guys. Paul describes his status as a Pharisee in a way that makes being a Pharisee sound like a positive thing. And even Jesus had some nice things to say about the Pharisees; he described them as sitting "on Moses' seat" (Matt. 23:2), and he ordered his followers to "do whatever they teach you and follow it" (Matt. 23:3)·

But if the New Testament provides a somewhat balanced view of the Pharisees, Christian history does not. Under Christian influence, "Pharisee" became synonymous with "hypocrite"; indeed, *Webster's Unabridged Dictionary*,[45] the *Oxford English Dictionary*,[46] and *The American Heritage Dictionary*[47] all give "hypocrite" as a *definition* of "Pharisee." Even if some of Jesus' opponents among the Pharisees were hypocrites, how did the word *Pharisee* come to be defined as the behavior of the group's worst members? Bart Ehrman has compared this to traveling into the future to find that "Methodist" has been defined as "liar" and "Baptist" as "adulterer."[48]

Christians have transformed the Pharisees into the "rhetorical Jew" par excellence, the ultimate insult in the "intra-Christian exchanges of anti-Jewish insults."[49] Martin Luther's ally, Philipp Melanchthon, described Luther's struggle against the Catholic Church as a triumph over law, works, and Pharisees.[50] Luther himself wrote in *That Jesus Christ was Born a Jew* that Jews had failed to convert to Christianity because of the teachings of "our Sophists and Pharisees"—that is, the pope and other officials of the Catholic Church.[51] But by far the most vicious Christian characterization of the Pharisees took place in modern times, among the influential German Protestant theologians of the nineteenth and twentieth centuries. Drawing on then-current anti-Semitic literature, these theologians wrote that the Pharisees "represent a wish to deceive oneself and . . . G[-]d," were "an abomination in the eyes of G[-]d," "hated [Jesus] with all their hearts," and were "religiously degenerate." As these scholars also considered the Phari-

---

45. *Webster's Unabridged Dictionary*, 2nd ed. (New York: Random House, 2001).

46. "Pharisee," Oxford Living Dictionaries," https://en.oxforddictionaries.com/definition/us/Pharisee.

47. *The American Heritage Dictionary of the English Language*, 5th ed. (New York: Houghton Mifflin Harcourt Publishing Company, 2013), available at http://www.yourdictionary.com/pharisee ("A hypocritically self-righteous person").

48. Bart D. Ehrman, *Jesus: Apocalyptic Prophet of the New Millennium* (Oxford: Oxford University Press, 2001), 108.

49. See note 29 *supra* and accompanying text.

50. Nirenberg, *Anti-Judaism*, 251.

51. Nirenberg, *Anti-Judaism*, 261.

sees to be the "Jews in superlative, the true Israel," it's easy to see the rise of German anti-Semitism reflected in this distorted image of the Pharisee.[52] Even after the end of World War II and the mass murder of six million Jews, some German religious leaders persisted in their abuse of the Pharisees, blaming the prosecution of German war criminals on the "Pharisaic self-righteousness" of the prosecutors.[53]

For me, it is tragic to see present-day Christians persist in using the term "Pharisee" to describe everything they most strongly oppose . . . particularly when I might otherwise join their opposition. It grieves me to find a LGBTQ-affirming website comparing Pharisees to churches that exile their gay or lesbian members,[54] and an Episcopal Church website proclaiming that "we are Pharisees if we participate in systems that allow poverty and suffering; systems that let children go hungry without feeding them,"[55] and a Christian Women's Resource Center site writing that "Christian husbands who beat their wives are akin to the Pharisees of old."[56] It is truly heartbreaking that Pope Francis has jumped into this conversation with a slur of his own. In a recent sermon, Pope Francis mentioned that many Catholics opposed Pope Pius XII when he eliminated the Eucharistic fast. How did Francis characterize these Catholics? As Pharisees.

> So many Pharisees were scandalized. So many. Because Pius XII had acted like Jesus: he saw the need of the people. . . . And these Pharisees [spoke about] "our discipline"—rigid on the outside, but, as Jesus said of them, "rotting in the heart," weak, weak to the point of rottenness.[57]

No, your Holiness. Not you too.

---

52. See Susannah Heschel, "The German Theological Tradition," in Jacob Neusner and Bruce D. Chilton, eds., *In Quest of the Historical Pharisees* (Waco: Baylor University Press, 2007), ch. 14.

53. Katharina von Kellenbach, *The Mark of Cain: Guilt and Denial in the Post-War Lives of Nazi Perpetrators* (Oxford: Oxford University Press, 2013), 194.

54. Kimberly Knight, "You might be a Pharisee if . . ." *Coming Out Christian*, September 1, 2013, www.patheos.com/blogs/kimberlyknight/2013/09/you-might-be-a-pharisee-if/.

55. http://www.episcopalcafe.com/woe_to_us_pharisees/.

56. http://www.spiritual-side-of-domestic-violence.org/id87.html.

57. http://en.radiovaticana.va/news/2014/12/15/pope_francis_rigidity_is_a _sign_of_a_weak_heart/1114830.

⌘

Let's leave this lachrymose discussion to the side for a moment, and focus on what might be the ideal posture for a Jew in Jewish-Christian dialogue. When we engage in interfaith dialogue, what postures are available to us?

I'll start with Catherine Cornille, who earlier provided us with the optimistic thought that dialogue should be positive and enlightening! In her book *The Im-Possibility of Interreligious Dialogue,* Cornille describes a three-step progression in how we might understand dialogue.[58] The first step is to see dialogue as "an exchange of information." We might then take a step beyond "accumulation of facts" and "include the possibility of learning from the other religion." A third possibility, the final step, is to view dialogue as "part of a continuous religious pursuit of truth . . . oriented to the possibility of change and growth."[59]

With this third and ultimate possibility of dialogue, Cornille demands a lot of us! Cornille expects us to come to dialogue with a strong religious commitment, so that our dialogue partner feels "effectively engaged in a dialogue with a genuine religious tradition."[60] Fair enough. But she also requires that we engage the other with due humility, notwithstanding her acknowledgement that "strong religious commitment coincides with religious intolerance."[61] More difficult still: Cornille adds the requirement that we enter dialogue with a radical openness to the possibility of personal change—a possibility so wide open that Cornille feels the need to discuss the question of conversion to the religion of the other. Cornille ultimately concludes that "to require openness to the possibility of conversion as a condition for dialogue may be both unrealistic and unnecessarily limiting."[62] I wish that Cornille had used stronger language here than "may be."

While there's much to admire in Cornille's program, ultimately her focus on religious "truth" and personal change makes me uneasy. I understand that Cornille is not speaking about "truth" in a rigid, narrow sense of who is right and who is wrong, or who is on G-d's side and who is not. I get that

---

58. Catherine Cornille, *The Im-Possibility of Interreligious Dialogue* (New York: Crossroad Publishing, 2008). Cornille's title suggests that she intends to explore both the possibility and impossibility of interreligious dialogue.

59. Cornille, *Im-Possibility,* 3.

60. Cornille, *Im-Possibility,* 67.

61. Cornille, *Im-Possibility,* 59.

62. Cornille, *Im-Possibility,* 90.

Cornille is talking about truth in a humble sense, as an understanding of a G-d beyond understanding. But fairly or not, my reaction to Cornille's focus on "truth" is colored by the Jewish-Christian history of disputation. I recall that during the worst of these disputations, at Tortosa, Rabbi Astruk Halevi voiced the following plea for tolerance:

> "I say that all disputation about a principle of religion is prohibited, so that a man may not depart from the principles of his religion. It seems that only science should be made the subject of dispute and argument, but religion and belief ought to be consigned willingly to faith, not argument, so that he may not retreat from it. When we say, 'We do not know,' and cease disputing, we are doing what is right for every religious adherent."[63]

Halevi's argument is that in any religious disputation, one will eventually reach bedrock principles of faith that are not open to question. In response, the Christian side at Tortosa argued for the rationality of religious belief and the need to defend one's fundamental religious principles.[64] Both arguments are sound—as Cornille herself said, "Religious convictions may be rationally argued and defended, [but] their truth is ultimately grounded in an attitude of faith . . . and set of beliefs that defy purely rational argumentation."[65] Ultimately, I share Cornille's desire to pursue the dialogue of personal growth. But so long as there is a stark disparity in Jewish and Christian power, and so long as some Christians seek to change Jews into Christians while there is practically no effort in the opposite direction, I don't consider "truth oriented to change" to be a desirable Jewish-Christian dialogue posture.

Instead, I turn to Martin Buber for my ideal of dialogue. Martin Buber is rightfully considered one of the giants of twentieth-century philosophy and theology, by Jews and Christians alike. His thought is frequently described as a "philosophy of dialogue."[66] In his classic *I and Thou*,[67] Buber outlines

---

63. Maccoby, *Judaism on Trial*, 86.

64. Maccoby, *Judaism on Trial*, 86–87.

65. Cornille, *Im-Possibility*, 90.

66. See, for example, Sarah Scott, "Martin Buber," Internet Encyclopedia of Philosophy; www.iep.utm.edu/buber/ and Michael Zank and Zachary Braiterman, "Martin Buber," *Stanford Encyclopedia of Philosophy*, December 4, 2014, https://plato.stanford.edu/entries/buber/.

67. Martin Buber's work *Ich und Du* was originally published in German in 1923. In the United States, it is more commonly known by the title *I and Thou*. There have been two important English translations of this work, one by Ronald Gregor Smith in 1937 (Charles Scribner's Sons, 1958), and another by Walter Kaufmann in

two primary postures we might take in relation to an other: either *I-You*, or *I-It*. The *I-You* posture is the more difficult one to achieve; it is dialogical, characterized by openness and mutuality, where we are available without limitation. The *I-It* orientation is the prevailing way in which humans interact with each other. *I-It* is utilitarian, limited by preconceived roles and by the benefit we seek from the other. In the *I-It* relationship, "we take care of business"; in the *I-You* relationship, we encounter the other "in the sense of his and her full humanity," and by doing so, "we encounter G[-]d."[68]

Buber's language for *I-You* is mystical and poetic:

> The basic word *I-You* can be spoken only with one's whole being. The concentration and fusion into a whole being can never be accomplished by me, can never be accomplished without me. I require a You to become; becoming I, I say You. All actual life is encounter.[69]

If all this sounds a bit too "new age," try this: imagine you're holding a newborn baby. The baby can provide you with no concrete benefit; not food, not money, not even praise. The baby is totally helpless and reliant on you. This relationship is *I-You*, just as the best moments with our closest friends and loved ones can be *I-You*. But when we order a meal from a waiter, this is *I-It*. My relationship to a waiter may be friendly, but it is also "defined and limited by specific roles we play and by benefits derived in the relationship."[70]

I said above that Catherine Cornille's idea of dialogue asks a lot of us, but certainly, Buber's concept of *I-You* requires even more. How can I continually be present, sincere, engaged, and open in dialogue, without limitation or expectation? It doesn't seem possible. Yet Buber is saying, in effect, that I engage in *I-You* all the time, routinely and spontaneously (if not continuously or even consistently), or else I would not even exist: "I require a You

---

1970 (Charles Scribner's Sons, 1970). For this analysis, I am relying primarily on Kenneth Paul Kramer and Mechthild Gawlick, *Martin Buber's I and Thou: Practicing Living Dialogue* (New York: Paulist Press, 2003). This work draws on both the Smith and Kaufmann translations. When I quote Buber herein, I will cite the page numbers from Kramer's book but indicate when I am using the Smith or the Kaufmann translation.

68. Rabbi David Rosen, "The Power of Interfaith Dialogue," *Vatican Insider* (2013), http://vaticaninsider.lastampa.it/en/inquiries-and-interviews/detail/articolo/tedx-religion-freedom-24236/.

69. Buber, *I and Thou*, 21 (Kaufmann, 62).

70. Rabbi William Plevan, "Martin Buber: The Dialogue with G[-]d," in *Jewish Theology in Our Time: A New Generation Explores the Foundations and Future of Jewish Belief* (Woodstock, VT: Jewish Lights Publishing, 2013).

to become," or as alternately translated, "I become through my relationship to the Thou."[71] In this, we see that Cornille's idea of dialogue is incorporated into Buber's. *Of course* I must speak and seek truth in an *I-You* dialogue— how else can I embody the presence and sincerity necessary to achieve this state of relationship with an other? But in Buber's ideal dialogue, the goal *is* relationship. Truth may be a prerequisite for *I-You*, and even a by-product of *I-You*, but *I-You* is not a truth-producing factory. If we approach dialogue seeking "output," then we're engaging not in *I-You* but in the utilitarian, benefit-oriented relationship of *I-It*.

Then again . . . there's a lot of Buber's philosophy of dialogue I do not understand. For example, Buber did *not* say that we should strive to live life exclusively in *I-You*. A good deal of *I-It* is inevitable, and necessary. More-over, *I-You* and *I-It* are related. I would think that we begin our relations with *I-It*, and as we grow in mutual trust and empathy, *I-You* would then become possible. But evidently, Buber thought that *I-You* comes first, and that *I-It* grows out of *I-You*.[72]

The pragmatist in me wonders how Buber fared in dialogue in the real world. From what I've read, Buber was a terrific conversation partner, but his efforts at dialogue did not always go the way he might have liked. Let's consider the dialogue between Buber and Karl Ludwig Schmidt in Stuttgart, Germany, in 1933. We might expect this dialogue to go badly, taking place as it did on the eve of Hitler's rise to power. But our attention should be drawn to this discussion, if only because of the quality of the two participants in this dialogue. Buber, we know. The Christian participant, Karl Ludwig Schmidt, was a New Testament scholar of international status, a prominent anti-Fascist and opponent of anti-Semitism,[73] who was forced to flee Germany shortly after Hitler became the German chancellor.[74] To his credit, Schmidt used the occasion of his dialogue with Buber to denounce German anti-Semitism, which he predicted would lead "directly to the de-Christianizing and the de-Churching of the German people."[75]

---

71. Buber, *I and Thou*, 21 (Smith, 11).

72. See the discussion in Kramer and Mechthild, *Martin Buber's I and Thou*, 42.

73. Paul R. Mendes-Flohr, *Divided Passions: Jewish Intellectuals and the Experience of Modernity* (Detroit: Wayne State University Press, 1991), 227.

74. Ekkehard W. Stegemann, "Martin Buber and Karl Ludwig Schmidt: A Jewish-Christian Dialogue on the Eve of the Shoah," *European Judaism: A Journal for the New Europe* 27.1 (1994): 11.

75. Maurice Friedman, *Martin Buber's Life and Work* (Detroit: Wayne State University Press, 1988), 179.

Sadly, Schmidt's contribution to the Schmidt-Buber dialogue is otherwise a disappointment. Schmidt opened the discussion by expressing his theological support for the mission to convert all Jews to Christianity, based on the church's exclusive claim to absolute truth. Schmidt did note that individual Christians could not be certain of their status within this absolute truth; for this reason, Schmidt stressed that Christians should live in a kind of fellowship with anyone who seeks G-d and G-d's revelation, especially the Jews. This was a brave statement for a German to make in early 1933. Yet Schmidt also stressed that the central question of this fellowship is whether Jesus is the Messiah;[76] as Jews rejected Jesus, it was G-d's will that Jerusalem be destroyed and that Christians replace Jews as "true Israel."[77]

Schmidt's position is reminiscent of that taken by church representatives during the medieval disputations, as subsequent scholars have pointed out.[78] How could Buber respond to Schmidt in an *I-You* kind of way? It would seem impossible. Buber declared after an earlier dialogue with a German Christian that "there is a boundary beyond which the possibility of encounter ceases and only the reporting of factual information remains. I cannot fight against an opponent who is thoroughly opposed to me, nor can I fight against an opponent who stands on a different plane than I." Still, Buber's reply to Schmidt was remarkable. He laid bare Schmidt's *I-It*, stating that the church's view of Jews as "an entity *rejected* by G[-]d" was grounded in Christian dogma and thus "unassailable." (Here, Buber sounds a bit like Rabbi Halevi at Tortosa.) Then Buber proceeds to a magnificently powerful demonstration of *I-You*:

> But we, as Israel, know Israel from within, in the darkness of knowledge from within, in the light of knowledge from within. We know Israel differently, we know ... that we who have sinned a thousandfold against G[-]d, who have apostatized from G[-]d a thousandfold ... we know that we are, nevertheless, not rejected. We know that this is an event which does not take place within the limited perspective of this world, but in the reality of the space between G[-]d and us. We know that there, within that reality, we are not rejected by G[-]d, that in this discipline and punishment, G[-]d's hand holds us and does not let us go, holds us within this fire and does not let us fall.[79]

76. Hans Joachim Schoeps, *The Jewish-Christian Argument: A History of Theologies in Conflict*, trans. David E. Green (New York: Holt, Rinehart and Winston, 1963), 147–48.

77. Stegemann, "Martin Buber and Karl Ludwig Schmidt," 6–8.

78. See Stegemann, "Martin Buber and Karl Ludwig Schmidt," 6n88 and the sources cited therein.

79. Schoeps, *The Jewish-Christian Argument*, 149.

Did Buber's response touch Schmidt? Schmidt told his audience that it did: "The depth of experience of a man living within the realm of Judaism by blood has been made clear to you."[80] Perhaps Schmidt *was* brought into *I-You*, for a moment. But evidently, it *was* only for a moment. Schmidt concluded his remarks with a chilling proclamation, made more ominous by our knowledge of the Shoah that was to follow:

> "Were the Church more Christian that it is, the conflict with Judaism would be sharper than it is now. From the very beginning of Christianity, this sharp conflict has existed. . . . We Christians must never tire of keeping this one conflict alive."[81]

Did I make a mistake, focusing here on ambitious conceptions of dialogue such as those of Cornille and Buber? Didn't Cornille warn me, with her title *The Im-Possibility of Interreligious Dialogue*, that her program for dialogue might indeed be impossible? If Buber himself struggled to achieve *I-You* in dialogue, what hope is there for me? Going back to the quote from Jeremy Cohen that begins this chapter . . . for some Christians, I *am* a "player on a theological stage set long before my arrival." How can I achieve *I-You*, if I'm expected to read lines someone else has written for me?

⚜

Where does this leave me, in my search for the right posture to take in Jewish-Christian dialogue? I'll return to where I started at the beginning of this chapter. Something like gravity drags me into the posture of Jewish victim, pushing Anthony into the reluctant posture of guilty perpetrator. In reality, Anthony and I are at worst distant relatives of victims and perpetrators; we don't belong in this posture. My search here for an alternative posture began with a sobering look at the history of Jewish-Christian relations. There are lessons to be learned from this history, one being that we don't have complete freedom (or should I say, power?) when it comes to posture. Choosing dialogue postures is in some sense a reciprocal exercise. If I choose the posture of victim, then Anthony's choice of a counter-posture is limited. If I speak to a Christian who sees me as a potential convert to Christianity, then my choices are limited as well.

---

80. Schoeps, *The Jewish-Christian Argument*, 150.
81. Quotation from Mendes-Flohr, *Divided Passions*, 227.

In a perfect world, I would strive for a dialogue posture of *I-You*. I think that in dialogue with Anthony, something like *I-You* is possible. But it's a tall order. *I-You* is not possible within the paradigm of perpetrator and victim, because *I* am not a victim and there is no *You* in my world that resembles a perpetrator. It seems embarrassingly fundamental to say this, but *I-You* dialogue is impossible unless we are committed to seeing ourselves and the other for who we really are.

If I had to name the single most pernicious threat to achieving *I-You* in Jewish-Christian dialogue, it is the persistence of Christian use of the "rhetorical Jew." At least when a Christian sees me as a potential convert, I *am* being seen—as an *It*, it is true, but at least I'm in the picture. But when Christians employ the "rhetorical Jew," I'm not being seen even as an *It*. The Jew in the "rhetorical Jew" exists for Christians in some shadowy way: lacking dimension, unable to speak or be heard, having no human character or content. Shadows lack posture. They mark a place where light doesn't reach.

When I call Christians on their use of "rhetorical Jews," I commonly hear in reply that these Christians "are not talking about Jews." In their mind, a modern Pharisee is a kind of bad Christian. If I've accomplished *anything* in this chapter, I hope it's clear that this kind of evasion doesn't work. It is anti-Jewish to use anti-Jewish slurs in any context, even if no Jew is present.

I have reached out to Christians who routinely use "rhetorical Jews" in their religious conversation, only to find that some Christians are more committed to their rhetoric than to fellowship. But not all Christians are like this. This leaves me in something of a posture conundrum, where I cannot find a single posture that works in all forms of Jewish-Christian encounter, and where I do not want to forge a different posture for each encounter. For me, a way out of the posture conundrum might be to adopt something like Martin Buber Lite. I'm not saintly enough to manage much of *I-You*, but I can come to dialogue first and foremost as myself. I may be the "Jew" in this book's title, but I'm only one Jew. In the unlikely event that there is such a thing as a typical Jew, I am not that Jew. Really, "Jewish-Christian dialogue" is a highfalutin term for what takes place between the covers of this book. Instead, what's happening here is an extended conversation between *a* Jew and *a* Christian. That's all it can ever be. Except . . .

Except there's a little matter of context. Step into a room as the Jewish representative in "dialogue," and watch yourself transform. You want to eviscerate thousands of years of stereotyping. You want to "represent." Careful now . . . or you'll end up unrecognizable, even by the modest standards of *I-It*.

Jalees Rehman, a Muslim active in interfaith dialogue, writes that when he speaks in terms of "as Muslims, we . . ." or "in Islam, it is important . . .," he is reluctantly speaking from Buber's *I-It*. Rehman worries that by so doing, he is failing to engage in authentic interfaith dialogue.[82] But just as I can't represent all Jews or Judaism, I can't entirely avoid the responsibility to represent responsibly. Anthony likes to tell me that many Christians have never met a Jew. If he's right, then there's the possibility I might be the only Jew some Christian ever meets. And what if I'm having a bad day that day? When asked why he always played baseball with such intensity, Joe DiMaggio replied, "There is always some kid who may be seeing me for the first or last time."[83] And I'm no more a DiMaggio than I am a Buber.

I'll return one last time to the legacy of the "rhetorical Jew." Amy-Jill Levine writes:

> At Vanderbilt I have been known to bring my son to my class. I introduce him to my students, and then I say: "When you speak of Jews [from the pulpit], picture this kid in the front pew. Don't say anything that will hurt this child, and don't say anything that will cause a member of your congregation to hurt this child." I grant that the move is theatrical and manipulative. It's also remarkably effective.[84]

The "theatrics" Levine describes are "remarkably effective" because, even if momentarily, they compel Christians to replace their imagined rhetorical Jews with real ones. I admit, I sometimes engage in similar theatrics. I have barged into Christian discussion of "rhetorical Jews" to proclaim that an actual Jew is in their midst. But my theatricality comes at a price: to strive toward a Jewish-Christian *I-You* relationship, we must emphasize authenticity, not theatricality. Granted, it *is* authentic for Jews to take a posture in dialogue that points out how we are authentically vulnerable. But dialogue provides the opportunity both to express this vulnerability and, in some sense, to escape from it to a place of relative safety and security. It also gives us the ability to see the vulnerability of our Christian dialogue partners.

An appreciation of our mutual vulnerability might serve as a starting point for a new kind of posture in Jewish-Christian dialogue. To repeat: whatever posture we might adopt in dialogue depends on our being seen for who we really are. There are no "rhetorical Jews" present for dialogue, and

---

82. Jalees Rehman, "Interfaith Moments," *Harvard Divinity Bulletin* 39.3, 4 (2011), http://bulletin.hds.harvard.edu/articles/summerautumn2011/interfaith-moments.

83. http://www.baseball-almanac.com/quotes/quodimg.shtml.

84. Levine, *The Misunderstood Jew*, 226.

the odds are stacked against there being any Christians bent on persecuting Jews. At the outset of Jewish-Christian dialogue, all you're likely to find are a bunch of nervous Jews and Christians, daunted perhaps by the history of Jewish-Christian recrimination. At this outset, we won't know each other well enough for anything like *I-You*—such knowledge may be the product of successful dialogue, but we can't base our initial postures on it. Instead, we might reach to a metaphor we've used with some success in this book, that dialogue is a kind of journey. We might take a posture toward each other as fellow travelers. Being different as Jews and Christians, we can nevertheless appreciate how our individual experience of dialogue is imperfectly reflected by what's being experienced by the relative strangers who have joined us on this journey. We are, in this sense, in it together.

Posture

Dialogue

Larry: I'll start with a simple question: Did you write the chapter that you were expecting to write when you suggested we write about posture?

Anthony: No, this chapter is much different from my first try. I wanted to talk about the difference between sitting down together versus taking a stand for something. I wanted to say that sitting together welcomes possibility, whereas standing up means you're advocating for a particular truth. This is the difference between what I think is an ideal posture in dialogue and how most Jews and Christians enter the room. The reason why my chapter evolved into something different was because I wanted to make sure I didn't frame this simplistically. I realized I couldn't say that "when you take a stand you're the problem, but if you're open-minded then you're part of the solution." What I ended up doing is finding a couple of examples, with Le Chambon and *han*, which allowed me to bring out cases where taking a stand was not just virtuous but necessary.

Larry: One thing you discussed that struck me was André Trocmé's most famous quotation, "I do not know what a Jew is. I know only human beings." When I read this quote, I felt grateful he saved so many Jewish lives, but I thought it would have been even better if he'd seen the people he saved as *Jewish* human beings. I like to be liked for what is particular about me.

Anthony: There's middle ground here. Trocmé valued all human life, and as an extension of this he could value Jewish life. For example, he ran schools where Jewish and Protestant kids were learning together, and he was adamant that he would not try to convert Jews attending his schools. Trocmé had experienced this same treatment as a youth—he was a Protestant, and his teacher was a French Catholic priest who was also firmly committed to not converting his Protestant students to Catholicism. When Trocmé began to ask his teacher about G-d, the priest would appear to Trocmé to be physically frustrated: he'd bite his knuckles or whatever, and he'd end up leaving the room! The priest feared that talking with Trocmé about G-d might result in his conversion to Catholicism. Trocmé adopted this concern when he became a teacher. So, clearly, Trocmé did see Jews as Jews, and he took on a special responsibility toward the Jews in his care. When it came to saving a person's life, however, he did so simply because the person was human.

Larry: I don't know much about Trocmé, but I imagine he was the kind of person who saw the humanity in just about everyone. But statements like Trocmé's will always make me pause.

Anthony: Trocmé's statement about not seeing a Jew but a human being could be seen as analogous to the idea I sometimes hear from white Americans that they don't see color or race. That creates problems for African-Americans, who can fairly say, "If you don't see black or white, you don't see me."

Larry: Exactly.

Anthony: Here's a story that might be apropos. I had lunch last week with an Italian friend, and if there are gradations of Italian, he's *really* Italian. By comparison, I'm mostly Californian.

Larry: Truth is, you're awfully Californian.

Anthony: [*Laughs*] Exactly! Anyway, I asked him, what do you write when you're asked to check a demographic profile on a government form? He told me that he clicks "Hispanic," because of the pattern of immigration his family took. I told him that I just click "Other." Neither one of us is comfortable clicking "White." I would imagine that lots of Italians feel the same way. The main reason is that "whiteness" is not our legacy. We don't want to claim that legacy; we've only been "White" for seventy years or whatever it has been. Yet it's important to realize that, outside of the company of Italians, for all intents and purposes we're white, and that's how people perceive us. But in our heart of hearts, when we're isolated and filling out these forms, we don't check that box.

Larry: Jews didn't used to be white, and now we're probably considered white, so what does that mean? We didn't change color. I'm laughing thinking about this, because I can imagine our parents and grandparents yearning for the day they could click the "White" box, and now you and I don't want to do it!

Anthony: [*Laughs*] That's interesting. Which box do you check? If there's a box that says "Jewish," I'm sure you check "Jewish." But there never is, right?

Larry: Well, there was. When my father's family emigrated from Germany in the 1930s, all the other Germans on the boat were shown as "German" on the U.S. immigration forms, and my father and his family were shown as "Hebrew." But I don't ever see an option like this, unless someone is specifically asking about religion. If they're asking about ethnicity, my choices are really "White" or "Other."

Anthony: And what do you choose?

Larry: [*Laughs*] I vary it. I'd like to check "Other," but it feels pretentious and dishonest, like I'm claiming the equivalent status of a Pacific Islander. "Other" means to me an ethnicity rare enough not to rate its own checkbox, but one we'd clearly think of as nonwhite. The world sees me as white, I have white privilege, who am I kidding?

Anthony: I know exactly what you're talking about, I know that feeling. But we should acknowledge that these forms are more difficult for some people than for others.

Larry: We need a box that says, "White but troubled by it." Or just, "It's complicated."

Anthony: This would make a great Key and Peele sketch.

Larry: If I don't have to check the box, often I'll skip it. And at a certain point, it starts to feel silly. Why don't I just say "White" and get it over with?

Anthony: Trevor Noah talks about growing up in South Africa, and never being black or white there. He was a hybrid, which is what they call "colored." But his whole life, he wanted to be black, and when he came to America, he got to fill out a bank form where he had to check a box. The woman at the counter told him, "You just choose the one you want." And he realized, for the first time in his life he could check the box that says, "Black." Then he realized, "If I can just check the box I want, I'm going to choose 'White.'"

Larry: [*Laughs*] Yes. I'll give you an example of the problem of box-checking in dialogue. I'm in conversation with a person I've met online who is affiliated with a Protestant evangelical college in the Midwest. This person feels a strong identity with this college, but she also identifies in some part with Catholicism. She's not a Catholic per se, but when she describes her Christian identity, Catholicism plays a big part. Now, this is great, of course! Except that Catholics can't teach at this Protestant college. This represents my experience in dialogue, in a nutshell. The Christians I talk to, almost always have checked boxes in addition to the Christian box. I do remember early in dialogue, thinking with some sense of frustration, "When am I ever going to get to talk to a typical Christian?"

Anthony: [*Laughs*]

Larry: I've kind of given up. If there are typical Christians out there, I'm convinced that part of what makes them typical is that they don't want to talk to me! Okay, I want to ask you about what you wrote in your chapter about the Korean notion of *han*. Does *han* help me understand my elusive typical Christian?

Anthony: I would say yes and no. This typical Christian you've never been able to find in North America . . .

Larry: . . . who probably does not exist . . .

Anthony: . . . this typical Christian has not experienced *han*.

Larry: And you have not experienced *han*.

Anthony: No, I haven't. My voice is a North American, Christian voice. That's the place where I communicate most often. And knowing that, I did make a conscious effort—and I think I've done this in other areas of my research—to put my voice in conversation with people from different geographies and socioeconomic backgrounds, and people with different racial, ethnic, and gender orientations and perspectives. Honestly, I think that this may help Jewish-Christian dialogue to be a bit more interesting; it will illustrate how very diverse global Christianity really is.

Larry: Yes, and I felt particularly grateful to have received that information. Are you trying to explain to me that American Christianity incorporates something like a *han* posture?

Anthony: No, not exactly. I wrote in my chapter that my understanding of *han* comes from the work of Andrew Park, and his work came out of his reading of a South American voice, really a Peruvian voice. These are examples of "liberation theology," and they express a Christian theology "from below." The expression "from below" is a historiographical term referring to the perspective of what I'm calling the majority world. Christian theology looks a lot different "from below" than it does from my vantage point. Liberation theology was adapted by James Hal Cone from and for an African-American perspective. So if you're asking whether *han* represents something about American Christianity, then this is absolutely true at my seminary. At my seminary, especially in the Doctor of Ministry program, my students are largely African-American. The Doctor of Ministry students I work with are specifically interested in African-American social justice in any number of areas. When we incorporate African-American and other diverse Christian voices into Jewish-Christian dialogue, then the dialogue takes a much different shape, and the victim-perpetrator posture we've both discussed is exposed as being *a* conversation point, but not the *only* posture available to Jews and Christians. It is only when the diversity of Christianity is recognized that we can shift these default postures.

Larry: One thing I noticed in your chapter is that you don't seem to think as much as much as I do about dialogue posture being mutually determined. Actually, you seem to think about this from a Jewish standpoint. You said that if Christians believe that Israel plays a role in the end of days, then you place certain expectations and limitations on any dialogue that follows. Perhaps you and I are both seeing something: that in Jewish-Christian dialogue, posture is initiated by the Christian. Do you agree?

Anthony: Say more about that.

Larry: Let's say I'm invited into Jewish-Christian dialogue with a group of Christians I don't know. Let's say that I don't know the group's denomination; all I know is that they are Christian. I'll sit down at the table with my notes and my cup of coffee and say, "I'm playing black in this chess game. First move is yours." Actually, chess is a pretty good analogy. The first move in a chess game is always made by the person playing the white pieces. White starts on the offensive. I think that Jews are playing black in this chess game. "What is your first move, Christian? I will adopt a posture accordingly." Which means, I guess, that my posture is defensive. I don't like this idea; I tried to come up with something else in my chapter. Rather than a defensive posture, I searched in my chapter for a reciprocal posture.

Anthony: Reciprocal is good, but you still need someone to make the first move. I don't know if we want to take the chess analogy too far; I'd like to think about dialogue differently than that. But as with anything that requires reciprocity, there is someone who takes the lead or makes the first move. And if I'm hearing you right, being the Jew in the room with Christians for the first time, you're kind of waiting to see what that first move is. Is that what you're saying?

Larry: I think so. I'm with you—I'm not comfortable with the chess analogy either, because chess has a winner and loser; it's kind of an idealized game of warfare. But to be honest about this, I don't want to come out of dialogue feeling defeated, and I do worry about that.

Anthony: You want to come out feeling like the winner.

Larry: No, I just don't want to feel defeated. I mean, what can I win? Friendship? Understanding? Knowledge?

Anthony: In all of those cases, you're sharing your victory with the person on the other side of the table.

Larry: You'd call that a win-win.

Anthony: You want a win-win in dialogue. You would lose if you walked away thinking, "I really won that argument." That would be a loss.

Larry: Right. I have no desire to convert the other.

Anthony: Okay, let me challenge you a bit on this . . . you used the phrase in your chapter, "eviscerate stereotypes." That's a scenario where you may want to win. If the Christian in the room believes you're trying to earn your way to heaven, and you can gently say that this isn't quite how Jews think about it, then you might have won an argument in a way, but it's different than defeating the other person. I think this is where posture helps us. You can win that argument in any number of ways. But you want to win in a way that reveals more of your own humanity to the other, and that allows you to discover your own humanity by being in conversation with someone who's equally human on the other side of the table.

Larry: Yes, but again, I don't know who I'm encountering until I encounter them. If it is just between two people, me and someone else, then if there's an argument, I don't care, I can lose the argument. But if there's a larger audience where it's between the "ism" I represent and the "ity" the other represents, then it gets uncomfortable. Because then, if I lose the argument, I feel like I'm letting people down. It's a problem; I think it's something I should let go, because I doubt anything I say has that kind of importance. But I do feel this way. It has something to do with what you said about standing and sitting postures.

Anthony: I recently met a Palestinian peace activist, and he says that dialogue is not the place where you agree; it's a safe place to disagree. It has to be more complicated than this, but there's some truth in this statement. By adopting a disarming posture, where both sides are comfortable sitting down and having coffee while you talk, that place might be a safer place to disagree, compared to two people in a formal debate in front of a thousand people and video cameras. There's something more at stake in the standing, debate context. That's not really a safe place to disagree, and I think part of what we want in dialogue is to create a safe place to disagree.

Larry: I agree with that . . . let's take an example that's as far from Jewish-Christian dialogue as possible. Let's imagine a Chinese-Tibetan dialogue about the future of Tibet and Tibetan independence. We want to make this a safe place for our dialogue participants, so they're both in seated postures. At the end, the Chinese dialogue partner says, "I guess we're going to have to agree to disagree." That's a very different agreement for the Chinese participant and the Tibetan participant. China can go back to oppressing Tibet, and Tibet goes back to being oppressed. I think the Tibetan participant might say, "I can't agree to disagree about this; that agreement does not reflect our relative positions here. You can afford to agree to disagree; this doesn't affect your homeland or your freedom. This doesn't impact anything that's nearly as important to you as it is to me."

Anthony: If the Chinese and Tibetan diplomats walk away agreeing to disagree, that's a win for the Chinese.

Larry: That's right.

Anthony: I readily acknowledge that this is a problem for this ideal posture I've constructed. However, I think creating a safe place to disagree is not the same thing as agreeing to disagree.

Larry: Yes. Arguably, in the example I posed, the space I imagined was unsafe for the Tibetan participant, not in the sense that she was going to face physical harm, but it was still unsafe, because agreeing to disagree is essentially agreeing to the status quo, and the status quo for the Tibetan is not safe. I agree that there are ideal qualities to that sitting posture you're talking about; but to get into that sitting posture, I think there has to be a stance behind it on both sides. Which is, "I will stand for your safety; I'll take a stance for your well-being."

Anthony: What you're saying may be overly idealized in the same way that my sitting-versus-standing metaphor is. Just being in the same room and sitting at the same table with an oppressive power is an accomplishment. There have been moments in history where people have fought and fought just to get a seat at the table.

Larry: Okay, let's try exploring this problem using a real-world example. I've taken a stance on my blog in favor of LGBTQ rights, and offline, outside of our conversations for this book, you've expressed some concern about this. I've found this confusing, because you feel just as strongly about this issue as I do.

Anthony: That's right, as far as the politics are concerned. We both feel strongly that LGBTQ rights are human rights, and this is the determinative factor for us. There may be some theological conversations worth having, but the human rights question is paramount.

Larry: Yet when I took this stance, it made you uncomfortable.

Anthony: Yes. But not for my sake. For your sake. Because you are committed to dialogue with Christians—and I know that this is something very important to you—my concern is that you are limiting several important political conversations with Christians, and I would like to see these conversations take place. But you are limiting these conversations by coming to the table as an advocate, rather than as a dialogue partner.

Larry: Is the problem being that I'm not going to end up talking to people I want to be talking to, because I'll drive them away?

Anthony: That's it. You have become vocal about LGBTQ rights, and this is a standing posture. Now, the Christians in the room may want to sit down and talk about this, and say, "Okay, I see you're taking a stand here. But sexuality is a lot more complicated, and it could be that your moral imperative is too simplistic." A statement like that can ring hollow, because it can sound like someone wants to have this nuanced conversation while there are people suffering. "Damn you and your roundtable discussion! Get up and take a stand, because we can't wait any longer for deliberation." I find myself torn. Even though I am staunchly committed to gay rights, I want to sit down with my brothers and sisters on the Christian side and have that conversation. But it's really difficult to have a conversation in public, because there's an accusation—and it may be justified—that there is no gray area on this topic to be discussed, that anything less than staunch advocacy is paramount to bigotry.

Larry: I'm glad you're bringing this up. I'm torn in way you described. When you and I sit down to Jewish-Christian dialogue, I'm hoping to be changed by it. I want to come to a better understanding of what's important to me. I look at the world and see that we need to be talking across differences. We've kind of lost the skill of being among people who are different from us and having civil relations with them. And then we come to something like the LGBTQ issue, where I don't know that I want to be changed. And that's an interesting question—why not? It may sound harsh to put it this way, but what if we're talking about my sitting down with a basic racist and having an open and honest conversation with them? That there's a small chance I'll come away thinking racism is not so bad? I can't do that.

Anthony: Let me say two things. One, I have friends I love deeply who are not advocates on either side of the LGBTQ debate; they feel internally conflicted, and they want to have a nuanced conversation about human sexuality, but they remain silent in public because they are afraid of both sides. They are afraid that they will be labeled as liberals by nationalist and politicized Christians, who are very loud and very destructive. But they're even more afraid of being called bigots.

Larry: Of course.

Anthony: That's not something you walk away from. Once you get that label, that's it! Bigots have no place in civilized discourse. So these people have chosen to remain silent, because they are equally—if not more—afraid of liberal advocates. The second thing I want to say is something very personal. When you say you're not interested in having your mind changed on the topic of racism, I feel just as strongly on the issue of pacifism. I don't mind having conversations about it, but I just can't imagine a world where I will come around to believe that nuclear proliferation or preemptive strikes are going to make sense in any context.

Larry: I'm not sure why you are bringing up pacifism in this context.

Anthony: I think that we have something in common in the way you deal with LGBTQ issues and I deal with pacifism, in that we are both uncomfortable discussing these issues from a "seated position."

Larry: When we discuss pacifism . . .

Anthony: It's a stance issue for me, right?

Larry: It's a stance issue for you. And I hate to say this, but you can be kind of violent in your defense of pacifism.

Anthony: [*Laughs*] I've never resorted to physical violence.

Larry: No, you never gone after anyone with a cudgel. Verbally, you've been aggressive. But you're right, this is a stance for you, and there have been times when this has caught me by surprise. I know a little better now, that this is an area of sensitivity.

Anthony: And I do too, by the way. I know this about myself a little better now. These discussions tend to follow a pattern. I will bring up the topic, and somewhere along the line I get offended.

Larry: [*Laughs*]

Anthony: This is just how it has gone. I'll get offended and suddenly I'll find myself outside of my normal, pleasant sitting posture, taking a stand about something I have some kind of emotional energy attached to.

Larry: Yes. When you've taken a stand on pacifism, sometimes it's a dialogue killer. "I can't talk to Anthony about this." Other times, I think we've had good conversations around the topic of pacifism. So yes, I've experienced the sitting-versus-standing Anthony. In a holistic way, I'm glad that both of those sides of you exist. A 100-percent-sitting Anthony would be not as interesting. But yeah, the sitting Anthony is a lot easier to talk to. Is that the point you're making?

Anthony: Here's the point I'm making: When you say you can't imagine sitting down with a racist and keeping an open mind, I understand that. That's kind of how I feel when I talk about pacifism. I don't think I knew this about myself until we ended up having those conversations. Actually, to be honest, I think that our conversation was like the third or fourth conversation I had about this topic since I moved to the Midwest. This came up a few different times, and you were someone I felt comfortable enough with to actually speak my mind fully. You probably heard the brunt of my frustration that had been building over a number of different conversations.

Larry: And in retrospect, I'm glad I got that. Maybe at the time, it wasn't so pleasant.

Anthony: So when you say that you're not interested in sitting down with someone who has a different perspective about racism or heteronormativity . . .

Larry: I'm interested in sitting down with that person, but not to change my mind.

Anthony: What you're describing is sitting down, but with an internal posture where you're taking a stand. That's what I'm trying to communicate. That's probably what happened when we had our heated discussions on pacifism. This is related to a really great article that Rowan Williams wrote about ten years ago when he was the archbishop of Canterbury. He was asked to talk about the division in the church over the LGBTQ issue. But he threw a curve ball. He said—and I'm paraphrasing here—he something like: *I can't imagine how any Christian could take the view that nuclear weapons are a good idea. How can you sit down and worship next to that person who has a different view on this, and call them your brother and sister in Christ, and find a certain amount of Christian unity with that person? That issue is almost unfathomable to me, but you've been able to do that. Christians have been able to decide to agree to disagree on nuclear warfare. If you're able to do* *that, you should be able to have some sort of Christian unity amidst a nuanced conversation about human sexuality.* I thought that was a very interesting approach to the topic.

Larry: Let me throw one other thing into the mix—not that this conversation isn't complicated enough, because I'm more willing to sit down in conversation with an anti-Semite that I am with a homophobe.

Anthony: [*Laughs*] Maybe you haven't met enough real anti-Semites in your life!

Larry: It's possible, but I'll make this statement in any event. And why is that? I'll draw an analogy. It's not like a lot of people approach me and say, "I hate Jews, want to dialogue?" But here's a conversation I have a lot. I'll find myself in the conversation with a Christian who's talking a lot about Jesus, and who will even express the hope that I'll find a belief in Jesus.

Anthony: That shouldn't be uncommon among Christians, I would imagine.

Larry: No, it's quite common, but what do I do with that? I'm not threatened by people who have that hope for me, but how do I respond? If I respond by expressing my admiration for Christianity and Jesus, I worry that I'm leading these people on.

Anthony: Are you saying this to yourself?

Larry: Yes. I tried something in a recent conversation. I said, "I need to be honest about this. I'm not saying that you're hoping to convert me, I'm not trying to look inside your heart, but I feel the need to tell you, I am committed to Judaism. This is who I am going to remain. I'm never going to have the belief in Jesus that you might hope for me. I love being in conversation with you, but I don't want to lead you on. I don't want you continuing this conversation with a false hope." This is the first time I've tried to say that.

Anthony: Can I make a parenthetical comment?

Larry: Sure.

Anthony: It occurs to me that maybe lots of American Jews don't know this about Christians: Very few of us feel comfortable with proselytization.

A lot of Christians look at it like an unpleasant obligation, like taking your medicine, but they feel commanded to do it. I will say this: There are folks who are gung ho for this, who get a thrill out of knocking on doors. But most of us have a very awkward relationship with this doctrine. I guess that maybe your friend is one of these people.

Larry: Jews definitely need to hear this. But I think it worked well to tell my dialogue partner that I'm not a candidate for conversion. She responded, "I'm glad you told me this. I want to tell you in the same spirit of honesty, I'm never going to stop hoping that you accept Jesus Christ as your personal savior."

Anthony: And how did you take that?

Larry: I took it positively. I'd told her who I am. And we've proceeded in conversation nicely since then, and she continues to tell me her hope for me.

Anthony: Don't you feel like, eventually, this will wear thin?

Larry: It might.

Anthony: That hope is a posture; it's a very common Christian posture, to have a hope that someone else will be transformed. I don't know if that's standing or sitting, I'm not sure.

Larry: I'm not sure either. It may be that she will lose interest in our conversation as it becomes more and more apparent to her that . . .

Anthony: Or, it may be that Larry Behrendt can only hear this hope expressed so many times before it starts to be off-putting.

Larry: Yes. That's possible, too. My point is, it's a different question of standing and sitting when you're standing and sitting for someone else. I'm not personally same-sex oriented; I don't personally identify as LGBTQ.

Anthony: So this is why you'd be more willing to have a conversation with an anti-Semite than someone who's pushing heteronormativity with a theological agenda?

Larry: Yes. My status as an ally for a different group is different from my status within a group. Nobody can take my Jewishness away from me. People may question how good a Jew I am, but I'm Jewish. My status as an ally depends in a certain sense on acceptance by a group to which I don't belong. So I need to worry a little bit. My willingness to sit down with a reasonable conservative on this issue—how will that be perceived by the group I'm allied with? Now, what I found is, my friends who are gays and lesbians tell me, "Go for it! Teach them something. We need people like you talking to people like that." But it's almost like I need permission. Some things sound better when they're said by an insider. This goes to what you're talking about. You can have the same kind of a conversation with me about pacifism as I can have with my friend about Jesus. Right?

Anthony: Right.

Larry: The chances are very small, practically zero, that during our conversation about pacifism, I'm going to talk you into buying an assault weapon. Right? That isn't going to happen.

Anthony: [*Laughs*] Right.

Larry: By talking to me, are you going to threaten your membership in the pacifist club? No! Talking with me about pacifism is a lot like my conversations with some of my Muslim friends about the State of Israel. There are certain convictions that are difficult to talk about with people who don't share some fundamental ground with you. Now if I were a pacifist, but a different kind of pacifist than you are, and I imagine there are different ways to be a pacifist, then it probably would be easier to have a conversation with me. But if I come to the table and say, "Look, I want to talk about pacifism, and the first topic I want to bring up is Auschwitz. And as far as I'm concerned, there's no level of weaponry I wouldn't be willing to use to liberate people from Auschwitz." What in the world are you supposed to say in response?

Anthony: I think that's right; this is important to nuance. I wouldn't call myself a radical or absolute pacifist. That's actually what got us into this question—me expressing some worry about this, because my pacifism was a conviction that limited me in my conversation about the State of Israel and the Shoah.

Larry: You are right.

Anthony: This really is a posture question. Because it depends on how you bring up a conversation. If you bring up the conversation by saying, "I hear you are a pacifist; what do you think about Auschwitz?" That way of framing the conversation immediately puts me on the defensive. I think, "How does either of us win in this conversation?"

Larry: It's lose-lose.

Anthony: It seems like a lose-lose proposition for me. So, yeah, you are right—there are certain topics that require a sitting position, and it may ultimately turn into two parties in a stance posture. But you don't want to limit the possibility of the conversation at the very beginning.

※

Anthony: In your chapter, you bring up the story from Dr. Jeremy Cohen, who taught a course on Judaism at a Christian seminary. He is happy to teach the course; he feels gratified by his contact with his students. But in his contact with other faculty members, he can't help feeling that he's being forced into a particular narrative. It's not a narrative of his choosing. It's some sort of mythological position, a certain cosmic street cred that Jews have among Christians. Sometimes this plays out in terms of Israel's role in the coming apocalypse. Sometimes it just comes out like you mentioned: you feel like you're in someone else's play, in the role of a people from the past, expected to act the part of . . .

Larry: Bible characters.

Anthony: Yes, right! Christians have a certain inclination to see Jews in this light. If that's the sense you get when you walk in the room, that limits the postures you can take. This is a point you made really well in your chapter. In my chapter, I'm talking about the problem of viewing Jews in one of two ways. The more positive way is a people especially close to G-d; so if I'm closer to the Jews, then I'm closer to G-d. That's actually dehumanizing, and it tends to be punctuated by the negative view, where Jews are demonized. Christians have a long history of doing one or the other.

Larry: But isn't there an easy way out of this? Haven't we learned by now to sidestep cultural stereotypes? I think we must be talking about something more than that here.

Anthony: We are certainly talking about something more than that. Because, it comes down to religion, it comes down to one's perceived place in the world, how one is reconciled with one's Creator. We are talking about things that are sacred, and my guess is that there are a lot more Christians than Jews in the world who look around them and see the supernatural.

Larry: This sounds like the worldview I hear on Christian radio.

Anthony: Right.

Larry: "G-d called me to be a vice principal." People really believe that the things in their lives that have worked out well for them—this wasn't simply a matter of G-d's general blessing, but G-d intervened specifically.

Anthony: Oh yes. And anything bad that happened is G-d closing a door, because G-d had something better in mind. This is what I'm talking about; this is the default position for many Christians. I am not a Deist; I want to believe that G-d acts in human history. But if my kid falls off the roof, I call 9-1-1 before I start praying. In other words, I am far more used to G-d's silence than anything else. But I have many Christian friends who attribute every twist and turn of the day to G-d's will.

Larry: There's something in that position of those Christian friends of yours that's going to make me feel shut out.

Anthony: Many other Christians feel the same way you do.

Larry: I'm sure of that also. But I guess maybe I don't hear those other Christians as sharply or pointedly as I might like. When I hear someone on Christian radio talk about how G-d directed him to answer a help-wanted ad because it is his calling in life, fine; but then he needs to consider some other people's stories. Such as, six million Jews were wiped out for no discernible reason. Christians who see the hand of G-d in ordinary events need to ask how G-d does not appear to be working consistently the way they find G-d working in their own lives.

Anthony: Two reactions. My own reaction is, there is a reason I don't want to believe that G-d opened a particular door so that your kid could go to private school. I just don't want to believe that G-d would do that—that G-d answered your self-involved, petty prayer—when G-d was ignoring the prayers of the Jews in Auschwitz. I acknowledge that there could be a G-d who would do this; I just don't *like* that G-d. But when I've said that to some of my Christian friends, and some of these folks are very intelligent, they'll say, "Yeah! G-d is mysterious, G-d is not consistent, and it doesn't matter whether you like the way G-d is or not." So, two responses, and I don't think either one of them is meant to be comforting. These are both troubling perspectives.

Larry: I'm not so much trying to make a theological point. I'm trying to say that I disappear in this particular worldview. I don't exist in it. Because the narrative is *not* consistently stated that sometimes G-d listens and sometimes G-d doesn't listen. This particular narrative seems to go that G-d is always there for some of us. It may come up as a secondary narrative, if it's pushed, that G-d is mysterious and inconsistent from our point of view, and that it's only sometimes that we're blessed to have G-d listen. But I don't hear that consistently as the main narrative, and since I don't, I feel like I'm being wiped from the main narrative. I'm not being seen. And this ties into the dualism we've talked about, the dualism where the Jews are either G-d's chosen or G-d's damned. Believe me, I'd rather be classified with G-d's chosen! But again, this narrative was written before I ever got here. It's not simply a matter of a distorted posture. It's that I don't have to be here for the narrative to go forward. I'm not needed. You don't need any actual Jews to put Judaism on one side or the other of this dualistic worldview.

Anthony: Let's make a distinction here. So, you're not being seen. Is it Jews *like you* who are not being seen, or real Jews at all?

Larry: Real Jews are not being seen.

Anthony: Then I have a question, and maybe a challenge. Are there Jews who would point to the Shoah and say that it was necessary in order to make the State of Israel possible?

Larry: There are Jews who say that the Shoah led to the formation of the State of Israel as a historical matter. That one thing led to the other, yes. But that this was G-d's plan, in the sense of a means to an end? I've read that there are Jews who see the Shoah as part of G-d's plan for Jewish redemption, but I don't know Jews who think like that. There are Jews who would say that we just cannot understand the ways of G-d. I mean, I think this is the mainstream Jewish response. If you believe in an almighty, perfect, just and loving G-d, then you have to say that we just don't understand how the Shoah could happen, and leave it there. For many other Jews, the Shoah is proof that G-d does not exist, and I respect that argument.

Anthony: That's a prominent thread of Holocaust theology. It's not the only thread. It's a completely understandable thread.

Larry: Right. I've come to a different conclusion, but it's not one that disproves the atheist argument. I see the arguments, and I have to live with a "this, and this," where I think G-d exists, and I think any effort to explain how G-d and Auschwitz exist in the same universe is hopeless.

Anthony: This is actually an interesting posture discussion. When you're talking about "this, and this," so you're holding two possibilities simultaneously in each hand, you might be more inclined to one possibility over the other, but that makes you a good conversation partner. This is a well-known rabbinic posture: *Let's explore different possibilities and see where the conversation goes.* I see this posture as almost essential for good dialogue. For me, this rabbinic posture is fundamentally different from the posture, "This is true, and I know this is true, so I'm here to convince you." For me, this posture of trying to convince the other is the posture of standing. And I think, in general, the rabbis I meet take a dialogical posture, and the preachers I meet tend to take a standing or sermonizing posture.

Larry: My experience is that Jews kind of revel in contradiction. I think there's something more going on than we're dealing with two possibilities that should both be explored, to see what happens. Somehow, there's the idea that the best point of view embraces two things at once that can't both be true. Or that, when you settle in an area where contradictions exist, you are closer to the truth than you are when there's only one obvious possibility. This has always been an area of Jewish philosophy I've wanted to explore. I roughly understand this in terms of "dialectics." Maybe it's just that I feel more comfortable thinking that the truth is ever bigger and more complicated. There's a show on Christian radio I sometimes hear called *The Narrow Path*. My reaction to this title is, "Yuck. How terrible!"

Anthony: [*Laughs*]

Larry: Who wants to be on a narrow path?

Anthony: But many Christians would say, "It has nothing to do with what I want!"

Larry: [*Laughs*]

Anthony: I don't choose the truth. The truth is just out there. Either I align myself with it, or I don't. That's the idea here.

Larry: It makes me feel uncomfortable. I like broader highways.

Anthony: I would like to point out two things. First of all, for some reason, we haven't been able to make liberal Christian radio work.

Larry: [*Laughs*] You are not broadcasting with many watts.

Anthony: I'm sure you can find some satellite radio station, but I haven't found it yet. Second, this is similar to what a rabbi I met in Israel said a few months ago: *A falsehood is only a partial truth masquerading as a comprehensive truth.* This is a great way to illustrate the Jewish dialectical, dialogical posture. And it's something a lot of Christians don't understand in terms of capturing something that is true about G-d and how should I live. I always get a particular question from my students in the middle of a class. So we'll be discussing something, and the conversation will be getting really interesting and complicated, and there's good back-and-forth, and one student will inevitably ask, "Yes, but how does this preach?"

Larry: How does this preach? I have never heard that question before.

Anthony: Oh, yes. This is common. What's behind the question is, "I need you to tell me what is true in a few sentences if I'm going to put this in a sermon." Because the purpose of the sermon is to communicate in a way that is unambiguous and inspiring. This tends to work sometimes, if there is a clear moral obligation. Example: "We cannot wait for white America to get on board with this; we are going to do it with or without you." There's a reason why Martin Luther King was a preacher, and why he used preaching. It was a way to communicate an actual cosmic truth: that G-d was actually on his side. Boy oh boy, does that work! *How does this preach?* There should be equality for all, that's the bottom line. But when we're wrestling with a question like theodicy (why does G-d allow evil and suffering?), where I think there is value in having a theological discussion even if there's no sermonic bottom line . . . when I feel that way, and someone asks me, "How does this preach?," I feel like they're trying to short-cut the conversation. They want something to preach from the pulpit, rather than what I think is the better academic position: to sit around the table and see where the conversation goes. For me that's the posture of sitting versus standing.

Larry: I think that's a great illustration of sitting versus standing. When you talk about, "How does this preach?," I think in more secular terms, "Will this be on the exam?" That's the question that kills every conversation in a secular classroom, right?

Anthony: Right. Or the question is, how do we reduce this to a sound bite, like a political stump speech? It's ten words or less that's going to be in the sound bite, and you have to figure out how to take this complicated economic policy and boil it down to ten words. It is so infuriating!

Larry: I don't want to overgeneralize, but I find that sometimes in my religious conversations with Christians, the assumption is that the answers to big questions are simple ones. And I respond, "No, they aren't!" These are the most complicated questions and answers that human beings can consider. When we're talking about G-d, there's nothing more complicated, there's nothing harder to understand.

Anthony: Let me end this discussion with one last question about Jewish identity, going back to our discussion of *han*. How do you feel about the association between *han* and the Jewish experience of suffering, in that there might be both constructive and destructive ways to express that experience?

Larry: That's something I thought about when I read your chapter. I thought of the Jewish experience of the Shoah, and that not every conceivable reaction to that experience is going to be positive merely because it is a reaction to oppression. When I read your chapter, I thought about the modern State of Israel. I wonder if in Israel we're laboring under something like a post-traumatic reaction to the Shoah and everything that came before it. Much of Israeli policy seems to be based on how we've suffered historically, so now we're justified in acting first and foremost to prevent any further injury. So, to answer your question, yes. You wrote about the historical experience of *han*, where an oppressed people later rises to a position of power, and they become the oppressor. And I thought, we Jews now have power in Israel.

We have the power to oppress. So while this isn't the time or place to express my misgivings about Israeli policy toward the Palestinians, there is at least the potential that we Jews will manifest our *han*-like experience in destructive ways.

Anthony: We might share something in common on this. This is not a new experience for Christians, to be disappointed with the way other Christians act. This is part of the marriage of religion and politics.

Conclusions

The Sacred Nature of Interfaith Dialogue

Larry Behrendt

O mankind! Truly We created you from a male and a female, and We made you peoples and tribes that you may come to know one another. Surely the most noble of you before G[-]d are the most reverent of you. Truly G[-]d is Knowing, Aware.

—*The Quran, al-Hujurat, 49:13*[1]

Two qualities mentioned in the title of this book might have caught your attention from the outset: *sacred* and *dissonance*. From my arguments with Anthony, you've probably figured out how we came up with "dissonance." But "sacred"? I admit it: inclusion of "sacred" in this book's title was my idea. I chose the word *sacred* to indicate a value I see in dialogue that I don't think is widely recognized. Whatever it is I look for in religion, whether it's enlightenment, or a sense of awe and wonder, or inner peace, or a proper standing with G-d, or a sense of belonging . . . I find these things in interfaith dialogue.[2]

---

1. Translation from Nasr, Seyyed Hossein, ed., *The Study Quran* (New York: HarperOne, 2015), 1262.

2. Some object to use of the term "interfaith dialogue" to describe Jewish-Christian dialogue. The objection goes to the question of "faith." Christian identity is primarily a question of faith: faith (for example) in the existence of a Trinitarian G-d and in the saving power of belief in Christ. But a person can self-identify as a Jew, and be recognized as a Jew by other Jews, in the absence of any "faith" or conventional belief. As we've discussed in this book, a person can be Jewish and also agnostic or atheist. This argument against use of "interfaith" for Jewish-Christian dialogue is ably set forth by Amy-Jill Levine ("Jesus in Jewish-Christian Dialogue," in *Soundings in the Religion of Jesus: Perspectives and Methods in Jewish and Christian Scholarship* [Minneapolis: Fortress Press, 2012], 185). But I am not persuaded by this argument, as I think any form of Jewish identity is based on some kind of

It's frustrating, then, that I've never been able to communicate this finding to anyone's satisfaction: not to my rabbis, or my other teachers, not even to Anthony. Not even my friends and family understand. Mostly, they treat my interest in dialogue with Christians as a harmless obsession, the way you'd regard the activities of an eccentric uncle who nails old license plates to his garage wall. I've been asked, now that I have devoted years to the study of Christianity, isn't it time to concentrate on something else, like the exclusive study of my own religion? One close relative worried that my interest in dialogue would lead me to convert to Christianity and abandon Judaism altogether. I typically respond with some weak justification of my love for this dialogue, figuring that perhaps the quality I find in dialogue can be experienced but never explained. But even here, I see a problem: many of the Jews I know who engage in interfaith dialogue don't seem to find the value in it that I do. Some regard dialogue as a job they have to do—a chore, not a joy.

So, to those who wonder why I do what I do, here is my explanation: I see a sacred quality in Jewish-Christian dialogue. I understand that this quality is not readily apparent. I understand that I face an uphill battle, trying to get others to see what I'm seeing. As my usual efforts to explain sacred dialogue have failed, I'll try here an unusual explanation, starting from an unusual place: the 1961 dialogue between the American Jewish theologian Richard Rubenstein and the German Protestant theologian Heinrich Grüber.

I warn you that there's nothing pretty in the dialogue I'm about to describe. At the center of this dialogue is the Holocaust, the Nazi mass murder of six million Jews and five million others in the machinery built by the Nazis for that very purpose. The dialogue took place in the center of Berlin, the city where the Holocaust was planned and administered. As the dialogue took place, the Berlin Wall was being constructed, making Berlin the center of a Cold War that threatened the annihilation of humanity. The dialogue was conducted in this "ground zero" by a pair of relative outcasts. Grüber had been rejected by some in Germany for his pacifism and his view that the

---

faith. For example: I believe I was "born Jewish" because my mother was Jewish, and her mother was Jewish, and so forth, extending down a long matrilineal line of descent. But as I cannot possibly verify the Jewishness of every female ancestor in my family tree, my belief in my Jewish ancestry is a matter of faith. More than this, I participate in Jewish life and Jewish-Christian dialogue based on a faith that my Jewish identity is really "there" and counts for something. The "faith" I bring to dialogue may be qualitatively different from that of my Christian dialogue partners, but it is "faith" nevertheless.

Germans bore collective responsibility for mass murder.[3] Rubenstein was about to be rejected by many Jews for the theology that emerged from his conversation with Grüber.[4] Both Rubenstein and Grüber would espouse a view of G-d that many (perhaps most) would find abhorrent and sacrilegious.

It is in this very unlikely place where I propose to locate and describe the sacred quality of Jewish-Christian dialogue. I'm doing so in part because the Rubenstein-Grüber dialogue *is* unpleasant and disturbing. Throughout this book, Anthony and I have made fun of what we've called "Kumbaya" dialogue, when different peoples join hands around an imagined campfire and, gently swaying, sing that we're all essentially the same. There's nothing wrong with these moments, and they may indeed be sacred moments, but it's *too easy* to see the sacred in the sweet haze that accompanies these moments. To keep our heads out of the clouds, I've chosen a dialogue that's far from "Kumbaya."

Before describing the dialogue, let's look at the two participants in this dialogue. Rubenstein first. Rubenstein is best known today for his contribution to theology of the Shoah, but back in the 1960s he was thought of as a Jewish voice for "death of G-d" theology. Indeed, this is how Rubenstein once saw himself. By "death of G-d," Rubenstein was not referring to something that had actually happened to G-d; he didn't think that G-d had succumbed to a disease or been fatally injured by a rampaging asteroid. Rather, the "death" Rubenstein spoke of was one he thought had taken place within humanity.[5] In the aftermath of the Shoah, Rubenstein found it impossible for humanity to believe in the G-d traditionally invoked by both Judaism and Christianity, a G-d who chose the Jewish people as a holy nation. The G-d who remained for Rubenstein might be characterized by "immanence." G-d might be present with us and within us, and care about us, but G-d for Rubenstein could no

---

3. Baruch Tenembaum, "Due Disobedience," The International Raoul Wallenberg Foundation, May 2, 2002, www.raoulwallenberg.net/saviors/others/due -disobedience/. In his testimony at the Eichmann trial, Grüber reported that he received hate mail and threats from his fellow Germans, both because of his willingness to testify against Eichmann and for the work he performed to help German Jews. "Eichmann Trial," Steven Spielberg Film and Video Archive, https://www .ushmm.org/online/film/display/detail.php?file_num=2155.

4. I address this more fully later in this chapter.

5. Richard L. Rubenstein, *After Auschwitz: History, Theology and Contemporary Judaism*, 2nd ed. (Baltimore and London: The Johns Hopkins University Press, 1992), xii. *After Auschwitz* changed considerably between its first and second editions. Elsewhere in this book, Anthony cites the first edition of *After Auschwitz*.

longer be "transcendent"—a G-d in control of human and worldly events.[6]
Rubenstein expressed the problem in characteristically blunt language:[7]

> If I truly believed in G[-]d as the omnipotent author of the historical drama and in Israel as His Chosen People, I [would have] no choice but to accept Dean Grüber's conclusion that Hitler unwittingly acted as G[-]d's agent in committing six million Jews to slaughter. I could not believe in such a G[-]d, nor could I believe in Israel as the Chosen People of G[-]d after Auschwitz.

In 1961 Rubenstein was invited by the West German government to visit prominent German Christians, and for Rubenstein the most important of these Germans was Dean Heinrich Grüber. Almost from the beginning of Nazi rule in Germany, Grüber had been a determined opponent of Hitler. His "Büro Grüber" tirelessly negotiated with Nazi authorities for the emigration of Jews from Germany. He was arrested in 1940 and sent to the Sachsenhausen and Dachau concentration camps, where he was brutalized and nearly murdered. After the war Grüber became dean of St. Mary's Church in Berlin, and he worked to better the lives of those few Jews who then remained in Germany. He was the only German witness against Adolf Eichmann at his trial in Jerusalem.[8] Before Grüber died, he received one of the highest honors in the Jewish world—he was named as Righteous Among the Nations by the Yad Vashem Shoah museum.[9] The Jewish people have rarely had a friend the likes of Heinrich Grüber.[10]

---

6. Rubenstein, *After Auschwitz*, xiii. In his autobiography, Rubenstein emphasized that he was not an atheist. He wrote that "we live in the time of the death of G[-]d," in that "radical cognition of G[-]d's absence as a cultural fact offers the only basis for theological speculation in our time." In other words, "death of G-d" is an expression referring not to the state of G-d, but to our own state; it represents a "collapse of faith." Richard L. Rubenstein, *Power Struggle: An Autobiographical Confession* (New York: Charles Scribner's Sons, 1974), 2–3, 8–9, 10.

7. Rubenstein, *After Auschwitz*, 3.

8. "Eichmann Trial - Session 42," United States Holocaust Memorial Museum, https://collections.ushmm.org/search/catalog/irn1001575; "German Church Leader Testifies Against Eichmann at Jerusalem Trial," Jewish Telegraphic Agency, May 17, 1961, www.jta.org/1961/05/17/archive/german-church-leader-testifies-against-eichmann-at-jerusalem-trial; Tenembaum, "Due Disobedience"; Rubenstein, *After Auschwitz*, 4–5.

9. "The Righteous Among the Nations," Yad Vashem, db.yadvashem.org/righteous/family.html?language=en&itemId=4043003.

10. At the Eichmann trial, Grüber described the Jews as his friends. "We trembled with our Jewish friends the night before every Jewish holiday," he testified.

Grüber and Rubenstein sat down for their 1961 conversation in the study of Grüber's West Berlin home. Afterwards and throughout his career, Rubenstein referred to this conversation as "unforgettable," "the most important theological conversation of my entire career," and "the basis of much of my theological writings."[11] But the conversation as reported by Rubenstein did not go as he might have expected.[12] After discussing the Eichmann trial and global responsibility for the Shoah, Grüber proclaimed that many Jews then living in Germany were "engaged only in making money," and were reinforcing German anti-Semitic attitudes. When Rubenstein questioned why Grüber should care so much about the behavior of a handful of Jews, Grüber responded that Jews are the chosen people of G-d and should behave in ways consistent with this Divine responsibility. "G[-]d says this in the Bible and I believe it!" he proclaimed.[13]

The question of the chosen-ness of the Jewish people was and is a problem for Rubenstein. Indeed, the problem of G-d's election has been a long-standing source of discomfort for Jewish sages of all kinds. Without knowing Rubenstein, comedian Jon Stewart encapsulated the problem beautifully, as part of his "Timeline of Democracy." Stewart's timeline includes this seminal event, circa 1300 BCE:[14]

> G[-]d gives Ten Commandments to Israelites, making them His Chosen People and granting them eternal protection under Divine Law. Nothing bad ever happens to Jews again.

Obviously, Stewart's tongue here is thoroughly in cheek. He's got in mind (as did Rubenstein) the rough road our people have traveled, from exile and through repeated persecution. As I've tried to stress throughout this book, there has been both joy and sorrow throughout this journey. We are quick to give G-d credit for the joy. But if G-d is a G-d of history, if

---

"I don't want to talk about my sufferings, but about the sufferings of my Jewish friends." "German Church Leader Testifies Against Eichmann at Jerusalem Trial."

11. Richard L. Rubenstein, "Berlin, August 13, 1961," *New English Review* (2011), http://www.newenglishreview.org/custpage.cfm/frm/95462/sec_id/95462.

12. Grüber later denied that he'd said what Rubenstein reported he'd said (*After Auschwitz*, 4). My description of the Grüber-Rubenstein conversation is the one reported by Rubenstein. To my knowledge, Grüber never published his own version of this conversation.

13. Rubenstein, *After Auschwitz*, 6–8.

14. Jon Stewart, *The Daily Show with Jon Stewart Presents America (The Book): A Citizen's Guide to Democracy Inaction* (New York: Grand Central Publishing, 2004), 4.

"He's Got the Whole World in His Hands," then isn't G-d responsible for the whole kit and caboodle, the good and the bad, both the elevation of Israel and everything the Jewish people have ever suffered? Rubenstein had raised this question in prior conversations with German Christians, and in each case those Germans had insisted that despite G-d's transcendence, G-d was not responsible for the Shoah.

So Rubenstein asked Grüber, "Was it G[-]d's will that Hitler destroyed the Jews?" Grüber responded with a passage from the Bible: "Um deine Willen warden wir getötet den ganzen Tag" ("For Thy sake are we slaughtered every day").[15] He went on:

> When G[-]d desires my death, I give it to him! When I started my work against the Nazis I knew that I would be killed or go to the concentration camp. Eichmann asked me "Why do you help these Jews? They will not thank you." I had my family; there were my wife and three children. Yet I said, "Your will be done even if You ask my death." For some reason, it was part of G[-]d's plan that the Jews died. G[-]d demands our death daily. He is the L[-]rd, He is the Master; all is in His keeping and ordering.[16]

Rubenstein responded that he'd choose atheism over belief in such a G-d.[17] But Grüber continued to press his idea of Divine punishment. "At different times," Grüber told Rubenstein, "G[-]d uses different peoples as His whip against His own people, the Jews, but those whom He uses will be punished far worse than the people of the L[-]rd." Grüber pointed to all the ways the Germans had suffered under and after Hitler; their military defeat, the destruction of their cities by the Allies, and (in 1961) the construction of the Berlin Wall. "We are now in the same situation as the Jews," Grüber told Rubenstein. "I felt a chill at that instant," Rubenstein later wrote.[18]

Grüber's reasoning may seem monstrous to us, but in no sense was he trying to excuse what the Nazis had done. He regarded the Nazis as thoroughly immoral, and believed that the Germans deserved their Divine punishment. And even if we disagree with Grüber (as I strongly do), his viewpoint is not without biblical roots. Nebuchadnezzar, the Babylonian king who destroyed Jerusalem in the sixth century BCE, is described in the

---

15. Rubenstein ascribed this quote to Psalm 44:22. See Rubenstein, *After Auschwitz*, 9. But it is also found at Romans 8:36.

16. Rubenstein, *After Auschwitz*, 9. Grüber was not alone in this belief; there were some Jewish voices saying the same thing, as I discuss later in this chapter.

17. Rubenstein, "Berlin, August 13, 1961."

18. Rubenstein, *After Auschwitz*, 10.

Bible as G-d's "servant."[19] Portions of the Talmud blame Rome's destruction of Jerusalem in 70 CE on the bad behavior of Jews.[20] Rubenstein cites the opinion of some Orthodox Jews, both during and after the Shoah, that the Shoah was G-d's punishment for Jewish "evils," including assimilation and the modern critical study of the Bible.[21]

Interestingly, Rubenstein never asked Grüber *how* the Jews had so failed G-d that the Shoah could have been a fitting response. Later, Rubenstein conjectured that Grüber must have been thinking of the Jews' failure to acknowledge Christ. It's possible, of course, that Grüber might have had other Jewish failures in mind. However, this is key: Rubenstein never even raised this theological question with Grüber.

But again, it's not the theology of either Rubenstein or Grüber that primarily concerns me. What I'm interested in is the *impact* Grüber's words had on Rubenstein. Keep in mind that in 1961, Rubenstein was already a rabbi and a PhD. Doubtless he'd already given great thought to the Shoah and the question of how a good G-d could allow for rampant evil. He had already studied with world-famous scholars such as Paul Tillich and Abraham Joshua Heschel. But Rubenstein's conversation with Grüber is the one Rubenstein cited as pushing him "to a theological point of no return."[22] "When I left Grüber's home," Rubenstein wrote, "something within me had changed irrevocably."

Why should this particular conversation have changed Rubenstein in a way he'd remember for the next fifty-plus years of his life? Rubenstein guessed that this change in him "had been gestating for a very long time,"[23] and I'm sure he's right. Rubenstein asked whether Grüber's impact was owing to his

19. Jeremiah 27:6.

20. See Air Z. Zivotofsky, "What's the truth about ... the Cause of the Destruction of the Beit Hamikdash?" Jewish Action, June 24, 2013, https://www.ou.org/jewish_action/06/2013/whats-the-truth-about-the-cause-of-the-destruction-of-the-beit-hamikdash-2/.

21. Rubenstein, *After Auschwitz*, 159–61. The topic of Orthodox Jewish views of the Shoah is discussed again later in this chapter. Elsewhere in this book, I indicated to Anthony that I don't know Jews who think that the Shoah is a part of G-d's plan for the Jews, in the sense of a means to the end of the formation of the modern State of Israel. To clarify: I am aware that some Jews see the Shoah both as divine punishment and as part of G-d's plan for the redemption of the Jews. However, I do not encounter such Jews except through books like Rubenstein's, and I believe that such Jews are far from mainstream.

22. Rubenstein, *After Auschwitz*, 3.

23. Rubenstein, *After Auschwitz*, 170.

being German, or their having met in "the former capital of the Third Reich during the week the Berlin Wall was erected."[24] My suspicion is that these factors played a part, but also that something more was involved.

Rubenstein fails to point out the obvious: he was a rabbi and Jewish theologian, in conversation with Grüber, a pastor and Protestant theologian. The two were discussing Scripture, the nature of G-d, and the responsibilities that Jews and Christians owe to G-d.

This is interfaith dialogue. Interfaith dialogue has a peculiar transformative power. I think this power derives from a sacred quality of this kind of dialogue.

❖

So far, I've argued that interfaith dialogue is sacred without asking what makes something "sacred." The question of what is and should be sacred is surprisingly complicated! Here, I find the dictionary definitions of what is "sacred" to be singularly unhelpful: these definitions describe the quality of things we've *already decided are sacred* ("worthy of religious veneration; entitled to reverence and respect; dedicated or set apart for the service or worship of a deity").[25] There is nothing in these definitions to help us determine what we *should regard to be sacred.*

To get a better idea of the meaning of "sacred," I've turned to the work of the great sociologist Émile Durkheim. Durkheim saw nothing of a sacred "inherent nature."[26] He wrote:

> The sacred character assumed by an object is not implied in the intrinsic properties of this latter: *it is added to them.* The world of religious things is not one particular aspect of empirical nature; *it is superimposed upon it.*[27]

If Durkheim is right, then recognizing the sacred is a bit like perceiving beauty: it is in the eye of the beholder. Indeed, this is the only way we can figure out what is sacred to someone we don't know; we have to ask them, or we have to pause and see what they treat as sacred. To do so, we might

24. Rubenstein, *After Auschwitz*, 169.

25. "Sacred," *Merriam-Webster Dictionary*, http://www.merriam-webster.com/dictionary/sacred.

26. Émile Durkheim, *The Elementary Forms of the Religious Life*, trans. Joseph Ward Swain (London: George Allen & Unwin Ltd., 1915), 200.

27. Durkheim, *Elementary Forms*, 229; emphasis added.

observe another's religious practice. Durkheim defined religion as "a unified system of beliefs and practices relative to sacred things,"[28] so it would be logical to look to a religion to define what is sacred to believers in that religion. But to this, we should add that the idea of the sacred persists even in our "secular age" where religion seems to be declining.[29] We continue to treat certain ideas as sacred (sanctity of life, freedom of speech, individual autonomy), even if we don't all connect these ideas to religion or G-d. We employ sacred-secular ceremony to create imagined and real transformations: civil weddings to become socially and legally recognized couple-units, graduations to pronounce our entrance into educational hierarchies, and funerals to achieve an accepted catharsis and closure after death. It is common to hear people say, "I'm not religious, but I'm spiritual." Which may be another way of saying, "I continue to partake of the sacred; I just don't look for it (or cannot find it) in organized religion."

We may not all feel a need for G-d, but we all seem to need the potential for sacred transformation. Again, a look at Durkheim is instructive. For Durkheim, the demarcation between the sacred and the profane is absolute. "In all the history of human thought there exists no other example of two categories of things so profoundly differentiated or so radically opposed to one another."[30] But while the sacred and profane represent wholly different worlds, Durkheim noted how we routinely pass from one to the other. We cross an invisible border into church . . . and we cross back again. We seek atonement for our sins . . . and then pass back into the profane world to sin again. But it's wrong to think that we pass unchanged between the sacred and profane worlds. Whether it's by rites such as baptism or a bat/bar mitzvah, we are (or imagine ourselves) *transformed* by the journey between profane and sacred. Through this passage, we may be "initiated" into the Jewish covenant with G-d, or we may become "reborn." Our state or status is changed.[31] For me, this is the most important quality of the sacred: it possesses a transformative quality.

Relying on Durkheim, I'll use the following quick-and-dirty description of "sacred": it involves (1) a passage into a religious or otherwise extraordinary space, (2) which passage contains within it the possibility or promise of

---

28. Durkheim, *Elementary Forms*, 47.

29. Phillip E. Hammond, ed., *The Sacred in a Secular Age: Toward Revision in the Scientific Study of Religion* (Berkeley: University of California Press, 1985).

30. Durkheim, *Elementary Forms*, 38.

31. Durkheim, *Elementary Forms*, 39.

transformation in a way that affects how we see ourselves in relationship to G-d or in some other sense that transcends ordinary experience.

Notice that I haven't asked whether a sacred transformation is positive. Once again, the quality of the sacred depends on who is looking for it. For people living in an ancient culture that engaged in child sacrifice, the sacrificial victim would have been regarded as sacred by them, but not by us. If a Christian converts to Judaism, the transformation might be regarded as sacred by a Jew but not by a Christian.

I was on the sidelines for my wife's conversion to Judaism. She needed a year's worth of instruction, then had to appear before a *Beit Din*—a Jewish court—for an examination. She immersed in a *mikveh*, a ritual bath. Finally, there was a ceremony in synagogue. She passed through religious, transcendent space, and the result? I've asked her; *she felt changed*. I can say this was a sacred process, without much fear of dissent.

Rubenstein went through something similar in his conversation with Grüber. The transformation he experienced is the one I described: the conversation was for him "unforgettable" and the basis for much of his future writing. The special "space" he passed through to achieve this transformation was that of Grüber's Berlin. For Jews of a certain age, such as myself (and probably including Rubenstein), post-war Germany was an extraordinary space, and not in a good way. I visited Germany in 1981, twenty years after Rubenstein, and I probably looked deep into the eyes of every German I met there who was over fifty, to silently accuse them. "Where were you forty years ago? What did you see? What did you do?" Everywhere I went in Germany, I felt the presence of murder. I visited Nuremburg, where so much of what had been destroyed during the war had been painstakingly rebuilt, but only a monument marked where the city's old synagogue had stood. I remember passing through a train yard outside of Munich and asking myself, "Why are there so many boxcars here? Who could possibly need all these boxcars?"[32] The young people I met in Germany—that is, people roughly my own age—were lovely, intelligent, sensitive, and caring, determined in their own individual ways to go forward and make a better world. But the four or five days I spent in Germany were filled with dread

---

32. For those who do not understand why I would be freaked out by boxcars: the Nazis made extensive use of their railway system to transport Jews to their death camps. Jews were loaded into boxcars, or cattle cars, "designed" to hold fifty people each, though many were loaded to twice this capacity, so that many died before ever reaching the death camps.

for me. I probably wouldn't feel the same way today—few Germans today were near-adult age during the Shoah—but I've never returned to Germany.

Sacred space is not always joyous space. A graveyard might be sacred, or a battlefield, or a concentration camp. Rubenstein and Grüber chose Berlin, a place with enormous symbolic significance, to talk about G-d, religion, and the Shoah. That there might be something sacred in this conversation and the transformation in Rubenstein that followed—well, hopefully, I've explained by now how I might see such a thing.

And if you're still not seeing any potential for the sacred in Rubenstein's dialogue with Grüber—well, I think we can understand this, too. The Rubenstein-Grüber dialogue set the stage for Rubenstein's "death of G-d" theology. The initial Jewish reaction to Rubenstein was "overwhelmingly hostile." Death of G-d? Jews urged other Jews to reject Rubenstein and retain belief in the traditional G-d who operated faithfully in Jewish history as the Bible promised.[33] Certainly I heard this sentiment growing up, that millions of Jews had died with the name of G-d on their lips so that I could be free and Jewish in a place like America, where I could fidget my way through High Holy Day services to my heart's content. This is a lesson I was taught as a child to learn from the Shoah: to hell with Hitler. He's dead. His Third Reich is dead, too. We have survived him. We must survive those who would follow him.

I don't think that Christians, or even subsequent generations of Jews, can possibly imagine the power this argument carried with Jews of my generation. We could muster the cynicism to laugh at this, that we were somehow Nazi-enablers when we skipped Sunday school (and believe me, I skipped Sunday school). But the thought was buried in our subconscious that we must remain faithful to Judaism because of Hitler, and this thought might emerge within us in unexpected ways. In my twenties I attended a bachelor party for a close friend who was Jewish but not at all religious. His bachelor party was at one of the older restaurants in New York City's Little Italy. There, amid the traditional fare, the chianti and manicotti and cannoli, my friend (drunk as a skunk) unexpectedly bore witness to his Judaism. "The Jews are still here!" he proclaimed to astonished Italian diners (none more astonished than me), as he stood on the seat of his chair. "The Jews are still here!" I had to take him home a few minutes later, three hours before the party had been scheduled to end. The accumulation of food, drink, and religious fervor

---

33. Zachary Braiterman, *(G[-]d) After Auschwitz* (Princeton: Princeton University Press, 1998), 88.

had done him in. It took him a day to sleep it off, and afterwards he swore to me that I had made up the entire story. "The Jews are still where?" he'd asked. "Little Italy?"

The Jews are still here. To be elsewhere would be to grant Hitler a victory after his death that he couldn't win in life. Hopefully, this helps explain some of the Jewish fury directed at Rubenstein. Rubenstein had dared to ask if we should keep the same faith after Auschwitz as before. He had asked if G-d had kept faith with us, and if not, why not? Rubenstein had the courage to ask before many of us were ready to hear the question, let alone his answer. But some Jews *were* ready and *needed* the question asked when Rubenstein asked it. One of my favorite theologians, Arthur Green, described the initial reaction to Rubenstein among his fellow students at the Jewish Theological Seminary: "Here was someone finally dealing with the issues—someone finally raising the questions we had been afraid to raise except to ourselves and perhaps to our closest friends."[34]

This is one way to think of Rubenstein in terms of the sacred. For many Jews, the central religious question of our age is: How can anyone believe in G-d after Auschwitz? (To this we might add, after Armenia, Cambodia, Bosnia, Rwanda, and so many other places that have experienced unthinkable genocide.) I do not argue with anyone who finds belief in G-d to be impossible. But a few brave souls like Rubenstein have attempted to rescue G-d from the ash heaps of the Shoah. Rubenstein (to my knowledge) is the first to phrase the G-d-question in the way I ask it to myself: Not whether belief in G-d is still possible for me, but what kind of G-d can I believe in?[35]

True enough, Rubenstein's G-d is not the one I learned about in Sunday school, the one that had "The Whole World in His Hands." Instead, Rubenstein's G-d is the source of life but not the sovereign of the living; Rubenstein's G-d does not (in Grüber's words) demand our death, but instead is "the primordial origin to which all lives ultimately return."[36] It's up to you to determine whether Rubenstein has answered his own question and described a kind of G-d you can believe in. What cannot be denied, I think,

---

34. Arthur E. Green, "A Response to Richard Rubenstein," *Conservative Judaism Journal* 28.4 (1974): 26.

35. Rubenstein, *Power Struggle*, 5.

36. Here, I am relying on Zachary Braiterman's summary of Rubenstein's theology. See Braiterman, *(G[-]d) After Auschwitz*, 95.

is Rubenstein's bravery (noted by Green and others) in publicly asking the question the way he did.[37]

If Durkheim is right and there's no intersection between the profane and the sacred, then on which side of the divide *should* one classify Rubenstein's search for G-d after Auschwitz?

I keep saying that I don't want to focus on Rubenstein's work, yet I keep doing so. Enough! Let's focus on what I want to focus on: Rubenstein's dialogue with Grüber.

⸭

Let's go back to the question I raised earlier. Rubenstein was thirty-seven years old when he met Grüber—roughly the age of my learned coauthor, Dr. Le Donne. In other words, Rubenstein was no impressionable kid, but he was still young enough to have a great deal of career before him. In 1961, Rubenstein must have already been interested in the question of *theodicy*: the justification of G-d, notwithstanding the existence of suffering and evil. I cannot believe that Rubenstein had not previously encountered the idea advanced by Grüber, that human suffering is part of G-d's plan. Nor can I say that Grüber articulated this idea in such novel terms, using such persuasive reasoning, that Rubenstein was simply dazzled by the brilliance of Grüber's thought. Indeed, Rubenstein himself noted that he found Grüber's argument to be incongruous and ironic,[38] and the theology Rubenstein developed after his conversation with Grüber (which I think is rightly described as *antitheodicy*, a system of thought where we in some sense refuse to justify, explain, or accept the relationship between G-d and evil[39]) is a thorough-going rejection of Grüber's thinking.

Instead, consider the impact Grüber had on Rubenstein in terms of Rubenstein's Jewish identity. Donniel Hartman says that all religions "live in a dialogue with a larger world" and are improved by this dialogue, "because new ideas, cross-fertilization, which would have never been a part of your

---

37. Braiterman noted that Jacob Neusner has praised Rubenstein as follows: "The abuse to which [Rubenstein] has been subjected [is] the highest possible tribute to the compelling importance of his contribution." *(G[-]d) After Auschwitz*, 89.

38. Rubenstein, *After Auschwitz*, 10.

39. Braiterman, *(G[-]d) After Auschwitz*, 4–5.

intellectual ghetto, are now part of your society."[40] If no religion is an island, then Judaism is possibly the best (or at least, the most acute) example of this: we are perpetually a minority religion, with a diaspora going back nearly to our beginnings. Our homeland in Israel was placed strategically on the cultural, economic, and religious crossroads of the ancient and modern worlds.[41] Even if we Jews desired nothing more than to be left alone, our circumstances (perhaps ordained by a transcendent G-d?) have forced us into dialogue with others. If Hartman is right, if dialogue has not merely changed but *enriched* Judaism, then surely the credit belongs to those who have constructively engaged in this dialogue before now.

Hartman mentions something else that's key to understanding the importance of dialogue. He argues that prior to modernity, Jews had a "singular identity" that defined every aspect of our being and provided our sole lens to view the outside world.[42] But as Anthony and I have discussed (in terms of the boxes we check on a standard form to describe our racial and ethnic make-up), we now have multiple, complex identities: I am Jewish, and American, and liberal, and a white person, and an attorney, and I feel equally at home in all of these identities, in part because I can choose which identities to personify in order to suit any situation.[43] Hartman talks about Jews who identify as Jewish a few days a year, maybe on Yom Kippur, maybe at Hanukkah, and on other days not so much, or not at all. I know Hartman is right; at times I've been the Jew he's talking about.

Complex identity poses a challenge: How do we retain Judaism and Jewish life when Jewish identity can be so fragile and ephemeral, and when it's so easy for Jews like me to blend into the American background? The nonsolution Hartman mentions is anti-Semitism, which eliminates complex identity in a hurry: to an anti-Semite, I am Jewish and nothing else. "If you made me feel a stranger," Hartman told a Gentile audience, "then my identity would be secure."[44] Obviously, Hartman is not seriously suggesting

---

40. Donniel Hartman, "Religion and the Challenges of Modernity" (lecture, 2009 Interfaith Dialogue Conference, Grand Rapids, Michigan), https://www.youtube.com/watch?v=jKGvsXbgn_E.

41. The Middle East is the only place in the world where three continents come together. See Phyllis A. Goldstein, *Convenient Hatred: The History of Antisemitism* (Brookline: Facing History and Ourselves National Foundation, 2012), Kindle location 332.

42. Goldstein, *Convenient Hatred*, Kindle location 332.

43. See the dialogue in part two of this book on borders.

44. Hartman, *Challenges of Modernity*.

that we move back to the ghetto. He's just pointing to the value of returning to something closer to a singular identity. And we have a means available to experience such an identity, through Jewish-Christian dialogue. In this dialogue, my identity is primarily Jewish. Christians don't come to this dialogue to hear my opinions on baseball, or single malt Scotch. They want to know about Judaism, and not merely about the religion; they ask me "what Jews think" about this or that; they want to know how it feels to be Jewish; they even ask why I'm not Christian.

In dialogue with Christians, I am asked to personify Jewish identity in a way I've never had to do before. It may sound odd to say this, but my Jewishness is not nearly as interesting to other Jews as it is to Anthony and other Christians. I've gotten used to how, with other Jews, I'm sometimes not Jewish in the right ways and in the right amount. But my failings don't appear to bother Anthony. He just seems to accept the entirety of my Jewishness as authentic. Paradoxically, this makes me want to be a better Jew, so that the Jewishness he accepts from me is a more committed and accurate version of Judaism. I say this is paradoxical, because I don't feel *nearly* this same impetus in conversation with other Jews.

But there's something else: it's one thing to identify as Jewish when I'm doing Jewish things with other Jews. It's quite another to self-identify as Jewish in a non-Jewish context: say, a wine tasting or holiday picnic in my new (and decidedly non-Jewish) home on Whidbey Island, Washington. I'm never sure what reaction I'm going to get when people learn for the first time that I am Jewish. Sometimes it's an effort at bridge-building. "Oh, I had lots of Jewish friends where I grew up in [fill in the city; probably some place like Boston or Philadelphia]." Or, "We LOVE Jews at our church; we give lots of money to Israel." Or even, "My husband was Jewish before I married him." But mostly, there is no reaction, or at least, none I can interpret, and I'm left to imagine what the other person is thinking: "I didn't ask you about your religion. I'm not particularly religious myself. I'm uncomfortable talking about religion. I don't know what you expect me to say. Are you accusing me of something? Why are you telling me this?"

Once I decided that Jewish-Christian dialogue would be a part of my life, I entered into a different relationship with my complex identity: my decision whether to self-identify as Jewish is now a *responsibility* as well as a choice. To an extent, this responsibility is one every Jew faces: if someone tells an offensive Jewish joke in our presence, not knowing we're Jewish, do we say something or let it go? But honestly, I hear very little offensive anti-Jewish speech. The question whether to self-identify comes up in benign contexts, where the speaker may not even be aware that they are invoking Judaism in a way that concerns me. Perhaps we're talking about illegal immigration, and I respond that my grandfather may have illegally crossed the German-French border in 1935 to escape arrest by the Nazis. Or someone mentions that peace in the Middle East is hopeless, and I reply that I have family living in Israel and cannot afford such hopelessness. Or I read a post online where a Christian describes his opponents as "Pharisees," and I respond that I'm a Jew who regards the Pharisees as my spiritual ancestors.

I don't always speak up. More often than not, I keep silent, not wanting to be seen as a scold or a troll. But with increasingly frequency, I do say something. I think it's good for Christians to know that we Jews are listening, that when they speak *about* us, they're also speaking *to* us and cannot avoid speaking *with* us.[45]

If Hartman is right that dialogue shapes what it means to be Jewish, then our future as a people depends on how we engage in dialogue with Christians and others. This, too, marks interfaith dialogue as sacred, because (as Rubenstein and Grüber both acknowledge) we Jews have traditionally seen ourselves as a sacred people, and thus the business of shaping and preserving a Jewish future is a sacred enterprise.

---

45. In his foreword to the collection *Anti-Semitism and Early Christianity: Issues of Polemic and Faith*, James Sanders describes the ongoing controversy over the "apparent anti-Jewish dimension" of the Oberammergau Passion Play. This passion play is performed every ten years in the village of Oberammergau, Germany. The play dates back to the seventeenth century, and efforts have been made over the past forty years to eliminate its infamous anti-Semitic elements. See, for example, A. J. Goldman, "New Kind of Passion in an 'Alpine Jerusalem,'" *The Forward*; May 26, 2010, http://forward.com/news/128345/new-kind-of-passion-in-an-alpine-jerusalem/. In his foreword, Sanders writes that "as long as only Christians witness such expressions of faith and obedience, they might themselves be encouraged in faith and heartened that humans were capable of such faithfulness. The problem was that the post-Holocaust world beyond the village of Oberammergau began to listen in, and what had surely been piety in its purest form for Christians only now began to be seen as the focused expression of parochial Christian anti-Semitism and anti-Judaism." James A. Sanders, foreword to Craig A. Evans and Donald A. Hagner, eds., *Anti-Semitism and Early Christianity: Issues of Polemic and Faith* (Minneapolis: Fortress Press, 1993), ix. Here, Sanders is expressing a point of view that is the opposite of mine. In my view, there is something potentially amiss with the "piety" of any performance that depends on it not being "seen" by a group characterized in and affected by the performance.

I am tempted to end here. Only I don't think I've gotten to the heart of what made (and makes) the Grüber-Rubenstein dialogue so powerful. I think something more was going on.

⌘

What strikes me about the Rubenstein-Grüber dialogue is this: if Rubenstein wanted to find someone to argue that the Shoah was G-d's punishment of wayward Judaism, he did not have to go outside of Judaism to do so. In *After Auschwitz*, Rubenstein described the thinking of a few Orthodox rabbis that the Shoah "was ultimately G[-]d's appropriate response against those who had proven unfaithful to His Torah"—in particular, secular and Reform Jews.[46] Yet this kind of Orthodox Jewish thinking seemed to have had little impact on Rubenstein himself, even though Rubenstein lived for a number of years as an Orthodox Jew.[47] It was only when Rubenstein was confronted with this same line of reasoning, this time from a heroic German Christian and not an Orthodox Jewish rabbi, that Rubenstein was shaken to his core. Why?

In *(G[-]d) After Auschwitz*, Zachary Braiterman discusses this question and proposes the beginnings of an answer:[48]

> Traditional assertions about G[-]d, covenant and suffering are not intrinsically problematic. They become problematic only insofar as they engender crippling feelings of collective guilt. In particular, they trouble Rubenstein when Christians, even sympathetic Christians, exploit them in order to fault the Jewish people.

As Braiterman sees it, what hit Rubenstein like a ton of bricks was a combination of message and messenger: the problem was not merely *the idea* of the Shoah as Divine punishment, but that *a Christian* (worse, a prominent German Christian) saw the Shoah as Divine punishment. If an Orthodox rabbi or two blamed other Jews for Hitler . . . well, that was obnoxious, and self-serving, and terrible theology, and nothing more, because not even the craziest Jew would seek the destruction of his own people. But Germans represented a different kind of threat to Jews, even in 1961.

---

46. Rubenstein, *After Auschwitz*, 159. Again to emphasize, it is Rubenstein's opinion, not mine, that the thinking he describes was ever typical of Orthodox Jewry.

47. Rubenstein, *Power Struggle*, 102.

48. Braiterman, *(G[-]d) After Auschwitz*, 91.

However, I think Braiterman is wrong if he thinks that Rubenstein's reaction to Grüber was primarily a matter of threat assessment. For one thing, Rubenstein expressed nothing but respect for Grüber, something you wouldn't expect if Rubenstein believed Grüber represented a danger to Jews. Rubenstein wrote after his talk with Grüber that Grüber was a "decent human being" who spoke with "consistency" and "admirable bluntness and candor."[49] Rubenstein recognized that Grüber's dogged determination to see the Jews through the lens of the Bible was the very quality that caused him to act as a righteous Gentile and oppose the Nazis.[50] Also, if Rubenstein's sole concern was with the malevolent ways that Gentiles could use Jewish doctrine against the Jews, then he needn't have focused solely on doctrines of election and chosen-ness. There's practically nothing in Judaism, from golden calves to the very idea of a Messiah, that cannot be used against Jews by Gentiles determined to do so.

Moreover—and this is critical—Grüber wasn't parroting the typical early twentieth-century Protestant critique of Judaism. He wasn't saying that Judaism was primitive, moribund, and superseded by Christianity, with no continuing relevance or reason for existence. Nor was he saying that Jews are perpetually "cursed."[51] Instead, Grüber was saying that the covenant between G-d and the Jewish people is very much alive. Remember, Grüber argued that G-d effectively seized the German nation to use it as a "whip" against the Jews.[52] In this view of the cosmic drama, the Jews are the central characters, and the Germans (and perhaps Christians in general) are merely a prop.

---

49. Rubenstein, *After Auschwitz*, 4, 6, 9.

50. Rubenstein, *After Auschwitz*, 13.

51. In his groundbreaking work *Paul and Palestinian Judaism*, E. P. Sanders wrote that the then-prevailing New Testament scholarly view held Judaism to be "at best an inadequate religion and at worst one which destroys any hope of a proper relationship between G[-]d and man." E. P. Sanders, *Paul and Palestinian Judaism* (Philadelphia: Fortress Press, 1977), 35. Sadly, this point of view was held by some of the best-known Christian opponents of the Nazis and anti-Semitism. For example, in 1935 Martin Niemoeller spoke of the Jews as a people that "can neither live nor die, because it is under a curse which forbids it to do either." And in 1933 Dietrich Bonhoeffer wrote that ever since the Jews had "nailed the Redeemer of the world to the cross," they had been forced to bear an eternal "curse" through a long history of suffering, one that would end only "in the conversion of Israel to Christ." See "The Poisonous Well of anti-Jewish Rhetoric," *Haaretz*, June, 11, 2009, www.haaretz .com/the-poisonous-well-of-anti-jewish-rhetoric-1.4664.

52. Rubenstein, *After Auschwitz*, 10.

Braiterman pays insufficient attention to something crucial: Grüber wasn't merely a "sympathetic Christian." He was a hero who had risked his own life to save Jewish lives. He had suffered and nearly died in the same camps where Jews had died in the millions. Even if Rubenstein assumed (perhaps wrongfully) that Grüber thought G-d had punished the Jews for their failure to accept Christ, Grüber had acted with unimaginable courage to save Jews from this punishment. He had risked *everything* in this effort, an effort I'm sure he felt was G-d-commanded. (There is a horrible irony in this: Grüber saw both the destruction of much of European Jewry, and his own personal efforts to protect Jews from this destruction, as mandated by G-d.) Grüber simply cannot be lumped along with other "fault-finding Christians."

No, Rubenstein's epiphany must have come from a place other than worry about what Gentiles might do.

Let's turn back to the thinking of Donniel Hartman, who says that in interreligious dialogue, "It's not an external critic who you listen to. You yourself are experiencing different modalities which end up enriching who you are."[53]

Grüber might fit the bill of an "external critic," but as Hartman suggests, it wasn't the "modality" of Grüber as critic that affected Rubenstein so deeply. But before we consider Grüber's other possible modalities, we should ask what Hartman means when he talks about modalities. Hartman has said that:

- Judaism itself "is primarily a modality of being and belonging" that "includes modalities of action and faith."[54]

- After the destruction of the Second Temple, "Jewish national life was divided into two distinct modalities: *galut* and *geulah*, exile and redemption."[55]

- "A time to remember and a time to forget" are distinct modalities.[56]

53. Hartman, *Challenges of Modernity*.

54. Donniel Hartman, *Putting G[-]d Second: How to Save Religion from Itself* (Boston: Beacon Press, 2016), 137.

55. Donniel Hartman, "Israel and World Jewry: The Need for a New Paradigm," August 24, 2011, https://hartman.org.il/Blogs_View.asp?Article_Id=1860&Cat_Id=273&Cat_Type=.

56. Donniel Hartman, "A Time to Remember and a Time to Forget," August 9, 2013; https://hartman.org.il/Blogs_View.asp?Article_Id=1208&Cat_Id=273&Cat_Type=.

In dictionary terms, a "modality" can be a way or mode in which something exists or is done, or a way in which something is expressed or experienced.[57] In a typical dialogue, there may be two people in conversation but many more modalities present, many more channels where communication is taking place. Consider for the moment some of the "modalities" Anthony presents to me. Many we share in common. We're both baseball fans, so Anthony might use baseball to communicate to me his ideas about devotion and identity. Anthony grew up in Sebastopol, California, which he describes as a "cultural satellite of Berkeley"; I was a student at the University of California at Berkeley in the 1970s. He's a political liberal; so am I. He teaches at a Methodist seminary and initially supported a Jewish candidate for president of the United States in 2016; I'm a Jew who supported a Methodist candidate in that same election.[58] We share so much in common, in fact, that we've sometimes asked whether our dialogue is less Jewish-Christian, and more a matter of two tree-hugging granola-eating hippie wannabees shooting the breeze.

But as Anthony and I intentionally engage in something called "Jewish-Christian dialogue," it's impossible for either of us to avoid stepping into other modalities. Some of these modalities may be relatively new—for example, the admiration I express for Christianity is a response to the late-twentieth-century thaw in Jewish-Christian relations. Anthony has privately told me that when I express positive feelings about Christianity, it enables him to express his own feelings with greater openness and honesty. Is there a "modality" connected to "being among friends"? I think there is.

Other Jewish-Christian modalities of dialogue are more ancient, and less friendly. I believe that centuries of Jewish-Christian recrimination and polemic have opened up modalities of accusation that operate without our even knowing they're there. When I've criticized a Christian dialogue partner (for example, when I've argued that Christians should not accuse others of being "Pharisees"), on occasion I've been met with the response, "I am not anti-Semitic!" Somehow, what seems to me like a gentle critique, or even

---

57. "Modality," *Oxford Living Dictionaries*, https://en.oxforddictionaries.com/definition/us/modality. The concept of modality in philosophy takes in ideas of what is possible, necessary or impossible. See "The Epistemology of Modality" in the *Stanford Encyclopedia of Philosophy*, http://plato.stanford.edu/entries/modality-epistemology/, but I don't think this is the sense that Hartman is using the word *modality*.

58. The Jew here is Bernie Sanders; the Methodist is Hillary Clinton.

a friendly piece of advice, can sound to my dialogue partner like a deadly accusation. How does this happen?

But I've seen this same phenomenon in reverse: a Christian may say something relatively innocent to me, and I hear things that were never said. Perhaps I'll be in a discussion about whether the Gospels are "anti-Jewish,"[59] and a Christian will argue that early Christianity was a Jewish sect, and that many (or most, or all) of the Gospel authors were themselves Jewish.[60] The idea of Jewish-authored anti-Judaism is certainly not unprecedented. But when I hear this particular argument, in this particular context, it triggers something for me. I think to myself in response, "What are you saying, my Christian friend? That the horrible history of Christian anti-Semitism was

---

59. I have placed "anti-Jewish" in quotes because it's not obvious what we mean when we ask whether a Gospel is anti-Jewish. Do we mean that the Gospel is critical of Jews and their leadership, or of Jewish practice? Or that a Gospel proclaims the end of the relationship between G-d and the Jews? Or that a Gospel maintains that Jews stand outside any hope of salvation? For a discussion of this question, see Amy-Jill Levine, "Anti-Judaism and the Gospel of Matthew," in William Farmer, ed., *Anti-Judaism and the Gospels* (Harrisburg: Trinity Press International, 1999), 12–14.

60. An example of this argument can be found in in the 1993 collection *Anti-Semitism and Early Christianity: Issues of Polemic and Faith,* supra note 47. In his Epilogue to this volume, Joel Marcus writes: "The central theme of this volume is that the polemic against Jews and Jewish institutions found within the New Testament is primarily an in-house phenomenon . . . mostly, in other words, a criticism formulated by Jews (i.e., Jewish Christians) against other Jews." Joel Marcus, Epilogue to Craig A. Evans and Donald A. Hagner, eds., *Anti-Semitism and Early Christianity: Issues of Polemic and Faith* (Minneapolis: Fortress Press, 1993), 292. To this, Craig Evans wrote in this same volume that the polemic found in the prophetic books of the Old Testament, and in the Dead Sea Scrolls literature of the Jewish community of Qumran, is more anti-Jewish than anything in the New Testament. Evans adds: "Never does the New Testament enjoin Christians to curse unbelievers or opponents. Never does the New Testament petition G[-]d to damn the enemies of the church. But Qumran did." *Anti-Semitism and Early Christianity,* 8. The arguments made by Evans and Marcus here are problematic, if only because the substantial presence of Gentiles in the early church makes it difficult to see the New Testament as a Jewish "in-house phenomenon." But I react to this argument emotionally as well as intellectually. The argument leaves me feeling that some Christians seek to avoid Christian responsibility for the legacy of anti-Judaism. In particular, I feel as if Evans is suggesting something he hasn't explicitly said, that anti-Judaism is an early Jewish creation ameliorated by later Christian ideas of love and compassion. To emphasize, I don't think it's fair to accuse Evans of any such thing, but it is difficult for me to read Evans without experiencing his argument through these modalities.

born of a Jewish self-accusation? That the centuries-long history of Jewish persecution is all, somehow, *our fault?*"

The point I'm making here is not about the origins of Christian anti-Semitism—instead, it's about how modalities of dialogue can twist our understanding of what's being said to us. Remember when Grüber told Rubenstein that G-d had used the Shoah to punish the Jews, Rubenstein assumed that Grüber meant "punished the Jews for Jewish unbelief in Christ." But Grüber never said this, and he may not have even *believed* this. Instead, Rubenstein may have unwittingly experienced Grüber through a modality of accusation and blame-finding. In a similar way, when a Christian dialogue partner points out that potentially anti-Jewish passages in the Gospels may have been written by Jews, my partner may be saying nothing more than what I frequently say in other settings; that Jesus and early Christianity must be understood in their Jewish context. But when this message is communicated in a discussion about anti-Judaism, these modalities of accusation can come into play for me, distorting meaning and pushing me toward the perpetuation of a legacy of recrimination.

When we enter into Jewish-Christian dialogue, we stand in the shoes of others whose words echo around us. We must be sensitive to this. We must modulate our speech accordingly, and listen to each other carefully, in due recognition of the modalities through which we communicate. But while certain Jewish-Christian modalities of dialogue are distressing, they can nevertheless lead to positive outcomes. Rubenstein's dialogue with Grüber led to his theology of the Shoah. As for me, my experience of negative Jewish-Christian modalities has led me toward the rejection of the dialogue of accusation.

Yes, Christians need to better understand their own anti-Jewish history. But there may be a limit on how hard Jews should pound the connection between Christianity and anti-Judaism. A pro-Jewish Christianity becomes impossible if Christianity and anti-Judaism become so closely associated that Christians are forced to choose between their Christianity and their friendship with us.

I return then to where I began this chapter: I feel that Jewish-Christian dialogue is a sacred practice, but I can't quite describe why this should be. But I no longer feel badly about my finding a sacred quality in an unexpected place. Indeed, we might incorporate the word *unexpected* into our definition of the sacred. The opposite of "sacred" is sometimes described as "secular," but it can also be described as "ordinary." We use holy places, times, and rituals to demark the sacred; but as we become accustomed to these spaces, they lose their power to move us. Somehow, the sacred must retain (or regain) the capacity to awe, meaning that we must invest the sacred with a capacity to surprise us, and even to make us uncomfortable.

In his most recent book, Anthony describes his experience with Jews and Judaism in terms of "journeys along Jewish-Christian borders." He writes that the best educations are acquired in proximity to a border, where we can see how our cross-border neighbors live and think.[61] He's right, and I think there's something more to it, because in dialogue we take up residence in border-land in conversation with someone (or someones) on the other side of the border. There's a partnership in this, a modality, a channel of communication that arises from our respective decisions to live near a border separating two religions, and not in the heartland of a single religion. Through this modality, Anthony communicates something of his lived Christianity, including its inherent sacred potential. I try to do likewise. This must be much of the reason to journey along Jewish-Christian borders, to glimpse the sacred on the other side.

There are words we can attach to this mutual sharing of the other's sacred: it's a gift, an act of friendship, even an act of love. I prefer other words, words that reflect an odd contradiction I also find sacred. You see, I am grateful for Anthony's presence near me in border-land. We're the kind of neighbors who, on occasion, cross the border—perhaps sometimes as tolerated trespassers, but more often as invited guests. I am grateful that we live along a border that's more open than it used to be and allows for such crossings. But when I return to my side of the border, and Anthony to his, I'm grateful for this, too.

In dialogue, we do not seek to eliminate the other's difference. We seek to draw closer to it. This difference is what attracted us to dialogue in the first place: eliminate it and the dialogue collapses. If Anthony ever converted to Judaism, I would gain a Jewish friend but lose a Christian friend, and I would grieve this loss.

I think, perhaps, the Quran quote I used to begin this chapter says it best. G-d created humankind as different peoples, different tribes, so that we might "know one another." Not "become like one another." Oh, to be certain, our more-open Jewish-Christian border allows some Jews to become Christians, and some Christians to become Jews. But that's only one possibility among many. The sacred nature of dialogue offers us the promise

---

61. Anthony Le Donne, *Near Christianity: How Journeys along Jewish-Christian Borders Saved My Faith in G[-]d* (Grand Rapids: Zondervan, 2016).

of personal transformation, without a guarantee of which path this trans-formation will follow. This might frighten us. But elsewhere in this book, Anthony quotes Christian theologian James Hal Cone to say that through G-d's love, we become who we already are in fact. Perhaps then, the dialogue G-d requires in the Quran provides us with the transformation we need to come closer to our true selves.

Pray that such conversations continue. Amen.

Encountering G-d as a Xn in Dialogue

Anthony Le Donne

To love another person
Is to see the face of G[-]d.

— "Epilogue," *Les Misérables*[1]

The biblical character Jacob—the man who is eventually named "Israel" (Gen. 32)—has always fascinated me. I have taught and preached on the stories of Jacob and Esau. But I never considered the significance of Jacob's story for interreligious dialogue until I heard my own pastor preach on the reconciliation of the two brothers.

Rev. Richard Baker preaches that when the estranged brothers are finally reunited, Esau is encountered as a person who reflects and refracts the light of G-d. Jacob, in the process of reconciling with his brother and enemy, says, "For truly to see your face is like seeing the face of G[-]d" (Gen. 33:10). Rev. Baker's message to us was that, with the right eyes, we encounter G-d's beauty in the most unlikely faces.

> Jacob said, "No, please; if I find favor with you, then accept my present from my hand; for truly to see your face is like seeing the face of G[-]d—since you have received me with such favor. Please accept my gift that is brought to you, because G[-]d has dealt graciously with me, and because I have everything I want." So he urged him, and he took it. (Gen. 33:10–11)

This encounter between estranged brothers does not undo Jacob's prior deception. Their reconciliation does not change the fact that Esau lost his

---

1. Claude-Michel Schönberg, Alain Boublil, and Victor Hugo, "Epilogue," *Les Misérables*, directed by Tom Hooper (New York: Universal Pictures, 2013), DVD.

father's blessing to his younger brother.[2] Indeed the giving and receiving of Jacob's gift—its significance and symbolism—makes sense only if both brothers remember what has been previously lost.

Jacob first says, *if I find favor with you.* The Hebrew is probably better translated, "if I have found favor *in your eyes.*" Jacob is first and foremost concerned with how he will appear to his brother. I believe that this empathetic posture of self-reflection transforms Jacob's own vision. As they stand face to face after years of estrangement, Jacob tries to see himself through his brother's eyes. In doing so, he encounters G-d in the face of his brother.

Things Rightly Named

Names like all words have power. I am convinced that language interprets and shapes our perception of the world, of each other, and ourselves. The words we use can change the way other people think about us. For example, when I hear Christians use the term "Second Testament" rather than the usual "New Testament," I tend to assume that they are doing so out of sensitivity for their Jewish neighbors. Or consider this example: when I hear a Christian use the phrase "the Jews" (complete with the definite article, "the") I tend to assume that this Christian lacks sensitivity to the variance, texture, and multiplicity of Jewish culture. Let me add very clearly and quickly that my assumptions often mislead me. Surely a person must be measured by more than first impressions![3]

In one of our earliest e-mail correspondences, Larry noticed that I often used the shorthand "Xn" for the word *Christian.* Larry wondered if there might be some parallel to the Xmas versus Christmas debate common among conservative, American Christians. Many Christians worry that removing the

---

2. Jon D. Levenson notes that Jacob "offers Esau a gift that is called a 'blessing' (*birkātî*), [but] he never returns the birthright [*běkōrâ*]." *The Death and Resurrection of the Beloved Son: The Transformation of Child Sacrifice in Judaism and Christianity* (New Haven: Yale University Press, 1993), 65.

3. I should probably note that I use the title "New Testament" rather than "Second Testament" and don't feel any reluctance to do so. I do appreciate, however, that the labeling of "New" and "Old" parts of the Christian Bible has contributed to the longstanding Christian notions that Judaism is something obsolete, incomplete, or (to the extreme) something to be done away with. I hope it goes without saying that these notions do not reflect my understanding of Judaism. I do, however, avoid the label "Old Testament" wherever I can. I prefer the less-than-perfect label "Hebrew Bible." I also realize that this is an inconsistency on my part.

name "Christ" from Christmas is a secularizing tendency. Perhaps then, Larry thought, my language was a nod to Jewish sensibilities. So he asked, "Do you use the 'Xn' abbreviation generally, or just with folks like me? For the record, I am not offended by the words 'Christ' or 'Christian,' though if you use 'Xn' out of sensitivity for my feelings, that's nice of you, and I'm fine with 'Xn' too."

I explained that I use "Xn" as shorthand, without ideological reflection, and regardless of company. (I use "Xn" rather than Christian for the sake of haste and laziness.) I might have also added "Don't flatter yourself" for good measure.

But, of course, because he called my attention to it, I began the process of self-examination. I am, after all, the sort of person who avoids "BC" and "AD" date demarcations out of sensitivity. I sometimes avoid vowels in certain words designating G-d as the referent. It is not beyond my concerns to choose my words carefully with an eye to how they might be heard by my Jewish friends. Larry was right to wonder whether I might be walking on eggshells for his benefit. He was also sensitive enough to me to assuage whatever worries I might have about his discomfort.

Upon reflection it occurs to me that oversensitivity can be alienating in a different way. If Larry senses that I am "acting a part" for his benefit, this has the potential of conveying a sense of my discomfort. Simply put, who wants to be the reason why a friend is walking on eggshells?

Something else occurred to me as I was thinking this over. Before Larry's e-mail, it had never occurred to me that anyone might try to *avoid* writing the word *Christian* out of sensitivity. Is the term "Christian" offensive to some people? And does that make me—a self-identified Christian—implicitly offensive? The enterprise of Christianity has been (historically and generally speaking) detrimental to Jewish well-being. No doubt the words *Christian* and *Christianity* scratch at old wounds for some people. I have tried in my writing to call out this legacy and to own it.

Still, there is something about carrying that legacy in your own name.

For all of his trickster tendencies, I feel for Jacob when his brother casts his name in a negative light: "Esau said, 'Is he not rightly named Jacob [יַעֲקֹב]? For he has supplanted me [וַיַּעְקְבֵנִי] these two times. He took away my birthright; and look, now he has taken away my blessing'" (Gen. 27:36). Here Esau suggests that his brother's name sounds a lot like the Hebrew word for "to supplant" or "to circumvent"[4] It may well be the case that Jacob is

---

4. It remains unclear if Esau's take on Jacob's name (connoting the idea of deception) is accurate. It seems that "Jacob" [יַעֲקֹב] is a play on the root for "heel" [עָקֵב].

rightly named from Esau's perspective. I feel for Jacob all the same. Such a name is a terrible burden.

In many ways early Christianity attempted to supplant Judaism. Christians (ancient, medieval, and modern) have tried to create a positive identity for ourselves by casting our Jewish siblings in negative relief. We have repeatedly tried to claim Abraham's blessing as our own.[5] As we expanded as a people and a political force, our Jewish neighbors retreated (and for good reason). Christians like me carry this legacy in our name. On this point, I am reminded of the different reactions to "the Cross" as observed by Rabbi Michael Cook:

> Ask a mixed group of Christians and Jews, "What does the Cross mean to you?" Christians may say that it signals Christ's incomparable gift of his life so that they might be saved; Jews may counter that it symbolizes unspeakable terror.[6]

Rabbi Cook speaks here of possibility rather than something generally true about Jewish sensibility. But the implication ought to be clear: the very thing that defines my identity can be terrifying to others. Moreover, naming myself as a Christian is going to offer a poor impression in some circles.

As I imagine myself through the eyes of those offended or terrified by my Christianity, I occupy some kind of middle ground. I find myself somewhere between *my agreement with them* and *my sense that they've misjudged something crucial about me.* I am divided, occupying a space of empathy with my religious neighbor but also a space of disappointment at the inevitable rift between us. So there are two rifts, equally problematic: (1) the default alienation that occurs between Christian and Jew; (2) the alienation I feel from myself as a mind divided. It is especially difficult to explain this second point. In owning the Christian legacy, I am internalizing it in a way. So there is a part of my identity that refuses to harmonize with the rest of me. This, I'm sure, adds further discord to my relationships with those beyond the borders of Christianity.

See Gen. 25:26. Whatever the case, the name continues to attract the popular definitions of "craftiness" or "deceiver" due in part to Esau's wordplay. Cf. also Gen. 27:35.

5. One could easily accuse me of appropriating Israel's legacy in these pages by drawing an analogy between the Christian identity and Jacob's. I must add that I do not intend any allegorical projection. I'm just saying that I can personally relate. Even then, I grant that my sense of relating might be misplaced.

6. Michael J. Cook, *Modern Jews Engage the New Testament: Enhancing Jewish Well-Being in a Christian Environment* (Woodstock, VT: Jewish Lights, 2012), 4.

And yet I only encounter G-d as a Christian. The label is not incidental or simply an accident of history. Christianity is part of me and I it. I don't claim to encounter G-d often. In fact, I rarely encounter G-d in a way that I would describe as a sense of Divine imminence. But in those rare and fleeting moments when I do, it is me-as-a-Christian who does. It is the same part of me that causes the dissonance.

Jacob Encounters the Divine

Jacob was born into dysfunction. There can be no doubt that he exploited his family dynamics to his advantage. He is justly marked by his role in the dysfunction. But we do him wrong if we fail to notice that his part in the drama was written up before his birth.

Pregnant with twins and sensing a conflict within her, Rebekah seeks Divine guidance. The L-rd speaks to Rebekah in an oracle:

> And the L[-]RD said to her, "Two nations are in your womb, and two peoples born of you shall be divided; the one shall be stronger than the other, the elder shall serve the younger." (Gen. 25:23)

So it seems that Jacob's part in the drama has been pre-scripted. He is part of a larger narrative that reaches back to Abraham and extends forward to tribal enmity. This scripted drama meets Rebekah most intimately. Sensing the discord within her, she asks, "If it is to be this way, why do I live?" One wonders if the oracle that follows is any consolation. I doubt it.

Walter Brueggemann explains Jacob's predicament like this: "The call of G[-]d places Jacob in a series of unrelieved conflicts. The entire narrative is marked by strife." Brueggemann gives the examples of Jacob's conflicts with Esau, Laban, Rachel, and even G-d. "Jacob is a man who will contest every step of the way with every party. But the dispute is not of Jacob's making. It is evoked by G[-]d's initial oracle (25:23). The narrative affirms that the call of G[-]d is not only a call to well-being. It may be a call to strife and dispute."[7]

Before I deal with Jacob's direct encounters with the Divine, it is important to recognize that his mother's encounter with G-d may be as important as any Jacob himself experiences directly.

---

7. Walter Brueggemann, *Genesis: Interpretation: A Bible Commentary for Teaching and Preaching* (Louisville: Westminster John Knox, 1986), 208–9.

After the successful con by Rebekah and Jacob, after Isaac is played for a fool, and Esau has stewed in his own defeat, the blessed, younger son flees for his life. Jacob's cover story is that he must visit his uncle Laban in Haran to find a suitable wife. But his underlying motivation comes from Rebekah's warning, "Your brother Esau is consoling himself by planning to kill you" (27:42). Indeed, the plot is seen through the eyes of Esau, "Now Esau hated Jacob because of the blessing with which his father had blessed him, and Esau said to himself, 'The days of mourning for my father are approaching; then I will kill my brother Jacob'" (27:41). So with his brother the hunter behind him and a life in hiding before him, Jacob encounters G-d in a dream.

It's difficult to imagine a more impressive epiphany. Jacob dreams of a great stairway (reminiscent of the massive ziggurat-styled structures of Mesopotamian temples). The vision suggests that Jacob has unwittingly rested in a place where heaven and earth meet. As if the pyramid-sized stairway pointing to heaven isn't revealing enough, Jacob sees that the top of it reaches *all the way to heaven* and "the angels of G[-]d were ascending and descending on it" (28:12). This is a gateway experience for Jacob. He glimpses the place and means whereby sacred and mundane merge to become something holy. The vision is also life-changing for Jacob. As such, it serves a gateway from his present life, fraught with uncertainty, to something as stable as a monument made of stone. In this moment, Jacob's legacy is established.

> And the L[-]RD stood beside him and said, "I am the L[-]RD, the G[-]d of Abraham your father and the G[-]d of Isaac; the land on which you lie I will give to you and to your offspring; and your offspring shall be like the dust of the earth, and you shall spread abroad to the west and to the east and to the north and to the south; and all the families of the earth shall be blessed in you and in your offspring. Know that I am with you and will keep you wherever you go, and will bring you back to this land; for I will not leave you until I have done what I have promised you." (28:13–15)

Perhaps the most striking feature of this vision is the proximity of G-d to Jacob. In other biblical theophanies, the Divine is too brilliant to look at. Sometimes the deity is represented by amazing but earthly phenomena: a burning bush, pillars of fire, a tornado, thunder. Some reveal the Deity enthroned in heavenly glory. In later apocalyptic literature, it is common for an angel to come alongside the seer to serve as an interpreter. In such visions, the Divine is something magnificent, nearly ineffable. Angels often function as intermediary agents. If indeed G-d is transcendent, an angel can get close enough to the human observer to explain what he is seeing. Not so in Jacob's vision. In Jacob's dream, the angels are part of the vision. In this case, "the L[-]RD stood beside him."

Here G-d is intimately conversant with Jacob. There is no mistaking who is speaking—the L-rd self identifies using specific ancestral names—and the meaning of the oracle is clear. Importantly, Jacob receives this oracle passively. He doesn't initially seek out a holy place, he doesn't pray, he doesn't even reply or ask for clarification once he hears the oracle. Jacob's only act of initiation is to fall asleep.[8]

Contrast this experience of Divinity with an altogether different encounter in the life of Jacob.

> Jacob was left alone and a man wrestled with him until daybreak. When the man saw that he did not prevail against Jacob, he struck him on the hip socket; and Jacob's hip was put out of joint as he wrestled with him. Then he said, "Let me go, for the day is breaking."
>
> But Jacob said, "I will not let you go, unless you bless me."
>
> So he said to him, "What is your name?"
>
> And he said, "Jacob."
>
> Then the man said, "You shall no longer be called Jacob, but Israel, for you have striven with G[-]d and with humans, and have prevailed."
>
> Then Jacob asked him, "Please tell me your name."
>
> But he said, "Why is it that you ask my name?" And there he blessed him.
>
> So Jacob called the place Peniel, saying, "For I have seen G[-]d face to face, and yet my life is preserved." (32:24–30)

If Jacob's first encounter with G-d seems dissimilar to other biblical theophanies, this encounter is altogether exceptional. This mysterious character is identified only as the "man" and avoids giving his name when asked directly. This man fights Jacob through the night but does not prevail. The man manages to put Jacob's hip out of joint (does this suggest that the man

---

8. Jacob then wakes, sets up a monument, and makes a vow to G-d. This encounter is reinforced in a later dream in which the Divine voice says, "I am the G[-]d of Bethel, where you anointed a pillar and made a vow to me. Now leave this land at once and return to the land of your birth" (31:13).

fights dirty?[9]) but still does not escape Jacob's grasp. Seeing that Jacob has proven the stronger of the two, the man pleads to be let go.

For the life of me, I cannot imagine why Jacob identifies this person as G-d. Indeed several traditional interpretations (both Jewish and Christian) assume that this "man" was an angel.[10] But Jacob—the intelligent and experienced man who has encountered G-d twice already—seems to be convinced that he has "seen G[-]d face to face."

I am struck by how immanent and intimate this exchange is. G-d and Israel continue a passionate love affair throughout the Hebrew Bible. This love affair is complete with jealousy, wounded rants, and trial separations. But nothing in Hebrew Scripture prepares us for the intimacy of this encounter: Jacob and the man he identifies as G-d—without warning—tangle themselves into pugilistic knots. The G-d of Genesis is never more anthropomorphized (portrayed in humanlike terms) than in this story. On the other hand, this mysterious G-d-figure is essentially veiled. His identity is concealed. The narrator fails to name him, and the "man" plays coy when asked his name. If indeed this character is G-d, it is a strange and estranging portrait. These are attributes that usually hinder intimacy.

In an odd bit of storytelling, the reader is left with more questions than answers. The only person confident that G-d was involved in this interface is Jacob. Whoever the nameless man was, it wasn't a dream. Jacob's limp is reminder enough that the fight did indeed occur. Jacob—now Israel—meets the sunrise, limping back to his brother, Esau.

This, right here, is where Jacob becomes my man.

When Jacob encounters a stairway to heaven, when the L-rd of his fathers sidles up to whisper in his ear, when the Divine voice promises him a world of blessing, I just can't relate. I do not have the imaginative capacity to envision myself in this scene. I have never encountered G-d with such clarity and certainty. My random and rare encounters with G-d lead me to ask stupid questions such as, "What is your name!" My encounters with the Divine tend to involve me fumbling around in the dark, fighting to maintain my grip on a mystery.

Bruggemann claims that our hero emerges from his fight a new man. He has a new name and a new walk about him. "He has penetrated the mystery of G[-]d like none before him."[11] Maybe. But I cannot help but notice that the narrator continues to refer to Jacob by his birth name.

---

9. It is possible that "hip" is a euphemism for genitalia.

10. Both Levenson and Kaminsky settle on the designation "divine figure."

11. Bruggemann, *Genesis*, 270.

Beyond Kumbaya Love

In his recent book, *The Love of G[-]d*, Jon Levenson reminds us that ancient conceptions of love differ from modern default settings. At the risk of oversimplifying a complex topic, the love between G-d and Israel was not unlike treaties between powerful kingdoms and less powerful tribes. In these political covenants, unequal parties were duty-bound to act out the details of the treaty. The more powerful party was duty-bound to protect the weaker party. Conversely the weaker tribe would be duty-bound to serve the greater kingdom. In short, the sort of love we read of in the Hebrew Bible is a political category. Israel shows love for G-d by "the performance of his commandments. Love, so understood, is not an emotion, not a feeling, but a cover term for acts of obedient service."[12]

This explanation of love is about as foreign to my experience as I can imagine. Levenson's observation doesn't help me put words to how I relate to my wife, children, or friends. My love for them is probably better related in Greek terminology, European poetry, or American storytelling. Understanding Suzerain treaties won't help me explain my love of chocolate, baseball, or Wes Anderson films. Levenson does, however, give me a better way to understand the character of G-d. The motives, logic, and works of G-d are altogether alien to me. When I repeat the very Christian mantra that G-d loves the world, I am speaking of a kind of love that is foreign to my experience. So I need better categories to explain it, and for that reason I am grateful to Levenson.

There is another factor here that is more personal. You see, I find it difficult to use the same word (*love*) for my experience of my most intimate relationships and also for a Divine figure who is most often silent, mysterious, and hidden. I know a thousand Christians who experience G-d's presence regularly. They feel touched by G-d during worship. They feel empowered and loved by G-d. I've had these experiences too, but my most prevalent and profound experiences have been of G-d's silence. I'm not complaining. I in no way suffer because of this. I still pray. I'm still moved by certain hymns and stained glass. I am grateful to G-d for my life. It's a good life. It's just that G-d's involvement is almost always invisible in my experience. So it is a bit difficult for me to relate to my fellow Christians who describe G-d's love

---

12. Levenson, *The Love of G[-]d: Divine Gift, Human Gratitude, and Mutual Faithfulness in Judaism* (Princeton: Princeton University Press, 2015), 4. Levenson also adds that affection can and does grow from this relationship.

as affection. I actually take comfort in the fact that many ancient Israelites thought of Divine love as a political category. Somehow it creates a category that makes room for me within the life of faith.

Most importantly, Levenson makes a suggestion that I find challenging and compelling. Encompassed within Israel's love-treaty with G-d are laws. While other nations expressed political faithfulness to each other (i.e., "love"), the treaty between G-d and Israel also includes day-to-day legal norms to reinforce the relationship.

> Those legal norms, of course, are in many instances paralleled in other collections of law, especially those from Mesopotamia, sometimes strikingly so. What is not paralleled there (as far as we currently can know) is the placement of law within a covenantal framework.[13]

Levenson suggests that the inclusion of community legal norms is crucial for understanding the Divine as a "personal G[-]d." Indeed it might be what makes Israel unique among other peoples of Mesopotamia. We may, in Israel's law, witness the birth of the concept of a personal relationship with G-d.

> The change is momentous. It means that the observance even of humdrum matters of law has become an expression of personal faithfulness and loyalty in covenant. . . . Israelites trying to heed those commandments and walk in G[-]d's ways face a far larger and more encompassing task than that of facing a minor ancient Near Eastern king trying to maintain faithfulness to the emperor with whom he is in covenant and whom he is commanded to love.[14]

In short, "opportunities to demonstrate their love for the L[-]rd are vastly more numerous, effectively encompassing the whole of their communal life." Every act of life within this political system was a way to reinforce the Divine love relationship.

If I were to bring this terminology into my own theology, I would say: *My life is duty-bound to G-d's love, both toward G-d and because of G-d toward others.* I am tempted to take this a step further: *The most tangible way to love G-d is to live a life of love that impacts community, society, and creation.* As a person who doesn't often feel a vertical connection to G-d, I am compelled to seek such a connection through my horizontal, flesh-and-blood

---

13. Levenson, *The Love of G[-]d*, 14.

14. Levenson, *The Love of G[-]d*, 14. He continues, "Another way to say this, however, is that the Israelites' opportunities to demonstrate their love for the L[-]rd are vastly more numerous, effectively encompassing the whole of their communal life."

relationships. Could it be that seeking the face of G-d requires me to seek the face of my neighbor?

I have found interreligious dialogue to be something of a spiritual exercise. I don't imagine that it will be experienced as such by every person. But seeking a connection with a religious "other" has become crucial for my edification as a Christian. It reinforces my vertical relationship to G-d.

Now, of course, I am in danger of sentimentalizing the human-to-human relationship. I do not envision a campfire-and-Kumbaya moment where we all gaze into each other's eyes and sing Don McLean. Remember, I am attracted to the theological/political conception of love. So allow me to fill out this discussion with a modern theological/political thinker.

James Hal Cone's theology grew out of the Civil Rights Movement of the 1960s. While many continue to think of his seminal work under the label of "liberation theology," Cone is a systematic theologian. As such, his work remains an important voice at the larger multiethnic and ecumenical table. Before I quote Cone on G-d's love, two points of relevance occur to me: (1) Cone's embrace of "Black Power" was a departure from (although not disjointed from) Martin Luther King's language. Cone acknowledges that Malcolm X's critique of America's "white Jesus" impacted his thought. So Cone's book derives from interreligious encounter. (2) Readers familiar with Martin Buber will hear echoes of his *I-Thou* and *I-It* paradigms. Cone most likely receives this language by way of Buber's dialogue partner: Paul Tillich. Cone writes:

> What does it mean to speak of G[-]d's love to man?[15] Man's response to G[-]d? His love of neighbor?

> For G[-]d to love the black man means that G[-]d has made him somebody. . . . He has worth because G[-]d imparts value through loving. It means that G[-]d has bestowed on him a new image of himself so that he can now become what he in fact is. Through G[-]d's love, the black man is given the power to *become*, the power to make others recognize him.[16]

Like many theologians before him, Cone believes that Christian love (properly conceived) is the secondary overflow from G-d's primary love. But not every people group experiences G-d's love in the same way. Cone expresses G-d's primary love as a uniquely black experience. This experience is mindful of a historic and systematic power disparity. It follows then that

---

15. Cone later acknowledges his androcentric language and regrets using it.

16. James Hal Cone, *Black Theology and Black Power*, 2nd ed. (1969; repr., San Francisco: HarperSanFrancisco, 1989), 52.

the secondary love (of neighbor) must be expressed differently as well. So he asks, "What does it mean for the black man to love his neighbor, especially the white neighbor?" Cone answers:

> To love the white man means that the black man *confronts* him as a Thou without any intentions of giving ground by becoming an It. . . . The new black man refuses to assume the It-role which whites expect, but addresses them as an equal. This is when the conflict arises.

> Therefore the new black man refuses to speak of love without justice and power. Love without the power to guarantee justice in human relations is meaning-less. Indeed, there is no place in Christian theology for sentimental love, love without risk or cost.[17]

Cone's notion of Divine love and love of neighbor is therefore not about reducing conflict and learning to get along.[18] Instead, he argues that the Christian acting along the lines of Divine love will address the historic power dynamics that make love of neighbor all but impossible. It must—to coopt Levenson's phrase—be an endeavor "encompassing the whole of their communal life." In other words, love of neighbor is a political endeavor: it seeks just relationships in all of the connections that govern social life. In a recent public lecture sponsored by my seminary, Cornel West put it this way: "Justice is what love looks like in public."

Larry Behrendt's brainchild—or at least one among his most compelling ideas—is the importance of recognizing "asymmetry" in Jewish-Christian relations. In an ideal world, I would like both Jews and Christians to come to the conversation table with equal levels of investment, purpose, expectations, and so on. But in reality, we experience our histories, our social placements, our spiritualities, our perceptions of the others (etc.) without symmetry. I would suggest that these asymmetries must be addressed along the lines Cone suggests if we are to see improvement in the Jewish-Christian relationship.

Esau Is Beautiful

I've never seen a vision like Jacob's sacred stairway. I've wrestled with G-d a few times, if I can use this story as a metaphor. I have concluded that

---

17. Cone, *Black Theology and Black Power*, 54.

18. I do not want to give the impression that Dr. King's notion of love was sen-timentalized and that Cone corrects this. It would be safer to say that the popular perception of Dr. King's message has been sentimentalized.

these struggles are sacred in retrospect, but they rarely feel sacred in the heat of the moment. Moreover, these moments, when I sense the presence of Divine mystery, are few and far between. Without being overly dramatic, let me put it this way: Most of my life as a Christian is lived carrying the troubling legacy of Christianity, while simultaneously negotiating G-d's silence. G-d's silence and the Christian legacy are not necessarily related problems. It's just that I continue to wrestle with both. For some, this might cause doubt. For me, it contributes to my sense of dissonance. But my life is not devoid of the sacred.

Jacob encounters G-d passively and definitively. Jacob also encounters G-d as aggressive and mysterious. But we must remember that Jacob also encounters G-d in a third way: as reconciliation with his estranged brother. Joel Kaminsky suggests that "if one hopes to see G[-]d's face and thus receive G[-]d's blessing, one must be reconciled with one's brother."[19] Paul Tillich defines love as "the reunion of the estranged."[20]

The reunion of Jacob and Esau is a sacred encounter, a Divine encounter. Rev. Baker's retelling of this story preaches to me:

> It is Esau's most beautiful moment. He's not a handsome man by the standards of his day or our own. But here, at this moment, he is beautiful. The glory of G[-]d, the mercy of G[-]d, and the love of G[-]d shine through his face. He is beautiful. And Jacob sees it. Jacob knows what G[-]d looks like. He has just seen G[-]d face to face for a whole night and he has lived. "For truly, brother, since you have received me with such favor, to see your face is like seeing the face of G[-]d." But now there's a difference. The night before, Jacob saw G[-]d as a mysterious man/angel of G[-]d, who is both adversary and bestower of blessing. But now, in the morning light, Jacob sees G[-]d as a brother and a friend, one who forgives him and now will journey alongside him. . . . Jacob at last finds his peace, his friendship, with his brother Esau.[21]

As I relate this story to Jewish-Christian interface, I am struck by the possibility of the sacred. I might not be able to predict (much less govern) when I will next experience G-d in a heavenly or mysterious way, but I can seek the face of G-d in this tangible way. My G-d is hidden, but

---

19. Joel S. Kaminsky, *Yet I Loved Jacob: Reclaiming the Biblical Concept of Election* (Nashville: Abingdon, 2007), 74.

20. Paul Tillich, *Love, Power, and Justice: Ontological Analysis and Ethical Applications* (Oxford: Oxford University Press, 1954), 25.

21. Rev. Dr. Richard L. Baker, Jr., "G[-]d's Light Refracted to Us and through Us: Jacob and Esau-Esau's Most Beautiful Moment (sermon, October 9, 2016).

those created in G-d's image need not be. Jewish theologian Arthur Green puts it this way:

> We cannot live with a faceless G[-]d. We will strive to mold ourselves over in the image of divinity. But in exchange we need a G[-]d to whom we can cry, with whom we can argue, whom we can trust and even love. For us, such a G[-]d needs to have a human face. So the face is our gift to G[-]d. But the light that shines forth from that face and radiates back to us with love—that surely is G[-]d's gift to us.[22]

As I seek the face of G-d in the face of my estranged neighbor, I encounter myself in dissonance. Because I am reminded of the discord I carry within me. I confess that I grow weary of it at times. I don't doubt that Larry has sensed my discomfort with the Christian legacy as we've argued and analyzed our historic defaults, postures, and asymmetries. Jewish-Christian dialogue is invigorating, transformational, and necessary. But it is not easy. For me it is worth it because it invites me into sacred space. In the reunion of the estranged, an encounter with G-d's love becomes possible.

---

22. Arthur Green, *Seek My Face: A Jewish Mystical Theology* (Woodstock, VT: Jewish Lights, 2003), 31.

Afterword

A Final Note

Émile Durkheim suggested that human beings are two-level creatures. For this reason he labeled the human as "homo duplex." Our base-level mind is occupied by biological needs and instinctual drives. At our base, we are creatures driven by self-preservation and primal appetites. Durkheim considered this level to be mundane.[1] The basic needs and drives on this level are just part of our ordinary, common life. But humans are also creatures that envision and enact higher-level needs and drives. This part of our mind is oriented toward community. When working at a higher, communal level, we are focused on the sacred.

The sacred elements of the human experience include shared morality, community building, and religion. Durkheim believed that the function of religion was to bring people together into a shared, sacred movement. Working from Durkheim's definition, Larry's previous chapter suggested that experiencing the sacred implies an extraordinary movement toward personal transformation. It is also important to underscore Durkheim's interest in the social nature of sacred experience.

Religion's purpose is to create a moral community. When people join a group around something sacred, they transcend the mundane world of simple self-interest. They find a higher level of consciousness within the group. They have become part of something greater than themselves, leading to the diminishing of self-interest and the elevation of communal well-being. While it is difficult to instill the codes and morals of collective conscience into the will of the individual, this can be done if the individual is joined to a group around something sacred.

---

1. As already mentioned by Larry, Durkheim used the word *profane*. It is worth noting, however, that profane is simply meant to refer to common life. It does not necessarily carry negative connotations.

In support of Durkheim, we could point to the experience of interconnectivity people sense when in heightened religious states. People who are uplifted by a religious experience sometimes feel a sense of harmony with humanity, nature, the universe, and/or G-d.

Durkheim is not immune to criticism. We could easily accuse him of modern bias. His attempt to explain religion as a detached observer limits him. Can all religions be reduced to the same basic principals? Doesn't his starting point assume Western individualism? Isn't religious experience more complex than a two-part model? And is there room for a real, living, and relational G-d in Durkheim's model? But for the moment, let's work with Durkheim's homo duplex explanation.

Think of it this way. Most of the time you are preoccupied with your most basic human needs. Sometimes you find a moment to forget about the basics and invest in something greater than yourself. You forget about your own personal cadence and begin to harmonize with others. This is the duplex experience.

So the title *Sacred Dissonance* might be a problem for Durkheim. If he saw the title of this book, Durkheim might (justifiably) declare it an oxymoron. Dissonance, because it resists harmony, is not sacred. In order for something to be sacred it must generate harmony, not dissonance. If indeed Larry and Anthony sense something sacred in Jewish-Christian dialogue, then Durkheim would expect Larry and Anthony to begin to harmonize. Or, conversely, if Larry and Anthony insist on preserving dissonance, then the dialogue must be something less than sacred.

In fairness, our dialogue is not a pure cacophony. During the course of this book, we probably agreed at least as much as we disagreed. So perhaps harmony *did* emerge in the course of this dialogue. It might be argued that Anthony and Larry came to this dialogue *already* sharing much in common: a mutual love of baseball, for example, as well as roots in California and an affinity for the comic strip *Peanuts*. That we are both political liberals is significant as this book was largely written during a U.S. presidential campaign. If we consider the perspective of intersectionality, where we describe interpersonal difference in terms of multiple factors, then we need to note other ways in which we do not differ: we're both men, for example, straight, abled, and cisgendered, living in an affluent country, and possessing elite educational credentials. From this perspective, we might be accused of having exaggerated the importance of our religious difference, and while we'd argue against this accusation, it's possible that the success of our dialogue (to the extend we *did* succeed) depended on what we share in common at least as much as on what divides us.

For example, having written this book during the campaign of Donald Trump versus Hillary Clinton, what would have happened if one of us was a political conservative? Could our dialogue have survived if it had taken place across a political as well as a religious divide? This question is far from academic, because we don't see much of the sacred in our current political dialogue. But if our thesis is right and sacred dialogue depends on dissonance, shouldn't there be an even greater potential for "sacred political dialogue," given the considerable dissonance existing between those on the Right and Left? If we don't see potential for "sacred" political debate between Republicans and Democrats, does this mean we can take the idea of "sacred dissonance" only so far?

This is not a book about politics. But we can note that in our present-day, politics is a highly partisan affair, where the goal is either to convert the other side to one's own point of view, or else triumph over the other side at the ballot box or in the corridors of political power. We've chronicled here how this kind of partisanship also used to dominate Jewish-Christian relations: for many centuries, the more powerful Christians sought either to convert the Jews or triumph over them. Thanks to a reconsideration of the Jewish-Christian difference that is (for the most part) less than one hundred years old, this kind of religious partisanship has receded quite a bit. Our dialogue is the stepchild of this reduction in partisanship. From the beginning of our dialogue, neither of us sought to emerge triumphant or to convert the other. For whatever it is worth, we don't see anything sacred in religious winning and losing, even if the silencing of a losing side produces a harmony by eliminating a voice not in concord with other voices.

Still, we'd push back against any suggestion that there's an *overarching* harmony at work in this book superseding the dissonant elements present here. At least, that's not our experience. During the course of our dialogue, we have not grown to believe that our religious differences are unimportant. We have not been tempted to suggest that, deep down, Jews and Christians are basically the same. While we have sometimes started singing the same tune, we experience that we are not members of the same choir.

We might try to describe this experience in terms of musical aesthetics: neither of us are fans of perfect harmony. We find barbershop quartets annoying, for example. Perfect harmony squashes any possibility of humor, which requires a well-timed injection of something unexpected. Conversations of complete agreement are generally boring. Or think of this in terms of friendship: If your closest friends always agree with you, shouldn't you be at least at least a little suspicious of their integrity? Returning to sociology, Durkheim saw religion as a way to transcend simple self-interest and take on a sense of communal well-being. But if all we sense is the well-being of our own group, then how far have we transcended self-interest?

Durkheim suggested that the higher level of human existence is the one oriented toward shared community. But our world is crisscrossed by difference. Earlier, Larry cited a verse from the Quran stating that G-d created human difference for a reason. The story of the Tower of Babel tells us the same thing. And while the community of Acts 2 is momentarily able to comprehend foreign tongues, their distinct languages remain distinct. The authors of this book are not equipped to tell you why G-d created the world in this way. We're just travelers along the borders that mark these differences. We find that dialogue helps us navigate these borders with more respect and better self-awareness. We find that Jewish-Christian dialogue helps us remember our sacred stories differently and more comprehensively. We find that interreligious dialogue has transformative power, as our internal and external postures reorient. At the end of the day, Larry and Anthony must return to our dissonant tribes. Returning to our respective religious cultures allows us to reflect and recharge so that all this work can continue.

We write this book confident that the positive qualities we find in dissonant dialogue are there for others to discover. We can't tell you how to do this. We present you with this book at a difficult time, when our ability to speak across differences seems to be narrowing, and the differences seem to be growing. We might naturally think that these two phenomena are related. Perhaps they're not. The Jewish-Christian difference has produced a historic dissonance that we've touched on frequently throughout the book; yet for all the dissonance, we have both found something sacred in the experience of dialogue. Because we are convinced that interreligious dialogue can transcend basic self-interest to create a sacred space, we suggest that dialogue is a special case of the sacred.

There's an old joke about a man who repeatedly crossed a national border on a bicycle. The officials who guarded this border knew that the man was smuggling something from one side of the border to the other, only they never could catch him at it.

Finally, one of the guards took the man aside and said, "Look, we're not going to prosecute you. I promise. Only please tell me: what is it that you're smuggling?"

"Bicycles," the smuggler answered.[2]

Not every purpose is hidden. It could be that the purpose of inter-religious dialogue is just in the talking. Maybe G-d just likes it when we're listening and talking, and listening some more.

---

2. In his book *Border Lines*, Daniel Boyarin tells the same joke, only he has the smuggler smuggling wheelbarrows instead of bicycles. Daniel Boyarin, *Border Lines: The Partition of Judaeo-Christianity* (Philadelphia: University of Pennsylvania Press, 2004), 1.

Acknowledgments

The process of writing this book has proved a blessing to both Larry and Anthony. Several mentors, friends, and family members were integral to this process.

Larry would like to thank his many faith conversation partners, including: Jonathan Aaron, Aneelah Afzali, Dave Baraff, Kerry and David Bar-Cohn, Sarah Bassin, Cynthia Beach, Judy Behrendt, Ann and John Brantingham, Tamar Chalker, Jo and Justin Scott-Coe, Niccolo Donzella, Chris Eyre, Josh Garroway, Laura Geller, Iris Graville, Joscelyne Gray, Andrea and Rick Grossman, Regina Manion Harris, Marie Hartung, Sara and Bill Heroman, Patrick Hurley, Chris Keith, Yohanna Kinburg, Todd King, Leah and Zev Kops, Ethel Krinick, Idit Lev, Kim Lundstrom, Bob MacDonald, Sara Maher, James McGrath, Christine Myers, Vivian-Lee Nyitray, Douglas Oliver, Claire Percival, Linda Peterson, Teresa Rogatz, Gwen Samelson, Aaron Smith, Cathee Weiss, Jill Zimmerman, and particularly Lillian Behrendt. Special thanks to the two people who continue to teach him how to write: Melissa Hart and Ana Maria Spagna. Loving thanks to his favorite editor, Stephanie Barbé Hammer.

Anthony would like to thank Leonard Greenspoon, Chris Keith, Lisa Hess, A.-J. Levine, Joel Lohr, Andrew Park, and Barry Schwartz. He is also grateful to Dr. Richard Baker for permission to use his sermon on Jacob and Esau. Acknowledgement is due to Zondervan/HarperCollins, as portions of the research on "borders" in this book were presented (albeit in a different form) in my book *Near Christianity: How Journeys along Jewish-Christian Borders Saved My Faith in God*. Early chapters of this book were presented to the students at United Theological Seminary and benefited greatly from these readers' reflections. Special thanks to Sarah Le Donne (my friend of virtue for twenty years).

Larry and Anthony owe a great deal to Carl Nellis, Patricia Anders, and the folks at Hendrickson. Thank you for taking this topic seriously and improving upon our final product. It has been an honor to work with you.